RUSI DEFENCE STUDIES SERIES

General Editor David Bolton, Director, Royal United Services Institute for Defence Studies

Questions on defence give rise to emotion, sometimes to the detriment of balanced judgement. Since 1831 the Royal United Services Institute for Defence Studies has been noted for its objectivity, independence and initiative, the views of its members sharpened by responsibility and experience. In continuance of the Institute's aims, the *RUSI Defence Studies Series* seeks to provide a wider understanding and better-informed debate of defence and national security issues. However, the views expressed in the books are those of the authors alone.

Published

Sir Ewen Broadbent
THE MILITARY AND GOVERNMENT: From Macmillan to Heseltine

Richard Clutterbuck
THE FUTURE OF POLITICAL VIOLENCE: Destabilization, Disorder and Terrorism

Christopher Coker
NATO, THE WARSAW PACT AND AFRICA
THE FUTURE OF THE ATLANTIC ALLIANCE
THE UNITED STATES, WESTERN EUROPE AND MILITARY INTERVENTION OVERSEAS (editor)
US MILITARY POWER IN THE 1980s

John Hemsley
THE SOVIET BIOCHEMICAL THREAT TO NATO: The Neglected Issue

Michael Hobkirk
THE POLITICS OF DEFENCE BUDGETING: A Study of Organisation and Resource Allocation in the UK and USA

Michael Leifer (editor)
THE BALANCE OF POWER IN EAST ASIA

K. G. Robertson (editor)
BRITISH AND AMERICAN APPROACHES TO INTELLIGENCE

Clive Rose
CAMPAIGNS AGAINST WESTERN DEFENCE: NATO's Adversaries
  and Critics

James Sherr
SOVIET POWER: The Continuing Challenge

E. S. Williams
THE SOVIET MILITARY: Political Education, Training and Morale

Forthcoming

Christopher Coker
US MILITARY POWER IN THE 1990s

Anthony H. Cordesman
FROM LEBANON TO THE FALKLANDS: The Lessons of Five Wars

Jonathan Eyal
THE WARSAW PACT AND THE BALKANS: Moscow's Southern Flank

Michael Hobkirk
DEFENCE DECISIONS: A Survey of Inter-Service Rivalry

Series Standing Order

If you would like to receive future titles in this series as they are
published, you can make use of our standing order facility. To place
a standing order please contact your bookseller or, in case of difficulty,
write to us at the address below with your name and address and the
name of the series. Please state with which title you wish to begin your
standing order. (If you live outside the United Kingdom we may not
have the rights for your area, in which case we will forward your order
to the publisher concerned.)

Customer Services Department, Macmillan Distribution Ltd,
Houndmills, Basingstoke, Hampshire, RG21 2XS, England

THE MILITARY AND GOVERNMENT

From Macmillan to Heseltine

Sir Ewen Broadbent
Retired Second Permanent
Under-Secretary of State
UK Ministry of Defence

Foreword by Harold Macmillan
first Earl of Stockton

First published 1988

Published by
THE MACMILLAN PRESS LTD
Houndmills, Basingstoke, Hampshire RG21 2XS
and London
Companies and representatives
throughout the world

Phototypeset by Input Typesetting Ltd, London

Printed in Hong Kong

British Library Cataloguing in Publication Data
Broadbent, *Sir* Ewen
The military and government: from
Macmillan to Heseltine.—(RUSI defence
studies series).
1. Great Britain. *Ministry of Defence—*
History
I. Title II. Series
354.41066   UA647
ISBN 0–333–43442–0

Contents

Acknowledgements

I should like to record my deep appreciation of the valuable views and advice offered to me by many civilian and military colleagues with whom I had the pleasure to work in Whitehall in the Air Ministry and the Ministry of Defence from 1949 to 1984. Their contribution has been invaluable.

I should also like to express special thanks for the willing and enthusiastic help I received from Mr John Andrews, Chief Librarian, Ministry of Defence and his staff, and for the patient and skilled typing of my script carried out by Mrs Jean Joss.

Finally I acknowledge with thanks the kind permission of the Right Honourable Michael Heseltine for a quotation from an article he wrote in 1980, of Jonathan Cape Limited and Mr Trevor Burridge for two short extracts from his book *Clement Attlee* and Messrs Cassell for a short extract from *The Central Blue* by the late Marshal of the Royal Air Force Sir John Slessor.

SIR EWEN BROADBENT

Foreword

During fifty years of public service I had the privilege of being associated in a variety of ways with the Armed Forces of this country and their tasks in its defence. In the First World War I saw at first hand the awesome demands and sacrifices expected of them, to which they responded so magnificently. In the Second World War I was involved at the political level with their equipment in the Ministry of Supply, with their operations when I was Resident Minister in North West Africa and with their administrations during an all too short a time as Secretary of State for Air.

These were impressionable and powerful experiences. They brought home to me the vital importance of each link in the chain which leads from the major decisions of the Cabinet to the fighting capability of the sailor, soldier and airman. When I was appointed Defence Secretary in 1954 the role of that small Ministry, separated as it was from the highly competent but unduly independent and inward-looking Service Ministries and the half-baked Ministry of Supply, did not seem to me to be adequate for the efficient discharge of its high responsibilities. I saw the need for change towards greater and clearer central control. But the timing had to be right.

I am proud that as Prime Minister I was able in 1962 to launch that change towards a unified Ministry. When I was about to start the process I wrote to Her Majesty the Queen, 'Somehow we have got to meet two needs. We must unify to be efficient and avoid waste. And we must diversify to keep alive the spirit of the men.' This was a difficult challenge. I was greatly helped by the constructive and far-sighted proposals drawn up by two eminent retired senior officers – Lord Ismay and Sir Ian Jacob. The outcome, thanks also to the drive of Peter Thorneycroft and the loyal support throughout of Lord Mountbatten, was the formation of a unified Ministry of Defence in 1964, to which the Aviation Supply responsibilities were added a few years later. There was thus created, and I am glad to see there still is, one centre for the major decisions, but the organism has been able to accommodate the three Services with their own vital traditions and skills.

I am sure that this overall structure is right. There can always be refinements and improvements. Many have been introduced in recent years. No doubt there will be more. By itself organisation does not solve the continuing major problems that face every Government over the roles, size, equipment and the ultimate test of the use in operations of our Armed Forces. But bad organisation can do much harm and this is truer in defence than in many other spheres. It is essential that Her Majesty's Forces are well administered and receive clear instructions from the Government. Without sound, practical and decisive policies their difficult and dangerous tasks would become impossible.

It is therefore important that all those concerned with defence, from the serving officer in the field to the Members of Parliament and Ministers who determine policies, understand how the Ministry works. This book describes the evolution of the Whitehall organisation in historical terms. It is important to see it in this perspective. It is equally important to understand, as is explained here, the parts that Ministers, officers, civil servants and scientists play within the whole. Their wide range of human skills must be used to maximise advantage, and good organisation can do much to facilitate that.

Defence is vital to the nation. A book which helps us understand better how the responsible Ministry works is a valuable contribution.

October 1986   HAROLD MACMILLAN
                                 (first Earl of Stockton)

Preface

Over the years at the Royal United Services Institute for Defence Studies there have been many presentations, lectures and discussions concerned with relationships between the military and government and, in particular, the function and organisation of the Ministry of Defence. It has long been a matter of consuming interest to those who work in or with the Ministry, whether they be politicians, civil servants or military officers. The political direction of the military, both in war and in peace, can certainly generate excitement for historian and practitioner alike.

With the competition for resources between government departments and, not least, the effect of success or failure upon the ambitions of the ministers concerned, recent years have seen fresh endeavours to make the Ministry of Defence more effective in its control of the military budget and the frequent belief that this might be better achieved by reorganisation within the Ministry. Over time and in turn, emphasis has been given to 'the Centre' and then the single Services. In the 1980s, the thrust has been towards strengthening the central and higher organisation of defence.

Leading up to 1980, and in that year itself, increasing concern was expressed over the Ministry's structure. It was argued that timely and specialist military advice to ministers was not being provided when it was needed, and that the management of defence resources could and should be tightened and improved. One cold winter's morning in 1981 a closed debate was therefore held in the RUSI. Selected officers and civil servants took part, both serving and retired, of two-star rank and above and including Chiefs of Staff. The outcome was agreement over the need for change but that the process should be evolutionary, albeit towards an eventual and fundamental restructuring of the Ministry. That debate was a factor in the reorganisation introduced by the then Secretary of State, Sir John Nott, and Admiral of the Fleet, The Lord Lewin, then Chief of Defence Staff. It also prompted the recognition in the RUSI that no concise reference existed of the many and various changes which had taken place since the formation of a unified Ministry of Defence. After the Falklands campaign in 1982 and then the further reorganisation of the Ministry by Michael Heseltine, the need became even more pressing. What was needed was someone who fully understood the system, who had worked in it, yet who could make an objective judgement of the political, economic and military issues involved. Sir Ewen Broadbent proved to be the ideal author. Lord Stockton too became attracted to the idea. This book is the result. It combines historical perspective and rigorous analysis with suggestions for prospective improvements.

DAVID BOLTON
Director
Royal United Services
Institute for Defence Studies

Glossary

ACDS	Assistant Chief of the Defence Staff
ADP	Automatic Data Processing
AEW	Airborne Early Warning
AUS	Assistant Under-Secretary
AWACS	Airborne Warning and Control System
AWRE	Atomic Weapons Research Establishment
CAPL	Chief Adviser Personnel and Logistics
CDP	Chief of Defence Procurement
CDS	Chief of the Defence Staff
CENTO	Central Treaty Organisation (Turkey–Iran–Pakistan–UK–US)
CER	Controller Research and Development Establishments
CERN	Controller Research and Development Establishments, Research and Nuclear
CIGS	Chief of the Imperial General Staff
CPL	Chief of Personnel and Logistics
CSA	Chief Scientific Adviser
CSCSE	Conference on Security and Cooperation in Europe
DCDS (P&L)	Deputy Chief of the Defence Staff (Personnel and Logistics)
DEPC	Defence Equipment Policy Committee
DOAE	Defence Operational Analysis Establishment
DRIRC	Defence Research and Intermural Resources Committee
DUS	Deputy Under-Secretary
FMPG	Financial Management and Planning Group
GLCM	Ground-launched Cruise Missile
GNP	Gross National Product
HMG	Her Majesty's Government
HOC	Headquarters Organisation Committee
MINIS	Management Information System for Ministers
MRCA	Multi-role Combat Aircraft

NDIC	National Defence Industrial Council
OKW	*Ober Kommando der Wehrmacht*
O&M	Organisation and Methods
OMB	Office of Management and Budget
PAO	Principle Administrative Officers
PEMB	Procurement Executive Management Board
P&L	Personnel & Logistics
PPO	Principal Personnel Officers
PSA	Property Services Agency
P&T	Professional and Technology groups
PUS	Permanent Under-Secretary
R&D	Research and Development
REME	Royal Electrical and Mechanical Engineers
ROF	Royal Ordnance Factory
RRE	Royal Radar Establishment
RSRE	Royal Signals and Radar Establishment
SAGW	Surface-to-Air Guided Weapon
SBAC	Society of British Aerospace Companies
SEATO	South East Asia Treaty Organisation
VCDS	Vice-Chief of the Defence Staff

Part I

Introduction

1 Setting the Scene

Organisation is often regarded as mundane, even tedious. Policies and personalities are what count. But in the field of defence this is not the case. The nature and adequacy of the higher central organisation of defence are critical for two fundamental reasons, which might in shorthand be entitled the efficient and the democratic. First, Armed Forces are now so complex and so technically advanced that if the central structure is not able to give clear directions and provide adequate resources the forces would rapidly become invalid and ineffective. Second, armed forces often form a potentially very powerful part of the state. Their existence has in the past called for and still calls for an organisation to control the armed forces themselves and for an arm of the state to decide upon their use. Sometimes, as in military dictatorships, the two strands have coincided. Sometimes there have been power struggles between two groups, in extreme circumstances leading to violent military revolutions. In democracies in recent centuries the relationships between the state and the armed forces have become increasingly stabilised and formalised. The nature of the form of defence of a country is an essential part of a government's overall policy, to be determined by a number of complex factors including its foreign policy and its economic circumstances. The armed forces for their part have both to respond to the political directions of the government and to advise the government on the degree of defence they can offer for given resources and treaty provisions. There must therefore be arrangements and structures which permit a continuous and effective dialogue between the politician and the military.

THE PLACE OF DEFENCE IN CENTRAL GOVERNMENT

The organisational shape that is adopted to meet this requirement has changed and evolved over the centuries. But, looked at from the broadest standpoint, there is a considerable similarity of pattern

3

between the solutions adopted in a wide range of countries. This is not surprising. Defence as an issue remains such a vital function of a modern state that it needs to be a core function of the central system of government of the state. Defence as a resource has become so complex and so demanding both financially and technologically that there has been a growing belief in the need to bring the various strands involved in defence together into some form of unitary central organisation of government. Each country has found its own detailed solution, influenced by its own traditions and its contemporary circumstances.

In the United Kingdom, political control over the armed forces was established as a principle some centuries ago and, unusually even for Western Europe, has never been seriously challenged. The organisational shape that this control took within the executive arm of the state was embodied in the two Government Departments of the Admiralty and the War Office. This structure changed little until well into this century, the creation of the Air Ministry amounting to no more in these terms than another copy of the same model. But from the middle of the century the political pressures and the pace of change grew. In London, as in Paris, Bonn, Washington, Canberra, Ottawa and many other capitals, a defence ministry as such was created, which became the focal point for both the formulation and the execution of defence policies, with the obvious key links of a political nature within the central government as a whole and of a military and executive nature with the armed forces and the associated defence-orientated industries. The structure of such a ministry has had to take account, as is the case with any major organisation, of both the policy issues and the people involved in their determination. In the Ministry of Defence the issues have been greater and the personnel interplays more complex than in the largest multinational companies or Government-run industries. The aim of this book is to describe how the organisational solutions have evolved in recent years. To understand this evolution it is first necessary to identify the main roles of the structure and the backgrounds of the people who make it work.

UNITY AND HOMOGENEITY

In the United Kingdom the Ministry of Defence, hardly now recognisable as the natural growth of the original child, has just passed its fortieth year of existence. In its more recognisable unified form after the embodiment of the former Service Ministries it will soon be twenty-five years old. There have been and are likely to be **no** celebrations. Other Departments of State such as the Home Office or the Board of Customs and Excise may feel confident and old enough to engage in such activities, which do at least generate a feeling of *esprit de corps*. But the Ministry of Defence still seems amorphous and in some ways impermanent, still in the process of settling down and yet constantly subject to change. It may have a logo and even a tie but it has no house style. Indeed, it has no house newspaper, which many major industrial and commercial conglomerates find to be of value, although the Procurement Executive did try for a short time. And yet within the Ministry of Defence itself there are strong traditions and loyalties. These are not just the basic loyalties that come from wearing the uniform of one of Her Majesty's Forces. There are loyalties within the sub-structures of the Ministry. The Royal Corps of Naval Constructors celebrated recently, with some pomp, their hundredth anniversary. On the second floor of the main Whitehall building hangs a board listing the Masters General of the Ordnance from 1414. The post has not yet been retitled Army Systems Controller. The members of the Admiralty Board still walk across Whitehall to meet round their ancient Board table and can look up to see whether the wind is set fair for sailing in the Channel. The professional civilian accountants have formed a thriving discussion society.

These are not meant to be sentimental or facetious examples. They illustrate the scale of the human as well as the organisational problems that were posed in 1964 and considerably added to in 1971 when first four and then effectively five ministries were brought under one overall umbrella. The Admiralty and the War Office in particular had long histories, strong traditions and clearly allocated and complementary tasks for their uniformed and civilian staff with their self-contained career structures. The loss of all these as a consequence of amalgamations was not welcomed. Certainly other such combinations of ministries occurred in the 1960s and 1970s when the macro-department became fashionable. The present Foreign and Commonwealth Office incorporated the Foreign Office, the Commonwealth Relations Office and the residue of the Colonial Office. The Departments of Trade and Industry and of the Environment likewise involved major change. But such changes were not so demanding as the unification of defence matters. The other ministries had a basic, indeed predominant, role of operating as a central department of government. In terms of staff numbers, though these ministries were high in the Whitehall league, they were smaller. Moreover their staff were less varied in their backgrounds and proportionately more of them were regularly working in a central government department. These factors call for elaboration.

THE VARIETY OF ROLES WITHIN THE CENTRAL DEFENCE ORGANISATION

At the level of the lowest common denominator, there is the unifying word, 'defence'. But, sub-dividing this generalised term only slightly, it can soon be seen that the roles that are carried out in the Ministry of Defence have great differences which have had major effects both on the shape of the organisation and on any desires or capacity for changing the shape, or, even within the basic shape, for delegating or hiving off major elements of work. These roles are usually simplified into three major groupings, each with a miscellany of sub-roles.

First, and most obvious, the Ministry is a Department of State. The vital importance of defence to the nation gives it a key place and status in Cabinet and Parliament. Its policy links with the Foreign and Commonwealth Office in international matters and with the Treasury in resource terms are very close and call for major and complex negotiations to hammer out policies. But its ramifications spread over virtually every Department of Government. A few illustrations will suffice; as an employer of a third of the Civil Service, it has a major input into the pay and manpower policies of the Manpower and Personnel Office; as a large owner of land and user of the surrounding air and sea areas for training, its activities greatly affect the Scottish and Welsh Offices as well as others; its purchasing policies, particularly in the fields of advanced technology, can help or hinder the sponsorship responsibilities of the Department of Trade and Industry; its many industrial-type activities as well as its firing ranges call for close consultation, required by recent legislation, with the Health and Safety Executive. Such examples can be multiplied many times over. Their relevance is not simply that staff in adequate quantities and versed in the administrative, political and legal aspects of work within Whitehall need to be available. They in turn need to have adequate lines of communication with the thousands of sites and units, distributed between the three Services and the Procurement Executive, manned by uniformed and civilian personnel including part-time auxiliaries and reservists and which are scattered around the country, or at sea or abroad. Nor is this all. There is one extra important dimension of advising and supervising visiting forces to this country in all these fields.

In addition to these lateral links the Ministry of Defence, as a Department of State, has to conform to the financial requirements of Parliament as expressed in the presentation of annual Estimates; the detailed procedure of the Public Accounts Committee; and the functions placed on Accounting Officers. At the mundane level the sheer scale of the annual expenditure calls for large financial and accounting resources. But the complexities go much deeper. The procedural requirements affect practices even in operational units, very remote in their nature from financial concerns. At the Ministry, the complexities of multi-million-pound contracts with development and production spreading over a decade or more and in fields that are up against the frontiers of technology, call for sophisticated skills in estimating, negotiating contracts and monitoring progress. Such contracts and associated delivery patterns do not fit in naturally with the annuality of the Parliamentary system. The last decade, with the highlight of the moratorium on defence spending in the latter months of 1980/81, graphically illustrated this problem. So too did the difficulty of securing even a modest degree of flexibility year to year which would assist the organisation to demonstrate that it had a degree of practicality and business acumen that its critics so often maintain it lacks. Many of these factors are common, to a lesser or greater extent, to all ministries. But the differences need to be stressed. The Ministry of Defence is much more an executive than a legislating department. Within this executive function it is much more directly involved and responsible than are such departments as the Department of Health and Social Services and the Department of Education and Science. While they sponsor large budgets for the Health Service and for schools and universities their controls are of a much more general nature. They do not need to have the whole panoply of financial, contractual, accounting, project management and staffing controls which the Ministry of Defence needs to carry out and monitor its programmes.

There is also the general accountability of ministers to Parliament. The task is common to all Departments of State and needs no elaboration. But it calls for an internal ministerial organisation which appears to make sense to Members of Parliament who wish to satisfy themselves that ministers are in a position to exercise effective control over their department.

The second major role is that of being the operational and managerial headquarters of the three Services. At the operational level the span of control extends from the nuclear deterrent, the links at governmental level with NATO in time of crisis, the political and strategic direction of national emergencies and campaigns such as recently in the South Atlantic, to the provision of a swift flow of information about, and on occasions control over the activities of the Armed Forces in support of the civil power. This last sub-role alone has a great range of its own, extending from Northern Ireland to Greenham Common and to the siege of the Iranian Embassy. Modern demands, particularly of the media, call for an instant flow of advice and information, often detailed, to ministers. Apart from the practical questions of communications facilities, such tasks always raise in an acute form problems of the balance between centralisation in Whitehall and delegation to the executive controlling formation. Some degree of centralisation is inevitable if adequate control and timely information are to be ensured, but clear and well-practised arrangements involving organisations in the Ministry of Defence, elsewhere in Whitehall and in external military formations have to be determined.

Operational effectiveness, whether in demonstrating the validity and viability of the deterrent forces or in carrying out military operations at whatever level, is the ultimate *raison d'être* of the Ministry. The cohesion of the trained battalion, squadron or fighting ship is achieved within the unit but is greatly dependent on the provision not only of clear executive orders, but also of manpower, equipment and total logistic support. This provision involves a two-way process. Bids have to be made for resources on whatever body has approving powers. Subsequently, all the processes for initiating orders for equipment and for recruiting and training manpower and then for bringing all these elements together in a timely and effective way, have to be undertaken and monitored. These processes were traditionally carried out in a single-Service environment because units were fighting in their own elements of sea, land and air. Increasingly, potential overlaps have arisen, notably in land–air and sea–air areas. Choices between competing ways of discharging particular functions need to be made on the basis of the most objective and comprehensive analysis of the facts that can be assembled. But, once made, nothing should cut across the clarity of operational orders and the purposiveness of the individual unit. Cross-over points between multi-disciplinary policy-making, which can involve scientists and administrators as well as all three Services, and clear executive operational hierarchies give rise to subtle and difficult problems which must be got right. Experience suggests that it is desirable to carry this out and find solutions at the level of the Ministry rather than between executive operational formations.

Organisational structure and tradition are interconnected. Tradition is a contentious subject which can be over-played or understated. It can result in fossilisation. It can, if handled with skill, be adapted to changing circumstances and demands. The restructuring of British Army regiments in the 1950s and 1960s is an example of successful adaptation. Across the Armed Forces and indeed between different classes within the Civil Service new patterns can achieve their own purpose and impetus. There can be a unity of function as well as of Service. All that needs to be said here, in the context of organisational patterns for efficient management in the Ministry, is that it is a factor which has to be carefully weighed when contemplating change, that it operates at all levels and that it requires time and skill to achieve successful reorientations.

The third major role of the Ministry is that of a huge business conglomerate. Its spending runs into billions of pounds a year, on the scale of the largest multinational corporations. But the complexities are greater than are theirs. It has not the same degree of choice in deciding what ranges of equipment it does or does not wish to purchase and stock. The degree of choice is somewhat greater, but often difficult to make, as between initiating research and development or buying off the shelf from abroad. It is often operating at the front end of the most complex technologies. It has to be involved throughout the whole life-cycle of equipment, from the initial concept through development and production to maintenance in rugged conditions beyond an equipment's cost-effective life. Recent years have seen some shift in aspects of research and development from intra-mural to extra-mural work, but policy direction and the provision and allocation of financial resources still have to be exercised. At any one time the Ministry is running dozens of very large programmes, each costing over their life-cycle hundreds or thousands of millions of pounds. Each is at least as complex as the most advanced and large civilian ventures such as power stations, oil refineries or the introduction of new car designs. A large and highly professional organisation is needed to handle such a programme. It has to be receptive to the needs of the customer: i.e. the Services. It has to negotiate with and monitor the suppliers who may be national, foreign or a complex collaborative grouping brought about for political rather than commercial reasons. It has to consider, more than would a commercial concern, the effects of its policies on national industry.

These few paragraphs have given a highly simplified and selective account of the major roles traditionally carried out for defence in central government. The purpose is to stress their magnitude and complexity, not as an apologia for the organisation but in order to bring out the variety of the work and the different backgrounds of the staff needed to carry out the work.

THE VARIETY OF STAFF

Policies and decisions flowing from these various roles are handed down to the staff of the Ministry from its political heads. The latter are few in number. They are almost certainly not expert in the individual subjects. In some cases they may even be antipathetic to the backgrounds and attitudes of the staff. But their policies will be made that much more effective if the response of the staff is enthusiastic and cooperative rather than indifferent or ineffective. They are therefore very dependent on expert, dedicated staff.

Such a capability is difficult to create and sustain in any large organisation. Motivation is a universally recognised problem. It is made easier when there is a clear yardstick, but in defence this is not always simple to establish. There is no generally applicable profit motive. There is no one measure of efficiency, though in operational units standards can be set and evaluated. There is no clear measure of cost-effectiveness, though many trials of instilling relevant financial yardsticks have been undertaken, most recently and extensively by way of responsibility budgets. But such yardsticks, where available, generally are more relevant to the Armed Forces and their supporting establishments in the field than to the work carried out in Whitehall.

This problem is compounded by the staffing patterns of the Ministry. For very sound reasons the staff need to come from a variety of backgrounds. Unlike civil servants the members of the Armed Forces do not join their Service with the expectation, let alone the desire, of serving in Whitehall. Such a posting takes them away from their primary task and from the application of skills which they have been accumulating over the years. While they may come to find the work to be intellectually challenging, a strange environment, different working methods and new colleagues have to be contended with and assimilated. Such considerations also affect many of the members of the Civil Service scientific and engineering staffs serving in the Ministry. They joined the Civil Service to do such tasks as research at Farnborough or warship repair in a dockyard. They too have major adjustments to make. It is therefore essential that the organisational structures which are adopted take account of the personal interrelationships.

ORGANISATIONAL CONSEQUENCES

This wide spectrum of roles and varieties of staff backgrounds may suggest that in principle it is wrong and is bound to be inefficient to try to combine them all in one ministry. But the unifying factors are even stronger. The three Services are interconnected and interdependent in their operational functions. A coherent policy for them is essential. There is a logical unity in the parliamentary accountability for defence. Equally in Cabinet terms defence is an identifiable subject like health and education. There are advantages in dealing with other countries on a broadly comparable structural basis. There are economies of scale from dealing with industry on a unified basis. There is a major benefit in handling defence equipment on a cradle-to-grave basis. In addition to arguments of principle there are pragmatic arguments of the economies and efficiencies that have been gained from rationalisation and unification in many areas of support and training over two decades.

What do these factors mean for the structure of the central organisation for defence? They do not point to a particular organisational solution. But their very complexity indicates certain very general principles which need to inform whatever organisational arrangements are selected. First, there must be clarity of purpose. Aims and policies must be clearly disseminated. Second, there must be a sense of unity. Staff need to see that there is a machinery for bringing together the various strands in a form in which all the key elements are represented. But the unity must not be repressive. Local, functional and professional loyalties need to be fostered, yet without allowing them to ossify. Competing views are healthy so long as they are not only heard but also debated and evaluated. Third, the very variety and complexity call for a high degree of personal professionalism among the staff. Fourth, this very variety and complexity also call for maximum simplicity and for economy in the numbers of staff. This is not a contradiction in terms. The less detailed work that needs to be done centrally and the more self-contained tasks that can be hived off without losing control over their policies or resource implications, the better. Fifth, given the complexity and technicality of many of the issues and the experience needed to make maximum use of a big organisation, greater continuity in staffing could pay dividends in greater efficiency. It is not always the organisation that is wrong if it fails to function adequately.

The preceding sections have suggested that the organisation for defence needs to be considered against the background of the roles that have to be discharged in central government, the people involved in the work and certain very simple but important principles that should be borne in mind. There is one other vital factor. The nation's defence capability must be a continuum. It cannot, like some organisations, stop and start again. Therefore the organisation has to be seen as a continuous thread; where it was is relevant to where it is now and where it may go. In analysing the changes in the central organisation of defence in recent years it is essential to take account of the inheritance. The four chapters in Part II accordingly summarise in chronological order the developments this century, though concentrating primarily on the more recent years. Certain common factors are then discussed in Part III. The chapters which then follow and make up Part IV analyse the significance of the changes in individual key functional areas. There is inevitably some duplication, but the standpoint in the fourth part is more that of the working effectiveness of the particular area rather than its wider political context. The last chapter then considers the reasons for the high level of organisational scrutiny and change in recent years, and, finally, speculates on the likelihood of and possible areas for further change and on its desirability.

Part II

Forty Years of Change

2 The Early Years

The earliest reference by those in authority to the need for formalised coordination between the Armed Forces of the Crown has probably not yet been identified. Certainly, Disraeli expressed the view. Somewhere there may be remarks by Wellington or Marlborough or Pepys. But the first organisational steps of significance were taken after the failings in the Boer War by the establishment in 1904 of the Committee of Imperial Defence. Its creation followed the report of a committee under Lord Esher.

1904–46

The Committee of Imperial Defence, and then in 1916 the War Cabinet – brought about by two years of experience in the First World War – were both operating essentially at the governmental and political level. They were not primarily directed at inter-Service planning. It was the creation in 1924, following a recommendation in the previous year, of the Chiefs of Staff Committee as a Sub-Committee of the Committee of Imperial Defence which first filled this gap at the professional level. During the next fifteen years, modestly supported by two sub-committees, it proved to be the main source of the military plans for the transition to and conduct of the Second World War. Somewhat surprisingly, at least on outward appearances, the appointment in 1936 of a Minister for the Coordination of Defence was not, as defined and operated, a significant step in organisational evolution. The post was not supported by any effective departmental structure. The Minister had no executive power, no clear responsibility to Parliament and no role in the allocation of resources between the three Services. His task was to assist the Prime Minister to oversee the rearmament programme. Given that limited basis, it is not surprising that it lapsed in 1940 when the Prime Minister assumed the additional title of Minister of Defence

15

and when a Minister of Production, with executive powers, was appointed.

Organisationally the wartime arrangements, as they were developed very much under the individual style of the Prime Minister, concentrated power in two bodies: politically in the Defence Committee of the Cabinet; militarily in the Chiefs of Staff Committee. The Service Ministries, headed by their Ministers, were responsible for the management of the Armed Forces, following up the central directions of the Chiefs of Staff.

THE FORMATION OF A DEFENCE MINISTRY IN 1946

The end of the war and the election of a Labour Government called for a fresh consideration of peacetime arrangements. The White Paper on Defence (Cmd 6743) which was presented in February 1946, announced the Government's intention of putting forward at an early date their proposals for a central organisation of defence (the phrase in itself is significant) which would embody the improvements suggested by the experience of the previous six years. There is no doubt that the Prime Minister's views had been shaped by still earlier experiences and ideas. In the later years of the pre-war rearmament period Mr Clement Attlee had been advocating, when in opposition and with only patchy and limited support from within his own party, the need for better coordination. His views had greatly influenced a report prepared in February 1939 by the defence group of the Labour Party which advocated the establishment of a Ministry of Defence.

It comes therefore as no surprise that the promised White Paper on the Central Organisation for Defence which was presented in October 1946 (Cmd 6923) advocated the appointment of a Minister of Defence, this time supported by a Ministry of Defence. Three main functions were envisaged for the Ministry. It would apportion in broad outline the available resources between the three Services, including the policy for research and development and the correlation of production programmes. It would settle questions of general administration on which a common policy would be desirable. It would directly administer inter-Service organisations.

In certain respects this White Paper marked a major and fundamental step. But it was one which was expressly taken with considerable caution and carefully inbuilt constraints. The White Paper discussed and rejected, at that point in time, the amalgamation of the three Services. It shied away from the creation of any form of combined General Staff, not only because of the recent antipathetic tones of the German Oberkommando der Wehrmacht (OKW) practice ringing in their ears, but also, as the White Paper expressly put it, for the positive reason that it was a cardinal principle of British organisation that those who are to implement the policy in the Service Ministries should be those who formulate it in the central machine. The White Paper similarly discussed and specifically rejected the idea of the appointment of an independent Chairman of the Chiefs of Staff Committee. There was a clear desire to maintain the high degree of direct contact between Ministers and the Chiefs of Staff and to continue the involvement of ministers collectively in major defence matters.

Underlying the proposed structure was a concept that the necessary improvements in resource allocation and moves towards inter-Service rationalisation (though the word had not yet appeared in its current sense) could be achieved essentially by coordination through the Chiefs of Staff machinery and through a small permanent central staff. A standing committee of the Minister of Defence and the Service Ministers would give directions on administrative matters of common concern. This machinery would operate independently of the Chiefs of Staff. The relevant Service Council or Board members, who collectively formed the Principal Personnel Officers Committee and the Principal Administrative Officers Committee, would directly serve the Standing Committee of ministers.

The problems of pre-war rearmament and wartime production were reflected in the considerable emphasis which was laid on the creation of a Joint War Production Staff working for a Ministerial Production Committee. A similar line of thinking led to the creation of a Committee on Defence Research Policy. Each of these two committees was to have a permanent chairman who, together with the Permanent Secretary and the Chief Staff Officer, were identified as the four principal advisers of the Minister. Looking ahead for a moment, after forty years those four pillars are still there in the forms of the Permanent Under-Secretary of State, the Chief of the Defence Staff, the Chief of Defence Procurement and the Chief Scientific Adviser, even though their relative and absolute powers have gone through several modifications.

The Paper still left the Service Ministers in the Cabinet and responsible to Parliament for the administration of their Services. It still left the Vote and programme responsibilities with the Service Ministries for their execution. Therefore, in practice, they remained in command of resources and manpower. As for the broad policy, it was intended that, via the Chiefs of Staff Committee and the Cabinet Defence Committee, a coherent scheme of expenditure would be drawn up which would 'give the country forces and equipment in properly balanced programmes'.

Over the next few years this new structure did not prove to be as effective as had been hoped. There were several reasons. It was perhaps unjustified to assume that the rather simple wartime arrangements could be applied equally successfully to a peacetime situation, when the conflicting demands between defence and other policies were greater and the priorities were less clear-cut. Initially the concentration of effort within the Forces was the run-down after the war and the transition to peace. Within the Government and markedly until 1951, the interest and thrust were on the massive economic and social problems of reconstruction. Defence matters became prominent only intermittently and then over such issues as the Berlin airlift and the atomic bomb, not so much over resource allocation. The Ministers of Defence themselves were on the whole not unduly powerful personalities or organisation men. When the Conservative Government took office in 1951 Mr Churchill's continued direct personal interest in defence matters tended to ride over normal organisational channels. But, as the 1950s progressed, the financial consequences of trying both to remain a world power and to carry out, independently, research, development and production across the whole spectrum of defence equipment became increasingly severe. They were in turn exacerbated by poor forecasts and estimates which led, almost inevitably, to a growing number of cancellations and programme changes, all of which exposed the Government to political criticism and budgetary problems.

THE INFLUENCE OF MR MACMILLAN

The latent dissatisfaction first voiced itself when Mr Anthony Eden became Prime Minister and Mr Harold Macmillan was for a short period of six months the Minister of Defence. Dissatisfaction grew and radical solutions were increasingly sought. If the period from 1947 to 1955 was static and quiescent, that from 1955 to 1963 was by marked contrast active and full of tensions. Both issues and personalities came vigorously to the forefront.

The whole range of issues, which had been identified and discussed in cool and considered terms in the 1946 White Paper, were debated once again and with more outward passion: a unified Ministry; unified Services; the role of the Chiefs of Staff and the place of a fourth Chief of Staff sitting over, in some form, his three single-Service colleagues; the method of resource allocation; the scope for administrative coordination or more radical change. In terms of public perception three figures stood out during this period: Mr Duncan Sandys in the first part; Mr Macmillan and Admiral of the Fleet Lord Mountbatten throughout. All, with varying emphasis, wanted radical change by moving in the same centralising direction. But they were not all equally successful in getting their particular solutions adopted. And such were the policy and programme difficulties at that time that other senior voices were also calling, though more behind the scenes, for major changes.

Mr Eden took over as Prime Minister in April 1955, and, as part of the accompanying reshuffle, Mr Macmillan left the Ministry of Defence, after a short and, what was to him, frustrating stay of only six months and was replaced by Mr Selwyn Lloyd. Mr Eden saw a need for greater and more sustained direction by ministers. He both added to the ministerial committee structure and strengthened the position of the Minister by giving him responsibility for the 'composition and balance of the forces'. There was little disagreement about strengthening the Minister's position, but the accompanying proposal to appoint a permanent chairman of the Chiefs of Staff Committee produced a flurry of concern and divided views among the Chiefs of Staff about the precise role and powers of the incumbent. After a hurried series of meetings Mr Eden accepted a compromise whereby the creation of the post of chairman was accepted but he was not made additionally the 'Chief Staff Officer' or the 'Chief Military Adviser' to the Minister.

1956 was dominated by the Suez crisis. Apart from its wider international consequences it had the effect of forcing up defence expenditure and precipitating an economic crisis. When Mr Macmillan suddenly became Prime Minister in January 1957 one of his first steps was to instigate a complete review of defence policy. He had already been looking during the previous year when he was Chancellor of the Exchequer for economies from defence. The need was now greater and his authority was stronger.

Mr Macmillan realised from his time as Minister of Defence that if his overall aim was to succeed he would need to appoint a strong minister and to endow him with clear and effective powers. The first conclusion was met by the appointment of Mr Sandys. The second was met not by formal organizational changes, which would be likely to take too long to bring about, but by the issue of a personal directive. As soon as possible, on 24 January 1957, Mr Macmillan announced that with a view to securing substantial reductions in expenditure and military manpower he had authorised his Minister of Defence to 'decide all matters of policy affecting the size, shape, organisation and disposition of the Armed Forces, their equipment and supply . . . their pay and conditions of service'. At the same time the Service Ministers were told that, in order to give reality to the formal 1946 structure they were to work through the Minister of Defence. The further step, discussed but not effected in 1955, of making the Chairman of the Chiefs of Staff Committee also the Chief Staff Officer to the Minister was now introduced.

Mr Macmillan was of the view that even with these changes the new system would depend, perhaps overmuch, on goodwill and cooperation to produce results, and that a complete reorganisation might be needed. In fact rapid and far-reaching results did emerge. Within a few weeks the Cabinet had approved Mr Sandys' plans. The White Paper, published on 4 April, based future policy on the deterrent power of nuclear armament. As a consequence it envisaged the end of national service after 1960, the reduction of the role of Fighter Command simply to the protection of the nuclear bases, a smaller Royal Navy, and many disbandments and amalgamations of historic regiments. But these conclusions were reached not so much through but rather in spite of the existing organisational system. They were brought about by Mr Sandys' willpower and strong views, reinforced by the knowledge of the Prime Minister's full support, and not by any classical use of the planning and coordinating machinery. Indeed, in the absence of any major body of central staff that he could feel to be his own, Mr Sandys used a personal 'cabinet' rather than the Chiefs of Staff machinery, and preceded by a series of often nocturnal confrontations. It was a particularly awkward time for the Service Ministers, who were half left out in the cold and found themselves in an equivocal position between the pulls of political and Service loyalties.

For Mr Macmillan the substantive outcome was satisfactory. His requirements for a fundamental review and the prospect of major reductions in defence expenditure were met. But he clearly judged that the results were achieved in spite of the organisation. He therefore invited Mr Sandys in May 1957, once his Minister had steered the radical White Paper through Parliament, to examine combining the headquarters administration of the three Services into a single integrated department which would also take on the functions of the Ministry of Supply. In contrast with the earlier review of strategy and resources this examination made slow, indeed imperceptible, progress. By March 1958 little had emerged. Mr Macmillan then appointed an *ad hoc* group of ministers to discuss the plans. There was little unanimity. The Chiefs of Staff were perturbed and divided.

Eventually in July 1958 a White Paper was issued on the Central Organisation for Defence (Cmnd 476). It said little new. Its substance was essentially a formal confirmation of the 1957 directive, with a limited degree of further tightening-up. There was no basic change in the structure of the five Ministries involved. The personal position of the Minister of Defence was strengthened and that of the Service Ministers reduced. It was now laid down that proposals made by them on any matter of defence policy were to be submitted first to the Minister of Defence. A Defence Board was created at ministerial level to assist coordination. The Chairman of the Chiefs of Staff Committee became Chief of the Defence Staff and was given a small staff of his own, but the Chiefs of Staff Committee in its collective capacity remained the source of professional military advice to the Government.

This outcome was seen in very different lights. To the Prime Minister it had been a Pyrrhic victory, conducted in an unpleasant atmosphere, and which left him unwilling to reopen the issue for some years. To some of the Chiefs of Staff it represented the maximum change they could tolerate. They attached the highest importance to the concessions they had secured about their continued right of access to the Cabinet and to the Prime Minister, and to their continued responsibility for operations. Moreover, it was their agreed advice which had to be tendered by the new Chief of the Defence Staff and, even when agreement was not possible, he had to report their views as well as to tender his own.

1959 saw two significant changes in appointment. Mr Sandys was moved to the Ministry of Aviation, the successor to the Ministry of Supply, and was replaced by Mr Harold Watkinson. As Chief of the Defence Staff, Admiral of the Fleet Lord Mountbatten took over from Marshal of the Royal Air Force Sir William Dickson, thus incidentally setting a pattern of the rotational filling of the post, which continued until 1985.

Mr Watkinson's period in office saw no significant attempts by him to make major changes within Whitehall. Whatever his own views may have been he was doubtless aware of the Prime Minister's disenchantment with the subject and of the other pressing calls on the Government's time. But Lord Mountbatten's position had already been made clear in the earlier rounds, moulded in part by his wartime experiences in Combined Operations and as an inter-Service Supreme Commander in South-East Asia, and also by a temperamental liking for personal authority and for the embodiment of decision-taking in one man. Essentially he favoured all advice on the key areas – defence policy, plans and operations, weapons systems – being channelled through the Chief of the Defence Staff to the Minister. As a consequence the Service Boards would be abolished and a functional structure created with functional ministers. But the steps he could take and get through on his own were limited. Within the Whitehall organisation he pressed through the appointment of a central Director of Plans who would also be the chairman of the Joint Planning Committee. His Chief of Staff colleagues agreed to a one-year experiment which began in September 1959 and which, on review, they subsequently agreed to make permanent. In the structure of the overseas Service Headquarters Lord Mountbatten was able to move further and faster. Political, strategic and diplomatic realities on the ground in the several major theatres where HMG still had commitments pointed to the need for a machinery to produce a coordinated policy and to be able to respond quickly to the requirements of London. The process began with the creation in 1960 in Cyprus of a Near East Command, followed by a Middle East Command in Aden in 1961 and a Far East Command in Singapore in 1962. The structure was headed in each case by a unified Commander-in-Chief who was given a small planning staff and who was placed over the single-Service formations. Thus the coordination of plans and operations could be achieved, but still basically using the large single-Service Headquarters which alone had the staffs for and retained responsibility for all personnel and logistic matters as well as the detailed conduct of operations.

The next major step was still to lie with Mr Macmillan. Just over four years after the 1958 White Paper he felt that the time was opportune to return to the issue. Progress had been made on other major national and international issues: in the defence area notably Polaris. He had replaced Mr Watkinson with Mr Peter Thorneycroft. Lord Mountbatten was still there and Mr Macmillan had the impression that the current generation of single-Service Chiefs of Staff was not all against change. He therefore decided that he would launch a new assault on the organisation. Indeed, intellectually, he could see a logical case for going beyond the organisation within Whitehall and creating one Service. But, at the same time, he recognised the importance and strength of tradition and local loyalties among servicemen. He summed up the task as finding a way to meet two needs: unification would increase efficiency and reduce waste (and he had in mind specifically such areas as stores, hospitals, transport and communications); diversity would keep alive the spirit of the men. In setting down these thoughts he concluded that if the will to cooperate were there, useful coordination could be brought about.

In December 1962, after some exploratory talks, Mr Macmillan was rapidly aware that there would be strong reactions. Taking into account the importance he attached to securing an attitude of mind that was willing to cooperate, he recognised the vital importance of getting the preliminary spadework done by people who would carry the confidence of the Services. He therefore looked outside the Ministry of Defence to two senior military figures who were by then detached from the hurly-burly but who were both held in high respect by the Services and who had deep experience of the subject – General Lord Ismay and Lieutenant-General Sir Ian Jacob.

From then on, the timetable was remarkably swift for a major reorganisation that was not summarily imposed but was the subject of internal and parliamentary discussion. Generals Ismay and Jacob reported by the middle of February. The Minister of Defence went to Cabinet and then outlined the Government's intentions to Parliament on 4 March. April and May saw detailed internal discussions during which the Prime Minister kept in close touch with his Minister of Defence, apprehensive that, notwithstanding Mr Thorneycroft's strong support, the changes might still be trapped by the weight of inertia which defeated him in 1958. The proposals were then embodied in a White Paper (Cmnd 2097) which was tabled on 16 July and debated on 31 July. (Its key organisation chart is at Appendix B in this volume.) Thereafter it was procedural and practical issues only which had to be settled: legislative changes; major accommodation requirements; postings; the discipline of the financial year. The outcome was an implementation date of 1 April 1964.

The Jacob/Ismay Report identified three broad possible courses of action: essentially the status quo with slight modifications; a fully integrated and functional ministry; and third, as a compromise but possibly also as a precursor to the fully functional solution, the subordination of the Service Ministries or Departments in a unified ministry with some changes but with these old Departments still retaining many of their previous functions. To point up the ultimate possibility their report outlined the concept of a single Service, and saw as a first step, or as a worthwhile measure in its own right, the creation of a single list for senior officers.

Tactically this approach with its several options was wise. It overtly placed the ultimate decision on political shoulders. By questioning the effectiveness of the first option, the report prepared the way for the middle course. Certainly it appeared as early as late February 1963 in talks with the Service Ministers and their Chiefs of Staff that there was a readiness to accept the middle course, even if, in the subsequent weeks, there was in-fighting over important details.

UNIFICATION

The opening section of the 1963 White Paper, it is interesting and not wholly surprising to note, sets out its fundamental aims in terms not very different from those of the 1946 paper. A unified ministry is essential if the defence budget is to strike a proper balance. Better arrangements are needed in the whole field of operational requirements and associated research and development. In certain administrative areas a common or major user approach may be desirable. But the separate identity of the Services will be preserved. In what way therefore did the changes embodied in this White Paper make it such a significant milestone? In some respects the most important changes were psychological and physical. All the staffs, with the exception of the very important area of those weapons systems still under the Ministry of Aviation, were to be in one ministry under one Secretary of State. To give this concept practical reality, large blocks of staff, primarily in the defence policy areas but including most of the senior officers, were to be accommodated in one building in Whitehall. Not only did this symbolise change, it had the practical effect that many staff, both military and civilian, were rubbing shoulders informally as well as formally with colleagues in related areas of work whom they had hitherto rarely, if ever, met. They could no longer unite so easily in opposition to the 'them' in the old separate Storey's Gate Ministry of Defence. They were now part of it. And with each round of postings the memories of separation would become weaker and unification would become the accepted norm. Collocation in the Ministry of Defence building was also applied to key Ministry of Aviation staff even though they remained part of a separate Ministry.

The keystone of the whole new structure lay in the position, powers and responsibilities of the proposed new Secretary of State. He was to have complete control both of defence policy and of the machinery for the administration of the three Services. In theory earlier ministers had this power: for example Mr Sandys had been given an all-embracing directive by Mr Macmillan. But there had been no associated machinery to make the power effective whereas this time it was to be a question of the control not just of the policies but also of the staff resources. The line of authority and responsibility was to run unbroken from him through all the military, scientific and administrative staffs.

In Cabinet terms the resources at the disposal of this one minister would be very great. But the wider considerations involved in determining defence policy and which were the primary concern of some other Government Departments were still just as valid and important. The White Paper formalised these in the creation of a Defence and Overseas Policy Committee, not dissimilar to the Defence Committee of the 1946 Paper.

Within the Ministry, the Secretary of State was to be supported by three Ministers of State and three Parliamentary Under-Secretaries of State, still with single-Service responsibilities as their primary function, but he was given the authority to delegate functions to them as he thought fit across the whole defence field. The seven Ministers, together with what the Paper described as the Secretary of State's three principal advisers – the Chief of the Defence Staff (CDS), the Chief Scientific Adviser (CSA) and the Permanent Under-Secretary of State (PUS) – and the three single-Service Chiefs of Staff were to form the newly created Defence Council, which was needed legally and which formally was to take over the powers of command and administrative control exercised by the Board of Admiralty and the Army and Air Councils. But the Paper recognised the large managerial responsibilities involved in running a Service. The long established Boards and Councils were to be continued much as before though formally they were now sub-Committees of the Defence Council. Linkage with the large responsibilities of the Ministry of Aviation and the Ministry of Public Building and Works in the defence field was to be achieved by the attendance of their ministers at the Defence Council for appropriate business.

Other than by this reference there was no other organisational provision affecting works matters. On the procurement side the problems were greater and the need for close working was recognised. Ministry of Aviation representation on the key research and development official committees was provided. But the Paper argued strongly that in the aviation field civil and military research and development were indivisible. To transfer all these responsibilities – taking into account the likely growth in civil aviation activities – to the Ministry of Defence would place on it a very heavy additional load, much of it outside the defence sphere.

It is understandable that Generals Jacob and Ismay did not themselves embark on this course. The absorption of the three Service Ministries was a big enough task, and the bulk of their effort and that of the follow-up teams went into the structures under the three principal official advisers.

THE NEW CENTRAL SUB-STRUCTURE

The changes in the area of military policy, comprising the existing small central staffs and the Naval, General and Air staffs, were carefully balanced, reflecting both the pressures for centralisation and the sensitivities of the single-Service Chiefs of Staff. The dominant principle was that the Chiefs of Staff Committee would remain in its existing form and would be the source of collective advice to the Government. A Defence Staff was created out of the Naval, General and Air Staffs together with the existing joint Service staffs, but this Defence Staff was to be responsible not to the CDS as his own staff, but to the Chiefs of Staff Committee. Some new central structures were created but the only area for complete integration was in the intelligence field. This compromise, weighted as it was towards the maintenance of the position of the single-Service Chiefs of Staff, was a somewhat surprising outcome given Lord Mountbatten's strong belief in much greater centralisation. It has to be interpreted, in part, as a reflection of the suspicions of him held by his Chiefs of Staff colleagues and of the extent of their independent influence.

The second area, that of the scientific staff, was, outwardly, less constrained by traditional single-Service loyalties. Technical change was becoming much faster. Costs and complexity of new weapons were increasing rapidly. These factors pointed to the key place of the CSA in the new structure and to a strengthening of the staff at his disposal. But, closely analogous to the arrangements within the new military Defence Staff, the majority of the scientific staff would be working in the single-Service departments alongside their military colleagues in the Naval, General and Air staffs.

The movement towards centralisation was greatest in the third major prong: that of the PUS's department. There was the initial advantage that, however great might be the ties of the administrative staff to individual Service Ministries in which most of them had spent their whole career, and consequently by association to an individual uniformed Service, they already all belonged to one corps, the Civil Service. The military problems of career structure and loyalty in the field did not therefore arise, but even so the traditional affiliations were strong. It was acknowledged that a long haul would be needed, helped by a mixture of cross-posting and the recruitment of a new generation of 'defence' civil servants, to break down all the prejudices. That the Government recognised the scale of the problem can be seen by the almost rhetorical appeal in the White Paper for a 'broadening of loyalties'. One organisational way of bringing this about was adopted in the key field of the formulation of the budgetary and political assumptions and policies. A sizeable civilian central defence secretariat was set up with three major sections for programmes and budget, for policy and for administration, each section covering all three Services, and each under the senior charge of a deputy under-secretary. These staffs were intended to play a major role in pulling together all the strands needed to achieve a balanced defence policy and to increase the coordination and cost-effectiveness of management policies. But the financial building-bricks still remained in the hands of the Service Departments. The Vote structure was still to be based essentially on the three Services and the Estimates for the three Services would continue to be debated separately. The new central programme and budget staffs were therefore short of tools that would give them the degree of power needed to match the intentions of the organisation.

3 Unification and the Healey Period: 1964–70

April 1964 saw a great game of musical chairs. Whitehall Gardens became the main Ministry of Defence building. Three thousand staff were concentrated there, many brought in from other buildings. Those who were already there were moved into new offices. The newly assembled staff were still finding their way around, and the paint was still new on the nameplates of the new-style ministerial appointments when the October 1964 election returned a Labour Government. This Government, re-elected with a larger majority in 1966, remained in power until 1970. During the whole of this period Mr Denis Healey was the Secretary of State for Defence, the longest ever occupancy of the head of this Ministry in any of its guises.

THE BACKGROUND ATMOSPHERE

This period of nearly six years saw major alterations by the Government in the country's social and economic policies, punctuated and disturbed by financial and economic crises. Defence as a major spender was constantly under the microscope. The repeated and sometimes very urgent demands for reductions in defence expenditure led to fundamental questions being asked about overseas roles; about the capabilities that the Forces should be given to carry out these roles, and about the selection of individual weapon systems to contribute to the effectiveness of these capabilities. There was a gradual and then accelerating pattern of withdrawal from the further overseas areas, and a move towards putting more emphasis in Europe, even if that raised balance-of-payments problems of its own. There was much controversy and doubt about the realism and cost-effectiveness of solely national production of the most sophisticated, technically difficult and highly expensive weapons systems, given added point by the inevitable fact that their very cost restricted them to short and therefore industrially uneconomical production runs. The dilemma of finding the right balance was brought out by Mr Healey in remarks towards the end of this period, when he laid claim to the value to the nation of a reduction of defence expenditure from over 7 per cent of GNP in 1965 to 5½ per cent by 1970 and a target of under 5 per cent by 1972, in releasing resources for housing, health, education and social security, yet at the same time stressed that defence expenditure was essential if security was not to be imperilled.

These pressures all focused attention on the key areas of resource allocation and equipment cost-effectiveness which had been identified in the 1963 White Paper – and indeed in earlier statements – as posing the greatest problems for the organisation. The adequacy of the 1963/4 changes was being quickly and severely tested before the new structures with their newly posted incumbents had time to settle down. The challenge would have been a great one at any time. The very speed and broad-brush nature of these changes made it almost inevitable that refinements and adjustments would be needed.

There was also the personality of the Secretary of State, heading, leading and sometimes fighting the organisation for the whole of this period. Mr Healey had prepared himself in opposition for the post: he was tough and intellectually capable of taking on the staff and staff advice single-handed. He would not be tied down by an organisation and was quite ready to improvise or ignore its procedures.

There was a further, third factor hanging over the organisation during this period: the shadow of the radical solution. The ultimate concept had been outlined in the Jacob/Ismay Report. The preference of Lord Mountbatten for a functional structure was known. Canada was embarking on fundamental changes in the structure not just of its defence ministry but of its armed forces. Mr Robert McNamara was seeking in Washington to solve the intellectual conundrum of resource allocation by the superimposition of an army of systems analysts. Then there were those commentators in the press and in Parliamentary Committees who held that the Ministry of Defence was simply too big and cumbersome and therefore by definition inefficient, and that its long record of alleged failures would never be rectified until, as it were, the three posts in each area of headquarters activity were wrapped up into one. There was considerable uncertainty in the air. It was clearly desirable to form a judgement within a reasonable period whether a further major change was desirable and, if so, how soon.

Looked at in retrospect there is a certain pattern to the period. A series of steps, taken at quite short intervals, all moved in the general direction of tightening up the effectiveness of the new structure, and in particular its ability to challenge itself, to pose options, to judge dispassionately. These various steps were all taken within the basic framework of the 1964 structure. There was, in the middle of the period, a deliberate decision not to change fundamentally the model, taken after considerable study and discussion. There is the often quoted '*bon mot*' attributed to Mr Healey about not removing a man's appendix when he is lifting the grand piano. It is a colourful metaphor but it probably conceals the fact that he had not been convinced that the case for major change had been shown to be of sufficient extra benefit to warrant the cost of upheaval. Furthermore, given his energy and intellectual self-confidence, he may have seen attractions in being in charge of a somewhat deficient organisation which would not be so capable of uniting effectively to defeat him.

If overall defence policy and consequent resource allocation dominated political thinking and consequently the scrutiny of the adequacy of the organisation, this period also saw a sustained concentration on saving money and increasing effectiveness in the administrative areas of the Armed Forces. Here, too, the pattern is of gradual change rather than major upheaval. This pattern was dictated in large part by the decisions not to alter the basic structure of the three Services and not to go for a functional organisation within the personnel and logistic areas of the Ministry. Therefore the approach was to tackle the problems area by area and to ensure that the higher organisation imparted sufficient drive to the work, rather than to try to solve the problems from top down by a fundamental change in the support structure.

THE INITIAL IMPLEMENTATION

The first step, taken immediately on the new administration coming into office, was to allocate the three Ministers of State across-the-board responsibilities – international policy; personnel and logistics; research, development and production – as well as their single-Service primary functions. This was done very tentatively, as it was made clear that they could not exercise executive responsibilities. It was stressed that this was no more than an interim step and that any further step would depend on wider changes in the structure. The

Minister of State for the Army, who was also appointed Deputy Secretary of State, was given the further task of looking at the whole structure in Commands as well as the Ministry headquarters.

The Government's first annual Defence White Paper in early 1965 (Cmnd 2592) concentrated on the train of policy studies it had set in hand to correct what it termed its legacy 'of seriously over-stretched and dangerously under-equipped forces'. Major equipment decisions had already been taken to cancel two new aircraft, the P1154 supersonic fighter and the HS 681 transport, both of which were at the early stages of development, and instead to look for off-the-shelf purchases. These and other big issues in the equipment field, such as the future of the aircraft carrier and of the TSR 2, led the Paper to stress the importance of the machinery, via a newly unified Operational Requirements Committee, for the closer scrutiny of new requirements. The Paper also announced the creation of a Defence Operational Analysis Establishment (DOAE) at West Byfleet, where a combination of scientists and military officers would, it was hoped, strengthen the data base at the disposal of the Ministry and, in particular, be a valuable tool for the Chief Scientific Adviser.

The Paper laid considerable emphasis on the opportunity afforded by the new organisation to consider a substantial extension of the arrangements for inter-Service cooperation in administrative areas either by unification, where lands and strategic communications were the first targets, or by rationalisation on a major user basis, starting here with accommodation stores, food and medical stores. To assist in this thrust toward common supply and logistic practices a new appointment of Director General of Supply Coordination was made.

1965 saw a continuous drive, carried out at a fast pace and against a tight timetable imposed by the Secretary of State, to study and determine future policies. In part, the new machinery was used and the areas of the Defence Staff and the Defence Secretariat were heavily involved. In part, *ad hoc* groups were set up to produce reports. The outcome was a series of decisions on the three fronts of commitments, capabilities and individual items of equipment. In Germany, while the forces were to be kept at their existing levels, conventional air capability was to be strengthened at the expense of nuclear strike aircraft. Outside Europe a general policy was formulated that HMG would not undertake major operations except in cooperation with allies. In specific theatres decisions were announced to withdraw from Aden after independence in 1968, to make reductions in the Far East as soon as conditions permitted, and to make substantial economies in Cyprus and Malta. Two major equipment decisions, which were attributed to these changes in commitments, were not to build the new aircraft carrier CVA 01 and to satisfy a minimum long-range air strike capability with the purchase of 50 F-111s from the USA, as a partial replacement for the TSR2.

One by-product of these decisions was the resignation not only of the First Sea Lord, but also of the Minister of State for the Royal Navy in 1966. Mr Mayhew's resignation undoubtedly pointed up the dilemma of the Service Minister, tied so closely as he sometimes became to the views of his particular Service.

These decisions were summarised in the 1966 Defence White Paper (Cmnd 2901) which once again gave a detailed analysis of the progress of individual areas of rationalisation, though this time they did not have any organisational consequences. But certain other changes, mostly modest but all towards the strengthening of the centre, were announced. A measure of unification was introduced in the areas of Security and the Defence Public Relations Staff. The Defence Intelligence Staff which had been created in 1964 was reorganised internally on to a functional instead of a single-Service basis.

Commenting on the efficacy of the organisation as a whole, the Paper confirmed the rightness of the 1964 unification, but acknowledged that the final organisational shape had not yet been determined. It reported that, following up the work initially carried out under the Deputy Secretary of State (Mr Mulley) who had been supported by a study by the Second Permanent Under-Secretary of State (Defence Secretariat), a special committee had been appointed in April 1965 to study the structure at all levels, both in the Ministry and in Commands. The Chairman was a Deputy Under-Secretary of State (Mr Geraghty, with whose name the Report was subsequently identified), assisted by representatives of the three Services, an economic adviser and an industrialist.

THE GERAGHTY REPORT AND THE HIGH POINT OF THE CONCEPT OF FUNCTIONAL UNIFICATION

The Committee reported a year later. Its work remains interesting and significant in that it represents the high point of thinking in favour of rapid change to a functional structure. It started from the premise that there was a strong and continuing groundswell towards such a development, based on the long-term thrust of the Jacob/ Ismay report; on the statement in the 1965 Defence White Paper that 'the question is not whether further changes take place but what changes, in what direction and at what pace'; and on the contemporary changes in Canada and the United States. The fact that the Committee's report was effectively buried from public gaze by not being published and by being dismissed in one clause in the 1967 Defence White Paper (Cmnd 3203) – 'These changes in organisation have been decided in the light of experience and studies over the last two years, including the work of the special committee which was appointed to study the structure at all levels' – has obscured its strengths and weaknesses and its importance in forcing major decisions. It showed great prescience in many specific fields. But the thinness of the argumentation in support of its sweeping conclusion, and the dubiousness of the assumption that those in the field were qualified to influence strongly the organisation of the centre, resulted, when taken together, in a search for more prag- matic, less doctrinaire solutions. Nevertheless, put at its lowest, it helped to provoke a series of measures many of which can individu- ally be seen to be aimed to meet its criticisms.

The Report saw four main needs: to be able to have a continuous defence review; to analyse systems and options; to exercise effective control over research, development and production; and to have maximum cost-effectiveness in administration. More generally, it saw the need for close political control of operations, and considered that national manpower trends, meaning as they would the availability of fewer, better-educated recruits, called for a unitary approach covering all three Services to ensure optimum use. The Committee brought back from their visits to overseas Commands the general message that the Services worked together well in the field in spite of what they called silly differences in their terms of service. There was no interest shown in the field in the MOD structure; those serving only wanted clear directions, quicker support and supply, and a recognisable head of each Service.

The Committee reviewed the various support areas. In the supply field they found in favour of integration rather than rationalisation, while recognising that it was a step in the dark which could involve loss of expertise and disturbance of Service loyalties. In the repair field they saw a need for centralised control even though they acknowledged the special problems of ship repair. As to personnel administration, they recognised the different patterns of work in the three Services but considered that some of the differences were no more than anomalies. They went on to assert that the Canadians had found it easy to resolve problems under their new integrated management – not a view that many would have shared some years later. They considered civilian labour was made a more difficult problem by the existence of three separate civilian labour sections. They saw little progress towards commonality in training being achieved as long as the approach was by means of rationalisation on a three-Service basis.

Other areas were similarly castigated. There was too much dispersal of effort in the three mostly separate scientific structures. There was inadequate control over resources, notably works services, in the management of major support units. The existing arrangements with the Ministry of Public Building and Works (which had been created overnight in 1962 for political reasons, with little attention being paid to the way in which the defence part of its responsibilities would be made to work efficiently with the quartering staffs of the Services) and with the Ministry of Aviation caused extreme dissatisfaction within the Services. Looking back over the recent defence review the Committee could identify no mechanism for giving ministers a full range of options, prepared and analysed on a valid comparable basis. In coming to this view the Geraghty Committee underline the experiences of the Templer Committee which had been set up in 1964 to examine the rationalisation of air power. Its work had been hindered by the problem of the production of totally different costings by different parts of the Ministry. These deficiencies were contrasted in the Geraghty Report with the USA's sophisticated use of systems analysis.

Their general conclusions were that the present system of organisation had a transitional air to it – they instanced the anomalies between the independence of the Principal Administrative Officers (PAOs) and the Principal Personnel Officers (PPOs), and the requirement placed on the newly created Second PUS (Defence Secretariat) to identify fields in which administration might with advantage be placed on a defence rather than a single-Service basis. Consequently the system would become progressively more uneconomical, being near as it was to the limits of its capacity for useful development.

Where then in the Committee's eyes should the organisation go?

They saw five theoretical choices. First, there could be a reversion to pre-1964. Second, the existing organisation could continue with a diminution of the Defence Secretariat role in the field of management, possibly by strengthening the position of the Deputy Chief of the Defence Staff (Personnel and Logistics) – DCDS (P&L) – as Chairman of the PPOs and PAOs. Third, the centre could be strengthened on American lines but, involving as that did the superimposition of large staffs over large Service Departments, they concluded that the UK could not afford the luxury. There remained, fourth, partial integration, or fifth, a totally unitary Ministry. They favoured the last because they believed that unification in such areas as personnel would be more efficient than single-Service management.

The method of organising the unitary ministry was somewhat cursorily described. Essentially, it would involve the creation of Personnel, Material and Supply Controllerates, with subordinate functional areas manned by tri-Service staff. The functional controllers would each report, in so far as their responsibilities to the user were concerned, to each of the three single-Service Chiefs of Staff in the latter's continued capacity as a Head of Service. Separately, CDS's position would be strengthened by having a DCDS (Systems and Requirements).

ALTERNATIVE MEASURES

The timing of the submission of the report was fortuitous. Defence ministers had been under continuous pressure for two years reviewing all aspects of the defence programme. Irrespective of the views of those in the field, they had themselves acquired considerable experience of the strengths and weaknesses of the new structure, and also of the pressures within Whitehall and more narrowly within the Ministry itself, on the basis of which they could judge the feasibility and acceptability of further changes. Over the following eighteen months there was a series of such changes and adjustments of some importance in several parts of the Ministry. It is idle to speculate about the proportionate contribution of direct experience, internal advice and the views of such specially appointed bodies as the Geraghty Committee. What is relevant is to note how many of the individual changes respond to the criticisms in their Report, even if the overall solution itself is different.

It is also essential to relate these changes to the wider national and international scene. Economic and financial difficulties were increasing and the pressures on the defence budget were consequently rising. Three Defence Statements over the next eighteen months, supplemented by interim special announcements, symbolise the pressure, even though the second of these Statements – the supplementary one of July 1967 (Cmnd 3357) – made the brave, if not foolhardy, assertion that this particular statement marked the end of the process of review which had been going on for three years. Such optimism was rapidly overtaken by the devaluation of November 1967 and by the February 1968 Defence White Paper (Cmnd 3540) which announced yet another acceleration in the speed of withdrawal from the Far East, as well as reductions in capabilities by such measures as the cancellation of the F-111 – ordered only two years earlier – and large reductions in the numbers of uniformed personnel and of air transport resources. (It is worthy of note that the organisation proved capable of handling efficiently the hurried series of withdrawals which were both logistically difficult and politically sensitive.) One overall effect was to concentrate the military effort more in Europe where the British contribution would be part of the NATO command structure, and thereby to reduce the need for unified military headquarters overseas and, consequently, their significance for the structure of the Ministry itself.

The first change to be announced was the appointment in January 1967 of two functional Ministers of State, one for administration and one for equipment, to replace the three Service Ministers of State. Thus, instead of having one central minister – the Secretary of State – and six single-Service orientated ministers, the balance was redressed to three and three. The single-Service Parliamentary Secretaries were to remain and to be the normal chairmen of the Service Boards. The 1967 Defence White Paper (Cmnd 3203) stressed the need for greater ministerial help for the Secretary of State in across-the-board matters. This was undoubtedly valid. But the change probably also reflected the unsatisfactory nature of the two-hatted arrangement for the Ministers of State introduced in 1964, the political lessons of Mr Mayhew's resignation and the views of such bodies as the Geraghty Committee on the need for greater control over the equipment programme and the greater drive in the search for cost-effectiveness in the support areas. This latter concern was also being met by the announcement in the Defence White Paper in the following month of the creation of a new and very senior military post in the centre, entitled the Chief Adviser Personnel and Logistics (CAPL), who would be the principal adviser to ministers in these fields and who would be the permanent chairman of the PPOs and the PAOs. This upgrading and strengthening of the DCDS (P&L) can be seen as an acceptance of the second of the Geraghty Report's five options.

The White Paper of February 1967 also announced another organisational creation, that of the Programme Evaluation Group. It could be regarded not unfairly as a poor man's American systems analysis structure. It responded to the criticisms voiced in the Geraghty Report and doubtless directly experienced by Ministers, that the existing staff systems, including the Defence Staff itself, were not producing enough options. Its function was to apply critical and constructive comment to those major proposals going to the Secretary of State concerned with future defence policy and programmes. It was a free-standing body with no executive responsibility, a position which gave it freedom but made it very dependent on patronage for its influence.

The fourth and last change announced in this Paper concerned the defence scientific staff. Here the change was possibly due only in part to the need for greater central scientific effort, but rather more to the need for a pragmatic solution to the replacement of Sir Solly Zuckermann who, as the Chief Scientific Adviser, had been identified in 1964 as one of the three principal advisers of the Secretary of State. The paper now announced a split into two posts: a Chief Adviser (Projects) and a Chief Adviser (Studies). Primarily pragmatic or not, the creation of the Chief Adviser (Projects) at least gave the new post of Minister of Defence for Equipment a very experienced adviser over the whole field of equipment hardware at Defence Council level.

The next twelve months saw further steps in the two directions of giving greater support to the two functional Ministers and of strengthening the powers and roles of central staffs. The Minister of Defence for Equipment was provided in August 1967 with a Deputy Under-Secretary of State (Equipment) to help him in dealing with general questions of research and development, procurement and production, and also sales, the latter task involving working with the Head of Defence Sales, another recent creation and filled from outside by a leading businessman. On the military side a Deputy Chief of Defence Staff (Operational Requirements) was appointed on CDS's staff. His main duty was to give added weight and thrust to the impartial assessment of proposed weapons systems concepts. There was also a significant change within CDS's staff in the field of planning, where the long-established joint planning staff was split into two, each under an Assistant Chief of Defence Staff, one to handle operations and contingency plans, and the other to formulate policies and plans including the fields of size, shape and deployment. The latter area was to absorb the functions of the Programme Evaluation Group which had lasted for only just over a year. The responsibility for providing ministers with an independent look at proposals and alternative options was thereby brought into the executive staff machine and embodied in CDS's staff and thus within the machinery of the Chiefs of Staff Committee.

Within the PUS's department, too, there were significant changes. The Geraghty Report had drawn attention to the inefficiency of having three civilian labour sections. In August 1967 a restructuring was introduced which not only rectified this but went further, in that the appointment of a Deputy Under-Secretary of State (Civilian Management) created a single civilian management organisation for all the civilian staff. There was also a major reorganisation of Accounting Officer responsibilities, designed to bring the structure more closely in line with the responsibilities of the two functional ministers. The three single-Service Second PUSs, who were the direct successors in 1964 of the Permanent Under-Secretaries of the former Service Ministries, were replaced by two functional Second PUSs, one for administration and one for equipment. While this change was to be introduced at the beginning of the 1968/9 financial year, it was recognised that they would have to function initially by using the relevant parts of the single-Service Vote structure. It was envisaged that the Vote structure would be changed by 1970.

The 1968 Defence White Paper (Cmnd 3540) explicitly stressed that these various changes in no way affected the continuance of three separate Services or of the detailed management of these Services by the Service Boards. But there were changes, some inevitable, in the composition of the Boards. With the creation of the two functional Second PUSs the senior civil servant wholly devoted to a Service Department was now a Deputy Under-Secretary of State (DUS) and he became a member of the Board with responsibility for financial and administrative guidance. But it was provided that the Second PUSs could also attend the Boards as appropriate. Conversely, the following year, 1969, saw the reduction of the military representation on each Board by one, as a result of the abolition of the appointments of the Deputy Chiefs of Staff. This step was basically taken for reasons of economy. The initial creation of the Ministry in 1964 and the subsequent strengthening in the centre had resulted in some growth in senior posts. The abolition of the single-Service Deputy Chiefs of Staff – as, for that matter, the reduction in Second PUSs from four to two by the combined measures of functionalisation and the abolition of the Second PUS (Defence Secretariat) – went some way to redress the balance. For the rest, 1969 saw a continuation of the process of bringing together civilian staff working in the same area in the three Service Departments. On the same lines as the previous unification of civilian management, unified directorates were created for statistics, management services, accounts and contracts. One unintentional consequence was that an organisational pattern was established, which lasted until the 1980s, and under which the degree of integration, rationalisation or just simplification which arose in these and other civilian administrative areas went much further than in the military and scientific staffs. This lack of structural balance created its own tensions and inefficiencies.

A FURTHER MAJOR REVIEW

By the time of the 1970 Defence White Paper (Cmnd 4290) the Government were entering their sixth year of office. During that time Mr Healey had presided over a steady evolution of the Ministry from a comparatively loosely knit federal organisation to one which, while still providing for the management of the individual Services on a single-Service basis through the medium of the Service Boards, saw a considerably strengthened centre and an increasing degree of functionalisation of activities on the civilian side. During that same time the Forces had been withdrawn from major overseas theatres, had contracted considerably in size and had seen a steady and large reduction in the percentage of GNP spent on defence. It was therefore decided to set up a Committee, this time under the chairmanship of the PUS himself (Sir James Dunnett), to see whether the organisation as it had evolved matched what was termed the new and less varied pattern of defence responsibilities. Responding to this framework the Committee was specifically charged to look at all areas of activity of the Ministry, and to consider the extent to which work was still needed to be done and whether the structure of consultation need be so complex, and to appraise the possibilities for devolution or delegation.

A basic assumption that was laid down was that the three Services should continue as separate bodies. Given this assumption, the Committee was asked to review whether the structure of consultation should be simplified, whether work had to be done within the Ministry or could be devolved elsewhere, and whether changes in organisation would aid efficiency. The Committee was also asked to take into particular account the studies already in hand under Sir John Mallabar's chairmanship into the Royal Dockyards and the Royal Ordnance Factories and the Army Department's internal study into the future Command structure in the UK.

From the start it was recognised that this would be a lengthy study, as it was intended to probe deeply into the practices as well as the organisation in all the large specialist areas: for example, contracts and audit. But a first report on the higher structure was submitted within a few months and decisions were conveyed in the February 1970 Statement on the Defence Estimates. Two recommendations were put into immediate effect. The CDS was given greater authority in his own right, as distinct from his position as Chairman of the Chiefs of Staff Committee. This greater authority took the form of giving him the authority to initiate work independently within the tri-service element of the Defence Staffs. There was a similar strengthening of the position and powers of the Chief Adviser Personnel and Logistics. He was given power to initiate and coordinate studies and other action on matters affecting the three Services, and the change was symbolised by dropping the word 'Adviser' from his title.

A third measure, also aimed at moving in the same direction of strengthening the central control of policy, concerned the ministerial structure. The Committee favoured combining the two functional posts at Minister of State level introduced in 1967 into one essentially coordinating deputy minister to be called the Minister of Defence for the Armed Forces. This post would be able to straddle all aspects of personnel, logistics and equipment concerning any or all of the Services, and thus avoid the weakness of splits at the ministerial level between requirements and logistics on the one hand and equipment on the other. A further proposal within the ministerial structure was the abolition of the Parliamentary Under-Secretaries of State with single-Service responsibilities and their replacement by one or more Parliamentary Secretaries covering all three Services. The

February 1970 Statement commented favourably on these proposals and stated that they would be introduced towards the end of the year, by which time the Committee would have been able to work out the consequent changes in subordinate organisation needed to support the new ministerial structure.

4 The 1970s: A Time of Consolidation

THE BACKGROUND ATMOSPHERE

This decade, if adjusted by a few months at its start and end, conveniently spans two administrations: the Conservative one under Mr Edward Heath from 1970 to 1974, and the Labour one under Mr Harold Wilson, succeeded by Mr James Callaghan, from 1974 to 1979. Lord Carrington was Secretary of State for all but a few weeks of the Conservative Government – Mr Ian Gilmour being in the post only for the first few weeks of 1974 – and Mr Roy Mason and Mr Fred Mulley shared the period of the Labour Government.

Organisationally, it was a time essentially of evolution and consolidation in the basic structure of the Ministry, with the very important exception of the fundamental changes of principle and approach in the procurement area. But even after leaving on one side the major study under Mr Derek Rayner of Marks and Spencer which led to the creation of the Procurement Executive within the Ministry of Defence, it was still a time of extensive and continuing review of the organisation of the Ministry. Two major committees reported: the Headquarters Organisation Committee in a report spanning three parts and over the period of 1969–72, and the Management Review in one document spanning 1975–6. Their method of conduct had much in common. Their working approach involved an extensive look at all areas of the Ministry and not just the seemingly more glamorous defence policy areas. They were each headed by the PUS of the day (Sir James Dunnett for the first, and Sir Michael Cary succeeded by Sir Frank Cooper for the second), with predominantly an in-house membership, though with one or two influential outsiders. They were both spread out over a lengthy period with much of the spadework being done by a full-time, mixed civilian and military secretariat. Other lasting features of the decade were the continuing pressures on two aspects of the Ministry's work: the drive for economies in the staffing both of the Ministry itself and of the command Headquarters; and the search for and conflicting beliefs in the scale of further savings that might flow from greater rationalisation.

THE 1970 CHANGE OF GOVERNMENT

In the previous chapter the setting-up of the Headquarters Organisation Committee (HOC) has been described. Its terms of reference and detailed method of working were, it was recognised, going to result in an extended period of working. Its initial report on the top structure was received before the change in Government. As described in Chapter 3, some recommendations were implemented forthwith. The one which favoured a further change in ministerial structure, away from single-Service affiliations, was viewed favourably by the Labour Government. It was not implemented at the time, avowedly because it was maintained that by the end of the year the Committee would have been able to work out the detailed changes in the sub-structures required to support the new ministerial arrangements. But it is highly likely that the avoidance of a ministerial shuffle shortly before the inevitable election was also taken into account. In any event the outcome was that this recommendation was not implemented. The perceptions of the new Conservative Government, and particularly of its back-bench members in Parliament, still favoured direct ministerial representation of each of the Services, and three single-Service Parliamentary Under-Secretaries of State were appointed, though, temporarily, under one Minister of State. The new administration also did not follow up another recommendation of the Committee which was linked, in part, with the abolition of the single-Service ministerial structure. This recommendation envisaged a tighter top structure with a small Defence Board (perhaps as small as four members: the Secretary of State, the Minister of State, the CDS and the PUS) giving policy directions to the Department, with, at the next level, Service Executive Committees under the chairmanship of their respective Chief of Staff instead of the Service Board with the single-Service Minister in the chair.

More generally the new administration set its aims and tone in two major statements in October 1970. The first, a supplementary statement on defence (Cmnd 4521), announced various changes of defence policy, all designed to retain rather than run down the overseas military presence outside NATO and to enhance the equipment and manpower levels of the Services. Among the major measures were a continued presence in the Far East, the retention of the *Ark Royal* and the Gurkhas, the acquisition of Exocet, and the collaborative development with the Germans and the Italians of the Multi-Role Combat Aircraft (the MRCA, to become the Tornado). Such and other similar measures would involve extra cost. The new administration therefore wanted the work of streamlining the Headquarters to be carried forward, still under the aegis of the Headquarters Organisation Committee appointed by the previous administration.

The HOC was also specifically charged with seeking improvements in management techniques. This was just one of the messages contained in the other White Paper presented in October 1970 (Cmnd 4506), and which was concerned with the principles and practices of organisation and management across Government Departments as a whole.

Two major themes ran through this White Paper. It was the time when the 'big' Department was in fashion. Functions should be grouped together so as to provide a manageably small series of fields of unified policy. The Ministry of Defence and the Foreign and Commonwealth Office were quoted as examples and the Department of Trade and Industry was created. But, at the same time, the White Paper recognised the risks of undue size and complexity within central government and consequently favoured two complementary steps. Some functions might be hived off from central government. Those which remained should, where possible, be so structured that accountable units of management would be set up with the maximum delegation of executive powers.

These potential conflicts and possible solutions were both highlighted by the question of what should comprise the total package of the new Department of Trade and Industry. The most difficult problem was what should be done about defence procurement, and particularly those fields, notably aviation, which after several changes were at that time located in the Ministry of Technology, itself a very recent concept. If they were all put into the Department of Trade and Industry they would increase its spread of responsibilities to an unacceptable extent. But the problem was even more complicated. These Ministry of Technology responsibilities in the defence field by no means embraced the whole of defence procurement. The Navy

Department looked directly after the design and procurement of its warships, though not the aircraft that operated from them. Much of the Army's equipment was supplied by the Royal Ordnance Factories, since 1959 likewise under defence management, and already the subject of a separate study.

THE RAYNER STUDY

The Government therefore decided on a two-stage operation. It would create, as a temporary measure, a new ministry, the Ministry of Aviation Supply, to be formed exclusively from the Aviation Group rump of the former Ministry of Technology. It would set up a project team to consider the future not just of this Aviation Group but of all defence procurement. There was one pre-condition incorporated in their terms of reference: the task would be how to organise the integration of all defence research, development and production under the Secretary of State for Defence. The ultimate recipient was thus pre-ordained. However, the project team under Mr Derek Rayner's leadership could consider the establishment of an agency within Government, a concept compatible with the principles of the White Paper on Government Organisation. The time-table laid down, contrasted with the continuing flexibility of the HOC, was tight and arbitrary. Recommendations had to be made in time for new measures to be implemented by the start of the 1972/3 financial year: i.e. by 1 April 1972.

Meanwhile the HOC continued with its review of all areas of the Ministry's activities. In 1970 it turned its attention to the relationship of the Ministry with Command Headquarters, concentrating on work until then done in the Ministry in the personnel and logistic fields. Recommendations about transfer of work to the provinces and delegation of work to Commands were accepted, accompanied by the expectation of savings of some 2000 Service and civilian posts in London. The Committee also reported on management practices and techniques in the accounts, audit and contract fields. Here again changes were recommended, including streamlining of procedures which produced staff savings. But, more important in organisational terms, another recommendation led to the creation of a Directorate of Internal Audit. Such a directorate, with wider critical powers than those exercised by the previous accounts staff, reflected recent management developments in the private financial sector. It was a stepping-stone to the creation in 1981 of a still more powerful and comprehensive Directorate General of Management Audit which played an important role in the reorganisation of the early 1980s.

Mr Rayner's Project Team worked very quickly, taking evidence not only in Whitehall but also from a wide range of British defence industries and in France and the USA. They reported on 31 March 1971. The Government, for its part, responded both promptly and positively. A White Paper (Cmnd 4641) was presented to Parliament in the following month, both publishing the report and endorsing its findings. The first executive step in the process of implementation was the dissolution, as early as May 1st, of the temporary Ministry of Aviation Supply.

The Project Team had clearly been influenced by the many criticisms of the disadvantages caused by the remoteness between the user and the supplying department, particularly in the field of aircraft and guided weapons, and of the weaknesses in securing effective control over industry's costs and delivery rates. They therefore sought a solution which, while recognising the professionalism needed to ensure cost-effective procurement practices in complex weapon systems operating at the frontiers of advanced technology, would at the same time establish a closer, contractual-type relationship between the user (the Armed Forces) and the supplier (the new structure in whatever form it took), and between the new structure in its other role as contractor and industry as the supplier. The ultimate solution also needed to foster good working relationships and create a sense of belonging to the defence world. Their basic organisational solution was accordingly not to create an Agency, as they did not see the particular circumstances of defence procurement as conforming to the agency concept as conceived in Cmnd 4506, but to form within the Ministry of Defence a self-contained department to be known as the Procurement Executive. At the head would be an official at Permanent Secretary level to be known as the Chief Executive.

Much of the thinking behind this concept reflected Mr Rayner's commercial experience that procurement was a highly skilled business calling for keen professionalism from its staff. Great stress was therefore laid in the Report on personnel management for the staff, directed at a full career in defence procurement. The top structure envisaged a Controller Personnel as one of the key management posts, operating at the Procurement Executive Management Board level.

On the hardware side the basic concept was that there was benefit to be gained from bringing all the Service procurement Controllerates together within the new Executive, where they could corporately develop their expertise, where international and industrial consequences could be looked at in their totality, and where they would benefit from having common staffs in the contracts, sales, quality assurance and procurement policy fields. For the RAF this was an obvious gain. They had felt, perhaps most markedly in the 1960s, that the succession of separate though changing Ministries handling their weapon systems were not always their agents but sometimes seemed to want to have a weapons policy of their own. But for the Royal Navy and the Army (and the latter had suffered some separation in the immediate post-war years at the time of the Ministry of Supply) there would be an apparent if not real loss of control when the Controller of the Navy and the Master General of the Ordnance were transferred away from their parent Service Departments into this new untried Executive. Much attention was accordingly paid to the form of linkage to be established between the new Executive and the single-Service Boards so as to achieve the desired close supplier/customer relationship. At the top level the linkage was to be achieved in two main ways. Under the Chief Executive the individual project managers – and the Report attached great importance to the high degree of direct management responsibility to be given to them – would continue to be grouped primarily round the three functional systems areas – sea, land and air – under the Controller Navy, Master General of the Ordnance and the Controller Aircraft. The very retention of the titles of the first two appointments underlines the importance attached to satisfying Service traditions – a microcosm of the struggle over titles in 1963. Second, these three Procurement Executive Board members would continue to be members of the respective Service Boards, thus offering both a formal linkage and a symbolic reassurance to the Services that this new monolithic structure would be responsive to their needs. The Report recommended a fourth Controllerate, that of Guided Weapons and Electronics, which was reflecting the current heightened attention to the rapid rate of change in these advanced technological areas. But its existence cut across the tidy linkage between the Procurement Executive and the Service Departments and, even in its own terms of new technologies, was logical only in the short term as it was clear that these techniques were going to permeate all weapon systems. The Report therefore favoured its early dissolution and absorption in the three other Systems Controllerates, hopefully solving any disadvantages of breaking up the technological unity by providing a continuation of the specialised expertise in the other new Controllerate proposed in the Report, that of Research and Development Establishments and Research.

The Project Team had to consider some other organisational issues. Civil aviation had over the previous thirty years stumbled round various Whitehall affiliations: pre-war linkages with the Air Ministry; subsequently a Ministry of Transport and Civil Aviation, a Ministry of Supply and a Ministry of Technology *inter alia*. The Report recommended a clear separation between the execution of research, development and production responsibilities which should lie, on an agency basis, with the Procurement Executive (thus providing at the working level for the easy harmonisation of work at such establishments as the RAE Farnborough), and the policy for civil aviation and associated research, development and production which should lie with the new Department of Trade and Industry. But even with such a clear split there would be a risk of failure of communication between the two Departments, and its avoidance was to be achieved by the establishment of a Ministerial Aerospace Board with the two Secretaries of State as members to give policy guidance to the Procurement Executive. This same Board, with extended membership, was also to be charged with handling space procurement policy which likewise straddled military and civil activities.

Another problem was that the creation of the new Controller of Research and Development Establishments and Research (CER) could have produced duplication with the senior scientist in the central part of the Ministry, who in his most recent manifestation as Chief Adviser (Projects and Research) had taken a particular interest in many activities now to be handled within the Procurement Executive. The preferred solution was that this top post, at Permanent Secretary level, which was retitled Chief Scientific Adviser with the arrival of Sir Hermann Bondi in 1971, should henceforth concentrate on studies, operational research and the broad objectives of the research programme, together with the formulation of operational requirements. The actual running of the research and other programmes in the Establishments would be the responsibility of the CER.

There remained the question of the financial arrangements. Here, too, as in the management of projects and the control of personnel, a structure was sought which would underline the direct financial responsibility of executive areas in the Procurement Executive for their programmes. The Votes were arranged so that each of the four Systems Controllers would have a Vote and would also be an Accounting Officer, with the Chief Executive being Accounting Officer solely for the headquarters administration costs and for the work of the R & D Establishments.

In July 1971 there was an interim report from the Mallabar study into Government Industrial Establishments, concentrating on the Royal Ordnance Factories (ROFs). It considered hiving-off not to be feasible and recommended the creation of a trading fund with the Managing Director ROFs as the accountable manager. This concept squared neatly with the Rayner Report's views on the position and accountability of the Systems Controllers and it prepared the way to tie the ROFs into the working practices of the Executive.

The Procurement Executive itself was formally set up on 2 August 1971. The process of creation was completed on 1 April 1972, the start of the next financial year, when the change in Vote structure could be tidily introduced. During this transitional period, following the demise of the Ministry of Aviation Supply, there was a separate ministerial post created in the Ministry of Defence in the form of a Minister of State for Defence Procurement. This post was short-lived and was dropped at the end of 1972 when the one remaining Minister of State took on procurement responsibilities at ministerial level.

Clearly, most of the Ministry's organisational and postings activities were concentrated in 1971/2 on creating the Procurement Executive and working out its interfaces with the rest of the Ministry, which for a time became known, rather unfortunately, as MOD (Main). The continuing activities of the Headquarters Organisation Committee were reported in very muted terms in the 1972 Statement on Defence Estimates as concentrating on management techniques and the handling of automatic data processing. The Statement also reported the intention of merging RAF Command Headquarters by the end of the year.

The Rayner Report, with its emphasis on a self-contained executive, staffed with sufficient and high-level expertise, and thus offering the continuity of experience and level of authority to hold its own with its customers, had created what some regarded as an unnecessarily lavish top structure. Apart from the Chief Executive and the four Systems Controllers, there were six other posts at Controller level (i.e. three-star) and above. The process of erosion began as early as 1972/3. Although the Report stressed the crucial importance of continuity of staffing to get the new organisation successfully under way, and specifically recommended the appointment of a Chief Executive for at least a three-year term, Mr Rayner returned to Marks and Spencer in October 1972. Two top posts were saved by absorbing the post of Controller Personnel into that of the post of Secretary, and by splitting up, as was admittedly foreshadowed in the report, the Controllerate of Guided Weapons among the three other Systems Controllers. On the other hand, the process of concentration within the Executive of all specialised defence procurement activities was taken one step further by the decision to transfer the Atomic Weapons Research Establishment from the Atomic Energy Authority into the PE as one of the Establishments under the Controller for R & D Establishments and Research. This was a loose end left over from the Rayner Report, the covering White Paper to which had identified the need for further study of this possibility.

WIDER ISSUES

During these first three years of Conservative administration, and leaving aside particular areas selected for study by the Headquarters Organisation Committee, the search for economy was initiated primarily on a single-Service basis. The absence of any central drive or direction was commented on adversely by the House of Commons Expenditure Committee. In their 1971/2 Report they recommended that in the training area, which they had picked out for detailed study, the central Committees should actively seek out areas for greater inter-Service cooperation and coordination. The Ministry's reply in February 1973 was lukewarm. While agreeing that the search for such areas should continue, it expressed the view that the field had been so widely reviewed in recent years that the scope for further action was unlikely to be large. The Defence and External Affairs Sub-Committee of the Expenditure Committee returned to the charge by collecting evidence on different standards and course lengths for the same trades in the three Services. They used this evidence to continue to press for a wide-ranging review directed at a common approach.

During this same period the Air Force Department carried out a major review of RAF manpower and support requirements aimed at an overall reduction of some 6000 posts, including posts within the Air Force Department part of the Ministry. Here, again, the

Expenditure Sub-Committee was disappointed by the absence of any active involvement on the part of the central staffs who should have capitalised on the success of this approach by initiating parallel action in the other two Services. This led the Committee in a subsequent report to express the view that the role of the central staffs should not be limited solely to the allocation of resources but should also be directed at obtaining optimum standards of management within the Services.

In the still wider fields of defence policy this period was one of consolidation of military capability and of reaction to national and international developments rather than of any searching for major new departures. The deteriorating situation in Northern Ireland was a major preoccupation. In the field of East/West relationships there was much consideration about initiatives such as Ostpolitik and, Mutual and Balanced Force Reductions, but there was no desire to alter the fundamental roles and deployment of the Forces.

THE INCOMING LABOUR ADMINISTRATION

The change of Government in March 1974 brought about by the early and swift election following the miners' strike, concentrated attention, once again, on the high ground of defence resources. The new Secretary of State announced on 21 March the initiation of what was called, perhaps somewhat ambitiously, 'the most extensive review of defence ever undertaken in peacetime'. The basic aim, very similar to that announced by Mr Healey in February 1970 but invalidated by the outcome of that summer's election, was to reduce over ten years the percentage of GNP spent on defence from 5½ per cent to 4½ per cent. By 3 December it was possible to indicate the main methods in a statement to Parliament. Cuts in the force levels of all three Services were to be achieved. Research and development effort was to be reduced by a tenth. Manpower was to be cut across the board: 35 000 uniformed personnel, which would call for a special redundancy programme; 15 000 UK-based civilians; 15 000 locally engaged civilians overseas.

THE MANAGEMENT REVIEW 1975–7

Such aims and intended scale of cuts inevitably focused attention, once again, on the role and size of the Ministry itself. Moreover, as one of the structural initiatives taken somewhat earlier by the comparatively new Civil Service Department (its creation was one of the outcomes of the Fulton Report commissioned by the 1964–70 Labour Government), a series of what were termed Management Reviews had been instituted to look in turn at the major Whitehall Departments. It was therefore decided that it was timely to carry out a management review of the Ministry of Defence, with in this case giving the review the specific task of adjusting the size and shape of the Ministry in the light of the recent defence review. The initiation of the review was announced in the March 1975 Statement on the Defence Estimates (Cmnd 5976). This announcement also conveniently enabled the Ministry shortly thereafter to reply to the Expenditure Committee and deal briefly with their recommendation about the strengthening of the central staffs by referring to the Management Review. The Committee's other main point of concern about training costs was dealt with by appointing an independent expert to inquire into the extent to which the Ministry could make more use of joint training.

Given the economic circumstances at the time of the Review it is not surprising that, unlike the previous major studies, its attention was directed specifically at economy as much as efficiency. The terms of reference set a target of a reduction of at least ten per cent on the numbers planned for 1 April 1979. The terms of reference also included Command Headquarters as well as all aspects of the Ministry, in this way both reflecting the earlier thrust towards greater delegation and facilitating the study of possible areas of duplication. A large full-time support team was provided, including Civil Service Department and private management consultant members. The Steering Committee, which although mostly comprised of Ministry members also included a representative of the Civil Service Department and Sir Derek Rayner, now back with Marks and Spencer. It was called upon to report by September 1976.

During the intervening year the country's economic situation deteriorated further. The Government found it necessary, notwithstanding the stringent nature of the 1974 Defence Review, to reduce planned defence expenditure further as part of its policy of a general reduction in public expenditure. Immediate steps were taken to make manpower savings as well as more general savings in the support areas. These savings anticipated and were then swept up in the economy part of the Management Review's tasks.

These new short-term pressures did not prevent the Review from taking a historical perspective over the developments since 1963 and assessing the validity and effectiveness of the Ministry's organisation as it had evolved in the intervening years. Coming as it does roughly half-way through the period on which this book is concentrating, it is interesting, both looking backwards to 1963 and forwards to 1985, to see on what areas the perceptions of 1975 led the Steering Committee to concentrate their attention, and where they judged change was or was not required.

The Review Team formed certain clear impressions about the relative successes of the evolution since 1964. First, they thought that the organisation had on the whole worked well. Second, they stressed the overriding single-Service content of much of the work of the Ministry. They reiterated, for example, the view of the Head-quarters Organisation Committee that in the logistics and personnel fields there was much more intra-Service rather than inter-Service activity, even at the Ministry level. In support of this view they considered that the military emphasis out in the field had shifted – because of the greater concentration since the early 1960s into NATO and Europe – from integrated tri-Service national overseas Commands to greater association with allies on a Service-to-Service basis. Their report, unlike some earlier and later expressions of view, had very little to say about inter-Service squabbles over resource allocation and consequently over the relative powers and positions of the four Chiefs of Staff and their defence policy staffs. Why this was not the subject of major comment was not discussed. It could be that the successful outcome, in political terms at least, of the recent 1974 Defence Review meant that Ministers had not felt themselves frustrated in their search for savings by this part of the organisation.

The Report favoured the continuance of the trend towards a more sharply unified Ministry. Steps to support this thrust were directed at three specific areas: the financial, the scientific and the procurement fields. At the centre of the Ministry the overall policy umbrella should be strengthened by a more regular and effective use of the already extant but hitherto largely neglected mechanism of the Defence Council. Even so – and thus consistently reflecting their views on the large intra-Service management tasks – it was expressly stated that the greater use of the Defence Council would not affect the work of the Service Boards, the Procurement Executive Management Board or, for that matter, the Chiefs of Staff Committee, all of which were seen as essential policy management tools in their own right. The one point of substance in the Report which was not accepted by the Government concerned the membership of the Defence Council. It was suggested that its size would be more manageable and thus it would become more effective in its enhanced role if the three single-Service Parliamentary Under-Secretaries of State were excluded. It is difficult to see how this exclusion could have been other than seriously harmful to their status and thus unacceptable to them so long as their posts continued. The decision in favour on their continued membership was conveyed in the Government's note of February 1977 to the Defence and External Affairs Sub-Committee.

Much of the Report was taken up with the evolution and effectiveness of the Procurement Executive in the four years of its life. The general conclusion was that the time had come for a series of changes all directed at integrating the Procurement Executive more into the Ministry so far as common services such as personnel management and finance were concerned, while preserving its professional independence to manage research and development work and monitor individual projects. The position of the Head of the Procurement Executive was strengthened, and his post retitled to that of Chief of Defence Procurement (CDP), by making him Accounting Officer for the whole of its work instead of the previous sub-allocations among the Systems Controllers.

In parallel, the position of the PUS was similarly strengthened by making him Accounting Officer for the whole of the rest of the Ministry's expenditure other than the specialised management areas of the Trading Funds for the Royal Ordnance Factories and the Royal Dockyards. As a consequence there was a two-way split of Accounting Officer responsibilities, between the PUS who would be responsible for the justification of the military requirement and the CDP who would be responsible for the efficient procurement of the approved requirement. This split was underlined by one other important conclusion. The Review confirmed the need for and the split between the two major central equipment Committees; the Operational Requirements Committee with its military and policy orientation and the Defence Equipment Policy Committee with its budgetary and industrial overtones.

But if there were no fundamental changes recommended in the whole organisational spectrum of the various separate staff areas concerned with hardware from the first gleam in the eye to the final delivery of the weapon system to a Service, that omission should not imply that the Review saw no scope for other improvements. It is, rather, that they saw improvements best being achieved by tackling methods and practices for the most part within the existing structure, rather than changing the structure. Thus they called for greater flexibility in the formulation of policy options which were to be supplied by the central staff of the PUS and the CDS working together at the two-star level. They saw a greater role for the Chief Scientific Adviser in the formulation of research objectives. They pressed for a broader and more coherent strategic background against which individual operational requirements could be considered and saw an important role for the recently changed Sea/ Air and Land/Air Committees to play. They favoured greater continuity in the staffing of the operational requirements branches. In sum, the emphasis was on practical, pragmatic improvements.

Another area of fundamental review was that of personnel and logistics. The early and mid-1960s had seen a great thrust towards rationalisation or even unification of particular activities. But, by the 1970s, the House of Commons Expenditure Committee was raising charges that the steam had prematurely gone out of this thrust and that there were still anomalies to be found and economies to be achieved.

Starting from the fundamental assumption of the continuance of three separate Services, the Report's consideration of the logistics area led to a reiteration of the view that while there was a prima-facie similarity between certain logistic activities of the three Services, and rationalisation might be justified in some areas, the overriding logical unity lay within the individual Service. The logistics of each Service were seen to be much more directly linked with, for example, its training and operational needs than with a similar logistic activity, where it existed, in another Service. On the personnel side they saw the same principle as essentially valid with perhaps a slightly different shade of emphasis as to where there was scope for rationalisation and where single-Service management should continue. The medical, dental and chaplaincy fields, for example, did not seem to them to have the same strength of internal unity as did postings, career development, manning, and even, despite the views of the Expenditure Committee, training.

AN AREA OF DISPUTE WITH THE HOUSE OF COMMONS EXPENDITURE COMMITTEE

At the same time, the Report acknowledged the need for an ability to search out areas for economy by the greater utilisation of common features. The organisational consequence of these conclusions was to support the continuance of the primary place of single-Service management under the PPOs and PAOs, but at the same time to see the need for a central capability for keeping policies and systems under review. In recent years this capability had been provided successively by a Chief Adviser and then a Chief of Personnel and Logistics (CPL), but the Ministry now doubted whether a separate four-star post was justified. Moreover, the combining of the post's responsibilities for logistics with those responsibilities exercised by the central defence staffs for the logistic and organisational aspects of defence plans and operations, was thought to offer military advantages. It was therefore proposed that most of the work of the CPL should be absorbed by the Vice-Chief of the Defence Staff who would, however, remain a three-star officer. Service pay posed particular problems, heightened by the greater role of the Armed Forces Pay Review Board and the Top Salaries Review Board. These two outside bodies both expected to get a coordinated expression of the Ministry's views from a central voice if possible. No clear-cut solution was put forward by the Review Team, but it was tentatively suggested that the necessary coordination could be achieved by bringing together in some way still to be defined the civilian single-Service divisions which dealt with pay.

Both the Management Review Report itself and the report by the individual consultant who had been appointed following the earlier criticisms by the Defence and External Affairs Sub-Committee, were sent to the Expenditure Committee in early 1977. Its Sub-Committee resumed their interest in the training field, and their inquiries that summer concentrated on that field, although their final session also took evidence on the wider issues discussed in the Management Review itself. The Sub-Committee were half persuaded by the arguments about the dominant effect of the individual nature of each of the Services, in large part because the independent review of training was able to point to only relatively few areas where further rationalisation might be feasible. But the Sub-Committee repeated its belief that the Ministry should take positive action to identify the scope for joint training by determining in what areas single-Service considerations were overriding. They believed that there still were anomalies. Central oversight remained important. They were dismayed at the proposed abolition of the Chief of Personnel and Logistics in favour of some unclear combination with the Vice-Chief of the Defence Staff, particularly as it was proposed that this post should stay at three-star level. It would thus be unlikely to have adequate influence over the powerful single-Service Principal Personnel and Principal Administrative Officers who were often very senior and four-star members of their Service Boards.

In November 1977, which was before the Sub-Committee formally reported but presumably after informal representations to Ministers by its members, the Secretary of State conveyed to the Chairman of the Sub-Committee a decision which effectively reversed the earlier conclusion. The argument now ran that, given the continuing import-ance of the current wide range of personnel and logistics issues – and it needed to be borne in mind that there was great pressure to find more economies in the support area – it was right to continue to have a post at four-star level operating in these areas. This post would also take over from the Vice-Chief of Defence Staff an overall responsibility for seeing that due weight was given to personnel and logistic factors when drawing up defence policy and operational plans. The post would be retitled Vice Chief of the Defence Staff (Personnel and Logistics), and its incumbent would be a member of the Defence Council. This change of attitude was influenced by urgent senior postings considerations as much as by the Sub-Commit-tee's arguments. This decision received a grudging welcome from the Expenditure Committee, who still believed that the combined post, notwithstanding its status, could not adequately compensate for the loss of a dedicated senior officer in each of these two fields.

A QUIET INTERLUDE

The 1978 and 1979 Statements on Defence Estimates were low-key documents in the organisational field. The major emphasis was on the achievement of the postulated economies. The Ministry was on target. It was considered that since 1964 major savings had been achieved in the support area. Lands, Claims and the Ministry of Defence Police were quoted as examples of successful unification, while rationalisation had been brought about in dozens of areas of activity. A word of caution was expressed about the scope for further major progress, particularly in the Ministry itself, in part because of the policy of dispersing large numbers of staff for wider social reasons to Cardiff and Glasgow. Internally, by way of implementing the Management Review's recommendation, a sustained effort was made to breathe life into the Defence Council which met regularly over this period.

5 1979–86: Conservative Ministers and Centralisation

THE BACKGROUND ATMOSPHERE

While the 1970s saw the creation and subsequent adaptations of the Procurement Executive within the Ministry of Defence, reductions in the size of the Ministry and a continuing search for targets for rationalisation, these years were, as the previous chapter describes, otherwise a low-profile period for the organisation of the Ministry. However, after the assumption of office by a Conservative administration in May 1979, the attention became much higher and the pace of change much faster.

Leaving aside the particular contributions flowing from the different personalities and interests of the three Secretaries of State in office from 1979 to 1985, there were several underlying reasons for this renewed emphasis.

First, the Conservative administration came into office in 1979 with the avowed intention of increasing the efficiency and reducing the size of the Civil Service. This drive has often been epitomised in the person of Sir Derek Rayner, working in Government once again, who both launched a wide range of studies and, as a deliberate policy to prevent them running into the sand, established a machinery and central staff structure for processing and implementing, against a deliberately tight timetable, the recommendations. These studies were but one approach to help meet the targets set for each Department for reductions in its size and specifically in the number of its top posts. The Ministry of Defence, as both the largest Department in central government and the biggest employer of Civil Service manpower – industrial as well as non-industrial with its major business and manufacturing activities in the form of dockyards, research establishments and ordnance factories – was in the forefront of such studies and pressures. While their initial thrust might have been directed at self-contained executive areas, the studies fed their way back into central organisation and the appropriateness of the work being carried out in the Ministry Headquarters. Furthermore, while it was not unusual for new Governments to come into power with sweeping statements of intentions to reform government machinery and modernise the Civil Service, the drive since 1979 has been sustained, somewhat exceptionally, at a high level over an extended period of years.

Second, notwithstanding the policy for steady growth in real terms of 3 per cent per annum up to 1986 in the defence budget in support of NATO aims and goals, successive Secretaries of State were being faced increasingly with an imbalance between available resources and the demands for resources. The reasons were various and were the subject of much political dispute. They focussed politically on the Trident programme once the decision to adopt this successor system was announced in July 1980, even though, for the first half of the 1980s at least, the Tornado programme, for example, was making much larger demands on the defence budget. It is also true that there were significant increases in the pay of the Services, even though, flowing mostly from the drive for administrative economies, the share of the defence budget that was spent on personnel continued to decline. But the dominant factor was that, across the equipment programme as a whole, costs were rising faster than inflation even after being topped up by the 3 per cent increase per annum in real terms, primarily because of the growing threat and the consequent need for greater performance from the new weapons systems. The ultimate consequence was to face Ministers, who were now working within the framework of an increasingly sophisticated ten-year long-term costings plan with its in-built rigidities as well as its planning advantages, with very difficult problems of priorities and choices. To help them in this task they wanted to be able to look to a Department geared to give them informed, objective, prompt and authoritative advice. And the Secretary of State also looked for a ministerial structure which would support him – and support him overtly and not just privately – rather than echo or reinforce the voices of the various single-Service lobbies.

Third, Ministers have been kept under greater pressure from Parliament both to account for their actions and to reply to specific recommendations as a result of the developments of the Select Committee system introduced in 1979. Both in 1981/2 and in 1984 the House of Commons Defence Committee paid close attention to, and offered a running commentary on, organisational changes that were being mooted or had just been introduced.

Fourth, and finally, the personality and background of Ministers played a significant role. Mr John Nott brought with his banking background a special interest in resource allocation. Mr Michael Heseltine, as a successful businessman and reinforced by the political success of the major innovations of techniques he had introduced into the Department of the Environment, brought a particular interest in systems of organisation. Both these Secretaries of State, while they had high regard for the professionalism of the Armed Forces in the field, belonged, in contrast to their predecessors, to a younger generation who had not been involved in the Second World War and whose emotional ties might have been less pronounced.

1979–81

These factors were not all immediately or equally dominant when the Conservative Government took office in May 1979. The Government had set itself as its immediate priorities in the defence field to review the defence roles of the country, including the question of GLCM (ground-launched cruise missile) deployment, and to 'put right' the pay of the Services. The new Secretary of State (Mr Francis Pym) had not been shadowing the Defence Ministry and had no preconceived views on the overall organisation or the ministerial structure. Therefore 1979 saw no immediate developments other than the launching of a number of Rayner studies. Nor did the 1980 Statement on the Defence Estimates (Cmnd 7826), while it referred to the continuing rundown of civilian numbers, to the scope for privatisation and to the progress on the several Rayner studies set in hand, give any prominence to higher organisational issues. But it is relevant to note that one of the Rayner studies of that time, which looked into the inspection and audit systems, resulted in the creation of an organisation under a new senior post of Director-General of Management Audit which was to become a very significant tool for Ministers in the 1982/4 period.

Policy and resource issues came increasingly to the forefront in 1980 when their potential incompatibility became more noticeable. The Government announced its decision to acquire Trident in July that year. While its effect on the defence budget, however debatable, was undoubtedly long-term rather than immediate, the Ministry of Defence found itself facing short-term financial problems in the autumn of 1980 derived from a rate of expenditure flowing well in excess of the provision contained in the arbitrary straitjacket of Annual Estimates. A swift, crude, but financially effective moratorium had to be applied, with severe effects on some defence contractors, and management inefficiencies for the Services in the field.

1981–3

This was the situation facing Mr Nott when on 5 January 1981 he succeeded Mr Pym as Secretary of State. Mr Nott soon decided that he had to take a fundamental look at the balance of the defence programme he had inherited, which seemed to be running into both financial and operational difficulties, notwithstanding the Government's reaffirmation of its commitment to the annual 3 per cent increase in real terms. His line of thinking was already apparent in the 1981 Statement on the Defence Estimates (Cmnd 8212), which reported that the cost and complexity of equipment were rising alarmingly and asserted that new ways must be found of coping with resource pressure. Successive budgetary difficulties had resulted in unbalanced cuts and as a consequence too much money had been tied up in weapon platforms and not enough directed at weapons themselves and sensors. Indeed it is clear that he had already by then formed his own view of the priorities which should shape the reallocation of resources and had issued on 16 March instructions on the basis for work on what was termed the 'Defence Review Programme'.

The outcome of this review was summarised in his statement to the House of Commons on 25 June 1981. Reductions in Service manpower and notably in the size of the surface fleet were among the major military consequences. Underlying the individual decisions was a key principle expressed by Mr Nott at the time in the terms that 'We must determine this balance in terms of real defence capability rather than as the outcome of a debilitating argument over each Service's budgetary share.'

In enunciating this principle Mr Nott was clearly implying that he had expected to get assistance from within the Ministry in reaching decisions that were based on more than crude equal misery for each of the Services. But the experience of his first few months had left him with the strong feeling that there were two key areas of the ministry where the organisation did not seem to be designed so as to give him the objective support and independent advice to he sought: the ministerial structure and the central military staffs under the Chief of the Defence Staff.

Ministerial structure, as experience across Whitehall has borne out over many years, can be changed overnight, even if the subordinate consequences take time for resolution. So, in May 1981, the structure of one Minister of State supported by three single-Service Parliamentary Secretaries which had survived in that precise form since 1972 (following the creation of the Royal Air Force in 1919 there had always been single-Service Ministers of varying rank and status), was replaced by a wholly functional structure of a Minister of State for the Armed Forces and Minister of State for Defence Procurement, each supported by a Parliamentary Secretary. Along with the change of organisation went a change of incumbency of most of the ministerial posts. The rationale for these changes was first set out in a paper sent in July 1981 to the House of Commons Defence Committee. When the Secretary of State appeared before the Committee on 11 November he elaborated on his reasons, stressing in particular that it was difficult for him to delegate effectively to junior ministers when they were so organised that they were bound to think not in terms of overall operational capability but in a single-Service capacity.

This reorganisation required a detailed allocation of functional responsibilities for each of the Ministers of State. The detailed arrangements were also set out in the paper to the House of Commons Defence Committee. This allocation had to try to make sense in terms of both internal coherence of subjects and of loading: for example the weight of ministerial correspondence was traditionally most heavy on Service personnel matters. The allocation was further complicated by the desirability of having one member of the ministerial team in the House of Lords. Inevitably there had to be compromises, not all of which outwardly seemed to offer the most efficient solution.

Mr Nott clearly also felt a comparable lack of support in the slowness of absence of collective advice from the Chiefs of Staff Committee. When he appeared before the House of Commons Defence Committee on 11 November 1981 he said that he was working on 'some evolutionary changes in the military area with the aim of giving the Chief of the Defence Staff a rather stronger voice whilst at the same time maintaining the authority of the single-Service Chiefs of Staff'.

Admiral of the Fleet Sir Terence Lewin, who was Chief of the Defence Staff during this period, likewise accepted that the organisation had not worked satisfactorily. He recognised that the three Services were too preoccupied in defending their own positions, and that the speed of events meant that, in his judgement, there had not only been a failure on the part of the central military staffs to grasp the essential problem of overall defence priorities, but also that, consequently, there had not been an adequate military input into the review. He therefore worked out proposals for strengthening the position of the Chief of the Defence Staff and his supporting central military staffs. It is to these proposals that Mr Nott was referring when he met the House of Commons Defence Committee on 11 November. Admiral Lewin later acknowledged that he had drawn up his suggestions without formally consulting his Chief of Staff colleagues.

During that winter Mr Nott defined the terms of such strengthening and secured the approval of the Prime Minister. Its precise form was set out in a letter from him of 10 February 1982 to the Chairman of the House of Commons Defence Committee and announced publicly on the same day. The key elements were that:

(a) The Chief of the Defence Staff, as the Secretary of State's principal military adviser, should offer independent military advice while at the same time reflecting the views of the single-Service Chiefs of Staff which he would obtain in the forum of the Chiefs of Staff Committee.

(b) The single-Service Chiefs of Staff would still be responsible for the conduct of single-Service operations and retain the right of access to the Secretary of State and the Prime Minister.

(c) To assist the Chief of the Defence Staff in proffering independent military advice, the central military staffs would be made accountable to and directed by him.

(d) The Chief of the Defence Staff would chair a Senior Appointments Committee, with the single-Service Chiefs of Staff as members, to review certain high Service appointments and promotions.

Mr Nott saw these changes as being directed essentially at resource allocation and balance of investment questions. Admiral Lewin considered them to be the most important change in the position of the Chiefs of Staff for over fifty years, and he attached particular significance to the new system for making higher appointments and promotions. As events turned out, any immediate effect on the allocation of resources was overshadowed, only a few weeks later, by the outbreak of the fighting in the South Atlantic which, as a combined operation involving all three Services, became a direct responsibility of the CDS. He therefore was the one senior officer who regularly attended the small 'War Cabinet' which was set up early on in the operations as the machinery of day-to-day policy control by the Government. Admiral Lewin considers that the arrangement worked well and that it would have been unnecessary and inefficient for the single-Service Chiefs of Staff to attend as well. Mr Nott, in responding to a letter from the Chairman of the House of Commons Defence Committee on 16 May 1982, stressed both the value of the leading role of the CDS in advising Ministers on the recent operations and the value of the corporate advice of the Chiefs of Staff Committee which had been meeting daily. But he went on to reiterate that in more normal times his main concern would be to have an organisation that would give prompter advice and clearer alternatives to Ministers in the field of resource allocation.

The South Atlantic operations delayed the publication of the annual Statement on the Defence Estimates (Cmnd 8529) until June 1982. Even then it did not, as would normally have been expected to be the case, expand on the detailed consequences of Mr Nott's letter of 11 February. The operations probably also affected the timing and emphasis of the Report of the House of Commons Defence Committee which was published in July 1982. Their Report welcomed the new emphasis on a functional organisation for minis-ters which should enable the 'management of the Armed Forces [to] be looked at in a comprehensive defence way'. The Committee also welcomed the stronger voice which was being given to the Chief of the Defence Staff whilst maintaining the authority of the single-Service Chiefs of Staff. They regarded the changes as being largely a matter of emphasis placing greater stress on the CDS's own advice and the machinery needed to formulate it.

Normally the associated changes in machinery would have been promulgated within a few weeks of the initial announcement, but the South Atlantic operations and their aftermath caused an inevi-table hiatus. It was not until 6 September 1982 that the central defence staffs were reorganised, with the creation of a new post of Deputy Chief of the Defence Staff at three-star level (Lieutenant-General Sir Maurice Johnston was the first incumbent) to coordinate the efforts of the central Operational Requirements, Policy, Operations and Signals staffs in a somewhat changed grouping. This new senior post was designed not only to recognise the close relationship between policy, resources and commitments, but also to provide at an effectively high enough level the desired degree of contact between central defence work and the single-Service Vice-Chiefs of Staff as well as the senior central scientists and administrators.

Notwithstanding these important changes in ministerial and senior military responsibilities and the consequences of the South Atlantic campaign, the House of Commons Defence Committee were preoccupied with defence procurement and the majority of its recommendations focussed on this subject. Some of them commented on studies, set up under the Rayner aegis, into methods of financial control and cash planning, and into the structure of committees for handling equipment requirements and development work together with the associated degree of financial delegation. Many detailed recommendations concerned improvements in the working relationships between the Procurement Executive and industry, spanning consultation on initial specifications, contract arrangements and wider industrial consequences. At the same time there were some recommendations which potentially had direct or indirect organisational consequences. The Committee favoured a strengthening and centralisation of operational analysis resources. On the assumption that the new central organisation could better handle the main defence policy objectives they favoured greater delegation within the Procurement Executive on individual projects. They recommended the creation of a ministerial Aerospace Board to achieve closer high-level coordination between the Ministry of Defence and the Department of Industry. In his response the Secretary of State set out the ongoing work in many of these areas, and concurred in the general thrust of the two main themes emerging from the enquiry: the emphasis on the role of the centre as a policy source coupled with greater executive delegation; the increasing need to have a more intimate association with industry.

It is noteworthy that neither in the Select Committee's Report nor in the Government's response was there any major critical reference to organisational lessons for the Ministry from the South Atlantic campaign. Its underlying political policies might have created much controversy. Militarily the operations might have cast doubt on some recent decisions about the long-term size and shape of the Royal Navy. The adequacies of a few individual items of equipment might have been questioned. Problems of public relations and censorship, always acute in a limited war, raised much heat and led to the setting-up of external reviews. But the campaign did not in itself cast doubt on the ability of the Ministry to raise, equip and train efficient fighting forces and to mount an effective campaign at the end of a singularly difficult and disadvantageous supply line. There was no groundswell of challenge to the organisation of the Ministry or its relationship with Command Headquarters flowing from the operation itself. Once again, as in the late 1960s, the Ministry's organisation was able to cope well with the central handling of the operations and the associated provision of support by the Services which called for many rapid and unforeseen logistic requirements. This ability contrasts with the repeated dissatisfaction at its alleged inability to solve problems in the fields of priorities and resource allocation.

Given the operational, personnel and logistic consequences of the campaign and the ongoing problems of maintaining the greatly enhanced military presence in the Falkland Islands, given the recent changes in ministerial duties and in the central defence staffs, and given the ongoing problems – in part still flowing from the moratorium – and alterations in practice in the procurement field, it might have been expected that 1983 would be a year which in organisational terms would be devoted to refinement and consolidation. That would probably have been the dominant collective wish of the Ministry. But January 1983 saw the departure of Mr Nott, prior to leaving active politics at his own request, and the arrival of Mr Michael Heseltine as Secretary of State.

1983 – THE ARRIVAL AND STANDPOINT OF MR HESELTINE

Mr Heseltine had become Secretary of State for the Environment in 1979. From his experiences in the private sector and from his time as Minister for Aerospace in the 1970–74 Conservative Government, he had clear and strong views about the managerial role of ministers. In 1980, when in the Department of the Environment, he wrote:

The management ethos must run right through our public life . . .
By management ethos I mean the process of examining what we
are doing, setting realistic targets, fitting them to the resources
available and monitoring performance . . . All the information
tools of management should be available to politicians and to civil
servants.

Had he written that article in 1983 he would surely have added, 'and
to military officers alike'.

Therefore, as a first step, and coincidentally at the same time as
the Ministry of Defence was launching one of its Rayner studies –
the scrutiny of the Department's staff inspection, internal audit and
central management services – Mr Heseltine instigated, similarly as
a Rayner exercise, a study of information requirements for ministers
in the Department of Environment. The particular system he
favoured, which flowed from information supplied by a large number
of section heads usually set at under-secretary level, was based on
reviews by ministers on an annual cyclical basis of the estimates,
priorities and tasks of each section together with their costs and
manpower resources. (The system became known as MINIS.) From
the ensuing comprehensive overview of the activities of the Department, ministers should be able to improve its operational efficiency
and make more detailed performance assessments. Though this was
a new approach on such a comprehensive basis in the public sector,
there was a large amount of written theory about, as well as experience of, practice in the use of management information systems in
the private sector.

At the start, the initiation of MINIS could have been regarded as
the individual approach of a particular minister to managing his
department, but the Treasury and Civil Service Committee
recommended in March 1982 that MINIS or its clear equivalent
should be adopted in all Government Departments. For his part Mr
Heseltine had earlier told the Committee that he would introduce it
in another department unless there was a system as good in operation. At that time the view was expressed by the Ministry of Defence
officials that the control systems already under development in that
department were perhaps more suitable than the importation of
MINIS. The Committee were not impressed. Behind this departmental thinking lay the parallel developments that were already
taking place flowing from the impetus of two Rayner studies.

The first, a scrutiny of the Ministry's staff inspection, internal audit and central management services in 1980 had led to the creation of a Directorate General of Management Audit, headed by an Under-Secretary, which by means of selective audits carried out by multi-disciplinary teams would review the resources – manpower, money and organisation – of specific areas of work. An essential tool would be the provision of staff budgets for individual areas. In time the whole would become greater than the sum of the parts and would provide an overview of the cost-effectiveness of the whole Ministry.

The second report in 1982 on financial accountability offered a further development with the scope for an associated greater degree of delegation in resource management arrangements. The tool for these developments would be the introduction of responsibility budgets, particularly for managers of large executive operations. Under this concept the managers would have to negotiate annually a level of performance to be achieved and the related level of resources. At the end of the year they would be called upon to account for the outcome. Such a concept presented large practical problems of sensible, flexible implementation for a department as heterogeneous as the Ministry of Defence. It was decided, dependent on the nature of the area of work, to subdivide the system into staff responsibility budgets and the more all-embracing executive responsibility budgets, and to start on the latter with a number of trials.

On his arrival Mr Heseltine had therefore to evaluate and inter-relate three main considerations: his personal commitment to the wider application of MINIS as a system within Whitehall; the steps the Ministry had recently taken down the road of greater managerial scrutiny, efficiency and accountability; and the problems posed by the biggest and managerially most complex department in Government. Moreover, the Ministry was unique in that it had at its sharp end as its *raison d'être* the operational units of the Armed Forces whose efficiency could not be evaluated solely in balance-sheet terms.

THE APPLICATION OF MINIS TO THE MINISTRY OF DEFENCE

The new Secretary of State soon decided that he would harness the Department's own initiatives to his own system. Within a month he announced in a Written Answer in the House of Commons on 1 February 1983 that he intended to introduce a management system for ministers into my Department very soon. The Ministry of Defence is a large and complex executive Department and I have not yet decided on the detailed application of the system. But it will complement and link with the management control, information and accounting systems which already exist in the Department.

He then asked the comparatively newly appointed Director General of Management Audit to set up a small MINIS Unit as part of his central Management Services and Organisation staff. Initially the Unit had to define which of the vast spread of areas in the Ministry should be covered by the process. The total ran into hundreds, even after eliminating front-line units, which, it was accepted, could and did have their performance evaluated in other ways, e.g. by NATO tactical evaluation staff.

The selected areas reported their data in April 1983. After they were analysed by the Unit, Mr Heseltine began in the summer an extensive series of discussions with their senior managers. He gave them sustained high priority over a number of months, but even so there were many more senior managers to interview than in the Department of the Environment and Mr Heseltine had severe problems in finding the time in his diary. However, by the autumn he considered that the areas he had cross-examined, together with his experience in running the Department in his initial months, provided him with confirmation that changes were needed in the top structure of the Ministry. The Procurement Executive was not involved at this stage, as the first round of MINIS interviews had excluded all that part of the Ministry.

The next few months were taken up with three stages of action: the drafting of general principles in the light of specific guidance from the Secretary of State; the publication of the proposals in the form of a consultative document together with a subsequent associated round of consultation; and the publication of the final plan together with an implementation timetable. The whole process was overlaid with one very marked difference from all the changes over the previous twenty years: the nature and degree of involvement of the Secretary of State. Clearly all previous changes were approved by Ministers and, sometimes, as occurred for example with the abolition of the Deputy Chiefs of Staff on the single-Service Boards in 1968, after direct personal involvement on the part of the Secretary of State. But the major changes in those two decades flowed from the initial advice of a committee (e.g. the Headquarters Organisation Committee or the Management Review) or from distinguished outside advice (e.g. the Jacob/Ismay and Rayner Reports). By contrast this reorganisation was led and carried out in detail by the personal intervention and determination of Mr Heseltine himself, as came out clearly in the evidence taken in July 1984 by the House of Commons Defence Committee only days after the publication of the White Paper giving the Government's conclusions.

This high degree of personal involvement had a marked effect on the machinery of work adopted for the three stages. Mr Heseltine had come to a view, perhaps as soon as the early autumn of 1983, although it was certainly refined by the ongoing MINIS process of area-by-area investigation, that the changes he required were not just changes of style and methodology but called for a different organisation of the top structure. In such circumstances his style of management, as he later explained, was to move on from a broad feel and enlist the support and expertise of those who would be involved in fleshing out the detail. At the same time he wished to maintain the impetus. His own procedural solution for the first of the three stages was to have the consultative document prepared with the drafting being carried out within a very narrow circle, effectively limited, with the concurrence of the PUS, to the MINIS cell initially created on his arrival. One consequence was that even the CDS – not to mention the single-Service Chiefs of Staff and the Chief Scientific Adviser – was not aware of the precise contents of the consultative Open Government document until forty-eight hours before its publication. This deliberate decision not to take them into his confidence caused some subsequent resentment and criticism. At the same time there can be little doubt that most senior staff, especially those who were in attendance at the series of the Secretary of State's MINIS meetings with the senior staff in their areas, would have had indications for some time of the nature of his dissatisfaction and of the trend of the likely changes.

PROPOSALS FOR REORGANISATION

Be that as it may, a Defence Open Government document was published on 12 March 1984, and on the same day Mr Heseltine made a statement to the House of Commons. Both the document and the statement were in some respects cautious and generalised in approach. Great stress was laid on preserving the separate identities and traditions of the three Services and the constitutional framework provided by the Defence Council and the Service Boards. Certain major fields of activity were effectively excluded from the proposals, at least so far as immediate organisational change was concerned. The whole area of procurement of defence equipment was reported to be under separate discussion with the National Defence Industries Council and under study by Mr Heseltine's recently appointed personal adviser, Mr Peter Levene. There was a general assertion that, there too, changes would be needed but that these could be pursued independently of the proposals for the rest of the Ministry. This could only be interpreted as implying that, somehow or other, they would not affect fundamentally the handling of the operational requirements responsibilities of the central defence staffs. There was a similar generalised expression of view that there might still be scope for further rationalisation of personnel and logistic functions, coupled here with an implication that such further work would not affect the basis of the role being allocated to each single-Service executive committee to manage these tasks in its own environment.

The basic thrust of the proposals was therefore centred on how to structure the Ministry so as to secure best value for money for defence, firstly in the determination of policies and priorities and secondly in the executive machinery for implementing the policies at both the Ministry and the Command Headquarters. In considering how to approach these issues the Secretary of State stated his conviction that:

(a) the span of command was too narrow and that there were too many senior posts;
(b) there was too much compromise in giving advice and taking decisions;
(c) lines of accountability were too blurred;
(d) a clearer distinction needed to be drawn between policy advice and management of the Services themselves.

These general conclusions were then translated into certain principles, still in quite broad terms, about the central machinery.

First, the responsibilities and lines of reporting of the most senior officers were to be modified so that formally the Secretary of State had only two principal official advisers: the Chief of the Defence Staff and the Permanent Under-Secretary of State. On the military side this would mean that both the responsibility for all operations and the task of advising the Government on the military aspects of policy and resource issues would rest with the CDS and no longer be the collective responsibility of the four Chiefs of Staff. Consequently, the principal concern of each of the single-Service Chiefs of Staff would become the oversight of the management of his individual Service. On the civil side this would mean that in addition to the normal administrative hierarchy, the other two principal civilian advisers, the Chief Scientific Adviser (normally an outside appointment) and the Chief of Defence Procurement, would formally report to the PUS.

Second, in order to give teeth to these two principal advisers, the document proposed major reshapings and revised reporting lines for the military defence staffs, comprising both the central staffs as restructured in 1982 and the Naval, General and Air Staffs, together with the associated civilian defence secretariat and budgetary staffs. Two major new blocks would be created. A unified and integrated Defence Staff would be set up which would comprise not only the four groups of military policy staffs but also the civilian secretariat staff dealing with the political aspects of defence policy. This unified Defence Staff would report jointly or severally to the CDS and the PUS, but all parts of the Ministry, including the single-Service Chiefs of Staff, could call on it for advice. As the primary aim of this grouping was to facilitate a 'defence' solution to major problems of a resource or operational kind, the posts of Vice-Chiefs of Staff in the Service Departments would lapse. Their major responsibilities would be transferred to the Defence Staff which would in any case need some reinforcement at the higher levels. The overall aim would thus be to reduce the involvement of the Service Departments in the allocation of resources at the macro level.

This outline concept for the central Defence Staff did not include the civilian programme and budget staffs, all of whom had formally been centrally located in the past, but some of whom had in practice worked most closely with the single-Service policy staffs on the costs of and options for their individual programmes. Clearly a vital element in the resolution of strategic priorities and resource allocations would continue to be their budgetary implications. One option, which the Open Government document did not however follow, would have been to take these budgetary staffs into the Defence Staff. Rather it proposed setting up under the Second PUS – who would report along with the Chief Scientific Adviser and the

Chief of Defence Procurement to the Permanent Secretary – an Office of Management and Budget. Behind this proposal lay Mr Heseltine's business and commercial experience. He likened this structure to that of the 'Finance Director' in a company and, continuing this line of reasoning, he saw the structure as designed to achieve stronger control over the Ministry's corporate planning. There might also have been the desire to generate some creative tension, but he recognised that the Defence Staff, the Office of Management and Budget and the single-Service departments had to pull together. He saw this being facilitated, *inter alia*, by the Head of the Office of Management and Budget being the senior civilian member of each of the Service Boards. Furthermore, in order to meet one of his other objectives of widening spans of control, he envisaged that this Office would also include all the other areas of central civilian administration work such as finance, civilian management and pay, legal and lands matters.

The Open Government document did not go into precise structures or terms of reference. That would be the next stage when, after consultation, a detailed organisation would be set out, thus identifying the savings in top posts it was stated would be achieved. Nor did it detail the nature and degree of delegation involved in the proposed responsibility budgets.

In the course of the statement made to the House of Commons on the day of publication (12 March 1984) the Secretary of State received a considerable degree of support for tautening the Ministry's organisation, on the understanding that it would do nothing to harm the separate traditions of the three Services.

Then began a hectic period of consultation. The Secretary of State invited comments from all members of the Ministry, the senior of whom he addressed, giving his thinking behind the document. In parallel a Steering Group on Defence Organisation was set up, under the chairmanship of the PUS and with the CDS among its members, to draw up precise proposals. Shortly afterwards the annual Statement on Defence Estimates (Cmnd 9227) was published, which stressed yet again the limits on resources and the need for rigorous scrutiny and flexible budgetary management. It also recapitulated the three main elements of the future: the combined Defence Staff; the Office of Management and Budget; and the role of the single-Service Chiefs of Staff, through the medium of the Service Departments, in the management of their Services, particularly in the direction of streamlining and delegation.

Meanwhile, public interest concentrated on the effect of these proposals on the position of the single-Service Chiefs of Staff as Heads of their Services. Apart from press correspondence there was an extensive debate in the House of Lords on 13 June in which several former ministers at the Ministry of Defence and former Chiefs of the Defence Staff took part. While there was a considerable degree of support for the strengthened powers of the Chief of the Defence Staff as introduced in 1982, there was concern, varying in degree, that the single-Service Chiefs of Staff would now be made so bereft of power because of the lack of staff and advice that they would be reduced to the role of 'Inspector-General'. They would not be able to discharge the responsibilities for the 'total fighting efficiency and morale' of the Services which the document stated they would still have. There was also some concern that the concentration of advice in two pairs of hands would reduce the scope for constructive debate and that the position and value of the Chief Scientific Adviser might be undesirably weakened. Given this interest and recognising the anxieties of the current single-Service Chiefs of Staff, Mr Heseltine suggested that, as part of the consultation process, all four Chiefs of Staff should see the Prime Minister. This meeting took place in early July.

THE PROMULGATION OF DECISIONS

On 18 July, some four months after the publication of the consultative document, the Government was in a position to issue a White Paper (Cmnd 9315) setting out its conclusions. (Its key organisation chart is at Appendix C in this volume.) They were in definite enough terms to enable it to announce that the implementation date would be 2 January 1985, while acknowledging that there were still ongoing issues to be resolved on the details of implementation.

The three basic building-blocks were confirmed. Much of the White Paper was taken up with details of terms of reference and the structure of subordinate parts of the three main areas. But there were nuances of importance that call for comment.

In his accompanying statement to the House of Commons on 18 July, Mr Heseltine took care to underline that the strengthened position of the Chief of the Defence Staff as the principal military adviser of the Government would not undermine unduly the contribution of the single-Service Chiefs of Staff:

The Government . . . attach critical importance to the role of the Service Chiefs of Staff in the maintenance of the fighting effectiveness and the morale of the Services . . . To exercise these crucial responsibilities the Service Chiefs of Staff will have full access to the Defence Staff, as well as retaining substantial staffs under their control. The Service Chiefs of Staff will continue fully to contribute to policy-making through their membership of the Defence Council, the Service Boards and the Chiefs of Staff Committee and will retain their right of direct access to the Prime Minister.

He also responded to anxieties about the Chief Scientific Adviser by saying:

Ministers need to be able to draw on independent scientific advice on long-term options and the scrutiny of major equipment proposals, and the staffs concerned are to be brought more closely under the direction of the Chief Scientific Adviser.

The White Paper gave greater precision to the specific changes. On the complex interrelationships of the four Chiefs of Staff it spelt out the main responsibilities of the Chief of the Defence Staff as being:

(a) tendering military advice on strategy, forward policy, overall priorities in resource allocation, programmes, current commitments and operations. In his advice he will take into account the views of the Chiefs of Staff and ensure that they are properly reflected.
(b) the planning, direction and conduct of all national military operations including the issue of relevant operational directives
(c) directing the work of the Defence Staff.

This wording confirmed and spelt out a considerable degree of centralisation in both the programmes and the operations fields. At the same time the White Paper not only confirmed that the single-Service Chiefs of Staff would have access to the Defence Staff, but that each Chief of Staff would have sufficient staff to enable him to 'direct the work of his Service including that of his Principal Personnel Officer and Principal Administrative Officer and their staffs'. The important word here is 'including'. In practice it meant, as became clear when the Secretary of State appeared before the House of Commons Defence Committee on 25 July, that there would be a two-star officer serving each Chief of Staff (two in the case of the Army, as the second was necessary to reflect HMG's commitment to the Territorial Army) with the prime responsibility of providing a focal point for access to the Defence Staff and thus ensuring the necessary linkage between policy-making and management. The precise number of staff from the existing Naval, General and Air Staffs who would not be transferred to the Defence Staff but would remain to serve these two-star posts was acknowledged to be unresolved at this time. Mr Heseltine wished to keep the numbers small, but it was suggested that it might be as many as 200 out of a total of 470.

As for the new unified Defence Staff three major specific points were clarified. First, the day-to-day direction of the staff would be under a four-star Vice-Chief of the Defence Staff who would be a member of the Chiefs of Staff Committee and the Defence Council. This level of rank and status was very important in underlining the authority and power of the unified staff and the thrust to 'defence' solutions. Second, the staff would be grouped under four three-star officers (one a Deputy Under-Secretary of State); the first covering strategy and policy; the second programmes and personnel; the third systems, including both operational requirements and command, control, communications and information systems; and the fourth commitments, which would cover both joint and single-Service plans. Third, while the 'defence-wide' basis and 'central coordination' were stressed, it was acknowledged that programmes would need to be looked at on a single-Service as well as a collective basis and that operational requirements would have to be organised – the White Paper said 'initially' – on a sea, land and air basis, thereby reflecting not only the existence of the three Service Departments but also the groupings of the Systems Controllerates within the Procurement Executive. Therefore, within the very significant step that the creation of this unified staff represented, there were elements of gradualness and realistic caution.

Within the Office of Management and Budget, three of the four groupings were incorporated without any change: finance, administration and civilian management. As for the area of Resources and Programmes, which was to be the budgetary complement and counterbalance to the Defence Staff, nothing was said about its internal structure or under what headings the budget would be broken down.

For the rest, the White Paper announced a miscellany of steps covering other areas of the Ministry. There was the creation of an independent Defence Arms Control Unit, deliberately kept outside the Defence Staff. The ongoing commitment to rationalisation was stressed: one further example was announced in the form of the creation of a single unified headquarters within the Ministry for medical matters which would control the three uniformed medical corps whose separate continued existence was confirmed. The basic soundness of the Procurement Executive was reiterated while stating that more effective competition for defence contracts and greater commercial professionalism within the staff of the Ministry would lead to better value for money.

The House of Commons Defence Committee had been keenly waiting to get their teeth into this reorganisation. They began to take evidence the day following the publication of the White Paper. In two intensive sessions they saw three former Chiefs of Staff (two of whom had subsequently become Chief of the Defence Staff), followed by the Secretary of State, the Chief of the Defence Staff (Field Marshal Sir Edwin Bramall) and the Permanent Under-Secretary of State (Sir Clive Whitmore). Much of the evidence concentrated on the Defence Staff and the changed position of the single-Service Chiefs of Staff. In the course of the exchanges it emerged that the Chiefs of Staff, given the option, would have preferred not to have had a hurried major reorganisation but to have tried to get more out of the 1982 changes. However, after discussions with the Secretary of State and then with the Prime Minister, who had assured them of the very great importance attached to the advice of the Chiefs of Staff both individually and collectively and who said that she would welcome a review of the reorganisation in about a year's time, the Chief of Staff considered that the 'safeguards', as it was put, were now adequate. One supporting reason that was given was that the organisation still contained provision for single-Service expertise. There would be both Systems blocks and Service blocks in the working arrangements of the Defence Staff. For example while all the size and shape dimensions were to be concentrated in the Office of Management and Budget, their structure would still be based on single-Service groupings. These divisions would therefore in their dealings with the Programme Staff of the Defence Staff and the Service Department still be able to present financial information in Service as well as functional terms.

In the light of their sessions of evidence the House of Commons Defence Committee reported in October. Their approach was to set the proposals in the context of the aims and organisational development over the previous two decades. The issues in the Ministry's documents covered well-trodden ground, and the Committee identified two main aims: economy, and the radical restructuring of the central staffs. In their judgement the economies flowing from reorganisation within the Ministry itself would not be significant. Therefore the benefits would have to be judged by whatever gains in cost-effectiveness in the defence programme were achieved, and the extent to which the new Defence Staff and the Office of Management and Budget could contribute to such gains. Better financial information should clearly be of value, but so too would be the provision of a disciplined methodology for resource allocation. On this point they remained disappointed at the apparent loss of status of the Chief Scientific Adviser and hoped that greater use would be made of the Defence Operational Analysis Establishment. The Committee supported the retention by the single-Service Chiefs of Staff of sufficient staff to enable them to make an input into policy and saw no harm in some healthy disagreement. They noted what they regarded as somewhat odd omissions or inconclusiveness: the absence of any reference to the importance of the changed appointments system introduced in 1982; the ambiguity over the role of the Defence Council; the vagueness over devolution. Their general tone was a mixture of moderate approval and mild scepticism.

Meanwhile work continued at a fast pace to achieve the target date of 2 January 1985. There was one unforeshadowed development in December 1984 when the post of Chief of Defence Procurement was sub-divided by the creation – also at Permanent Under-Secretary level – of a second post of Chief of Defence Equipment Collaboration. But this was not basically an organisational issue; indeed the subsequent 1985 Statement on the Defence Estimates (Cmnd 9430) reiterated the basic soundness of the Procurement Executive, and justified the additional post on the grounds of the increasing importance of collaboration.

More generally, the 1985 Statement reported that the new structure had come into effect as planned and was working successfully. The Statement went on to underline the continued role of MINIS in the search for efficiency, and identified three areas – the responsibility budgets; the rationalisation of support; and the delegation in the field of defence research – where efforts would be concentrated.

1985 passed without any major operational crises or public expenditure pressures which would have called for a major review of defence priorities. The new organisations were therefore not subject to severe pressures in their infancy and they had a period of grace to settle down and evolve good working relationships. January 1986 saw the sudden resignation of Mr Heseltine but, looked at purely in the context of the organisation of the Ministry, he had stayed long enough at least to see the Headquarters changes he had so energetically pursued reasonably bedded down into the system.

1986 AND A NEW SECRETARY OF STATE

It was therefore not surprising that the first formal stocktaking (Cmnd 9763) of the new organisation by its new Secretary of State, Mr George Younger, pointed the way to a period of consolidation. The new organisation was reported to have worked successfully in its first year. No major changes were foreseen, though clearly there was scope for refinement in particular areas. However, there were rather more specific comments in the procurement field. Again this is not surprising. Mr Heseltine's original consultative document acknowledged that much less work had been done on the procurement of equipment and that this whole field would be looked at separately. Furthermore, by 1986 the new Chief of Defence Procurement, Mr Peter Levene, the first to be brought in from the private sector since Mr Rayner's initial filling of the post, had had over a year's experience of the system. In addition, that period had seen much public criticism of defence procurement policies, notably the continued rumblings about the correctness of the 1978 decision to go for the national manufacture of an early-warning aircraft and its associated radar rather than an off-the-shelf purchase of the in-service American AWACS, and the challenge about the basic design of the Royal Navy's frigates and destroyers – the fat-versus-thin controversy. Therefore the White Paper, apart from announcing that a small team would be set up internally to look at the organisation for procurement, detailed a number of measures that were to be taken within the framework of the organisation to improve its efficiency.

In the course of 1986, several defence issues gained high political prominence. The issues of nuclear disarmament and the future of Trident, vital and major though they both are, did not have any organisational overtones. Two other contentious issues were both in the procurement field: the future of Westlands which led to the resignation of Mr Heseltine, and the future of Nimrod AEW. The House of Commons Defence Committee carried out an enquiry into the Westland affair, and in their subsequent report (H.C. 518 of July 1986) commented adversely on the relationships between the Ministry of Defence and the Department of Trade and Industry. Once again, as in their 1981/2 Report on Defence Organisation and Procurement (H.C. 22 of Session 81/2), they went back to the recommendation of the Rayner Report, which favoured the creation of a Ministerial Aerospace Board and which had not been implemented. Once again the Government in their reply (Cmnd 8678) stated that the relationships, both formal and informal, between the two Departments were excellent, and expressed the view that the quality of the relationships would not be enhanced by imposing on them the formal structure of such a Board. Here, at least, there has been no change. When, at the end of the year, the selection of the American AWACS was announced, initial attention was focused on the decision-making processes within the Ministry of Defence and the relationships between the Procurement Executive and British Industry, rather than on the relationships between the Ministry of Defence and the Department of Trade and Industry. The criticisms were of procedures and alleged incompetence rather than of organisational systems.

Part III

Factors of General Influence

Part III

Factors of External Influence

6 Factors of General Influence

GENERAL CONSIDERATIONS

The chapters of Part II have given a chronological account of the evolution of the organisation of the Ministry. Part IV will consider, in more depth, the particular issues and problems in each of the main functional areas of groupings within the Ministry. Before turning to this detailed analysis it is first necessary to see whether certain general factors have had significant effects either on the general shape and speed of change in the Ministry or, more specifically, on individual areas within it.

Five such general factors are discussed in this chapter. First, there is the changing position of the UK, coupled with the range and size of its military commitments and their consequences for the range and complexity of the work carried out within the Ministry. Second, there is the all-pervasive matter of finance and the handling of the defence budget, coupled with the extent to which practical realities in these fields may have acted as a constraint on radical organisational change. The third factor is the very size of the Ministry: how far has this been a political and budgetary issue in its own right which has in turn led to intensifying the search for particular organisational solutions. The fourth and fifth factors are of a rather different nature: the one dealing with the relationship between ministers and senior military officers and the question of any changes in the balance between them, and the other dealing with relationships with other Government Departments and within central government as a whole.

(1)THE WORLD SCENE AND THE UK's PLACE

The decades since 1945 have seen major changes in the balance of power and in the UK's perception of its place and role in this changing scene. The main landmarks are easily identified: the UK's position alongside the USA and the USSR in the peace negotiations of 1945; the formation of NATO; the withdrawal from Empire; the extended retention of Treaty obligations in the Far East, the Middle East and the Near East; the development and changing natures of the Commonwealth and the European Economic Community; the 'special' relationship with the USA, including the particular military dimension of nuclear weapons cooperation; the declining but still not wholly extinguished colonial obligations. This is not the place either to explore this complex history and the many reviews of defence policy required to adapt to these changes, or even to consider their consequences for the size, shape and equipment of the Armed Forces. But there are certain factors which can be identified as having very general but at the same time profound effects on the size and shape of the Ministry.

First, for the NATO role successive Governments have considered that the UK, as a major European member and moreover as one in a special position as a nuclear power, should contribute the complete spectrum of military capabilities spanning strategic nuclear and conventional forces, with these forces deployed on the central front, on the flanks, in the maritime roles in the Atlantic, the Channel and the Mediterranean, supplemented by a significant air and amphibious reinforcement capability. Furthermore, in the policy and planning fields it should be able to make a significant and constructive contribution across the fields of strategy, of force levels including disarmament aspects, of logistic rationalisation and of equipment policy. The UK has tried to make its influence felt not only through normal NATO machinery but also both bilaterally with the USA and by initiating special European groupings within a rather flexible European framework.

Second, notwithstanding the withdrawal of forces from many theatres and the dissolution of such Treaty obligations as CENTO and SEATO, HMG still has commitments outside the NATO area scattered round the world, including such sensitive areas as Belize, Cyprus, the Falkland Islands and Hong Kong. This type of global commitment has called, over the decades, for considerable staff resources to be located centrally in the Ministry in what is now the Defence Staff and the associated Defence Secretariats in order to provide political and intelligence assessments, to define appropriate force structures, to draw up contingency plans and to provide either direct control of, or information about any operations all within a coherent policy for operating outside NATO. There is a related need for a wide spread and depth of consultation with the Foreign and Commonwealth Office, and for adequate machinery to bring issues promptly and efficiently before Ministers collectively. While the likely frequency and geographical spread of military operations may have declined greatly compared with the 1950s and 1960s, there is still a desire, encouraged by Governments, to maintain contacts and provide a flow of information on a worldwide basis. Special links with old Commonwealth partners are preserved. Contacts with emergent independent countries are fostered, particularly in the fields of training, military assistance and the supply of defence equipment.

This worldwide range of commitments or interests has had major effects on the make-up both of the front lines of the Services and of their equipment programmes. The variety of the tasks has called for the provision of virtually every form of military capability. Some European land powers may have found it possible to concentrate on land and related air roles. Some maritime powers may have looked to a sea–air emphasis. British Governments have continued to cover the whole spectrum of sea, land and air capabilities including such sub-specialisations as amphibious and airborne forces, capped with the strategic nuclear deterrent. Occasionally there have been fierce debates about the retention of every capability (e.g. the carrier debate in the 1960s), but the usual result, when faced with budgetary pressures, has been for Governments to reduce the size of individual elements rather than eliminate a capability. Even where radical decisions for future phasings-out were taken, as over aircraft carriers in 1966 or the amphibious capability in 1981, they were soon modified. Therefore, within the Defence Staffs and Service Departments and the Procurement Executive, provision has had to be made for operational planning, for staff training, for specialised manning, for supply and support and for specifying and providing new equipment for this total range of capabilities.

This spectrum of capabilities, coupled with our perception of our manufacturing interests poised between self-sufficiency, Europe, the USA and the Commonwealth, have greatly complicated defence procurement policies. Staff had not only to specify a wide range of requirements but they were continually considering, often it seemed from scratch, whether to go it alone on production, or collaborate, or buy off the shelf. Much staff work was required internally to arrive at a Ministry of Defence view from often competing military, financial and scientific arguments. Discussion also had to be joined within HMG and the economic and trade Departments and separately with NATO allies or other potential partners or suppliers. The issue is still very much alive: the controversy over the selection of an early-warning aircraft is the most recent example.

All these factors have tended to conspire together to have a similar and cumulative effect on the Ministry. First, by virtue of the range and complexity of the tasks allocated to the Services, they have been used as justifications, and validly so, for the continuation of comprehensive staff resources within the Service Departments. Second, they have called for the provision of special cells in such areas as overseas training, defence sales, allied liaison or tactical doctrine. Third, they have added to the burden of central coordination and policy determination. Finally, they have added, quite significantly, to the burdens placed on the senior staffs. Ministers are involved in a wide range of bilateral and multilateral talks and frequent overseas visits. Senior military staff have to maintain relations with dozens of foreign forces. Procurement staff find themselves caught up in major issues of principle and consequently time-absorbing discussions with British industry and foreign interests on most large equipment projects. On top of all this, by virtue of the multiplier of complexity, the sum of the whole is greater than the parts in the demands it makes on the organisation. The range and nature of the tasks and problems are probably greater and more complex in 1986 than in 1946.

(2) CONTROL OF EXPENDITURE: THE SEARCH FOR SIMPLE PERFECTION

The opening chapters showed that the high costs of the defence programme have lain uneasily and threateningly behind many of the organisational changes in recent years. The later chapters, particularly those on the functional areas of Procurement and the Permanent Under-Secretary of State's Department, will detail the organisational changes that have been made in specific fields such as the defence budget, the estimates, functional costings, financial control, accounts, contract and audit.

Taken together these various fields span the whole subject of expenditure from the inception of new requirements for manpower, equipment or logistic support to the checking of the value and efficient use of the resultant in-Service activity. Much attention has been devoted to the adequacy of the financial systems in all these areas. They have been subject to much criticism. Some of it has been directed more towards the techniques used and the degree of professionalism of the staff – e.g. in the project management, contract and accounts areas – than towards the organisation as such. In other areas, attention has been concentrated on the degree of objectivity and authority enjoyed by the staff – e.g. in such fields as manpower control, systems audit and the scrutiny of new requirements. This has led to pressure towards centralisation on a unified basis as a way of ensuring greater independence from the executive management areas of the Service Departments and the Systems Controllers in the Procurement Executive.

But it is in the field of the defence budget and the most cost-effective allocation of resources at the macro level that the critical voices in the outside world have been the most strident and have from time to time found an echo in the views of ministers. The main thrust of the criticism has been that in some way reorganisation, coupled with changes in the method of production of the financial information, should help to achieve a more efficient allocation of resources than has resulted from the alleged self-perpetuating carve-up between the three Services. In support of this charge the pattern of the allocation of the defence budget over the years is cited as evidence to support the contention that the variations in the shareout of the defence budget between the three Services has been minuscule. The table at Appendix F gives percentage shares over a period of years. Not unexpectedly, the figures are open to differing interpretations. Some will argue that the shifts are very small, thus supporting the earlier contention. Some will argue that, given the in-built stability of manpower costs for some years ahead (unless there is a massive redundancy programme or marked changes in recruitment policy), and given the significant proportion of the budget that is taken up with recurring routine costs in such fields as works maintenance, supply, repair and unit running costs, the changes are in fact significant. Others will point out that big shifts can occur only as a result of major changes in foreign policy with consequent changes in strategies and basic roles. Therefore, so long as the UK regards its roles in NATO as requiring a considerable sizeable land and air presence on the mainland of Europe, a major naval contribution in the Atlantic and Mediterranean, the air defence of the UK base and flexible forces to operate on the flanks, the case for a large continuing contribution from each of the three Services is inevitable and self-evident. A steady pattern, so this line of argument concludes, is therefore logical and by no means a sign of weaknesses in central policy direction. It will be noted that the figures have been steadier in the 1980s (after the various measures to give more power to the Centre) than in the 1970s, which could be taken to indicate that external international or economic factors have more influence than the internal power balance within the Ministry.

Wherever the balance of truth may lie, there still remains a considerable school of thought that it would give greater credence to the objectivity of the system if, somehow, the resource allocations could emerge, as it were, pure and undistorted from a central source. Such data, it is accepted, would have to be in such a sophisticated budgetary framework that they could be susceptible to permutation in accordance with alternative policy options without undue interference from the individual Services with their arguments of self-interest.

The feasibility of such a concept is fundamentally affected by three considerations: the framework in which the data can be produced; the sources from which the data has to be drawn; the locations of the staff who are best able to interpret and adjudicate on them.

As to the form of presentation, it has long been recognised that the needs of Parliament for Estimates based on inputs and prepared for the following financial year were not relevant to the control of a massive long-term programme which needed to be viewed much more in output terms and over a cycle of something like ten years at least. Since the 1950s, various new techniques and methods of presentation have been introduced, undoubtedly with considerable benefit. There has been the policy, gradually applied across all major spending Government Departments and embraced in the Public Expenditure Survey, which set firm ceilings and associated policy assumptions over a three-to-four-year period. In the Ministry of Defence this was extended by the introduction of a ten-year Long Term Costing. Furthermore these longer-term figures were also translated, and on a steadily more refined basis, into a series of costs based on functional programme headings, thus giving a picture based on output across the major strategic functions. It is interesting to note that over the same period the US Department of Defense was wrestling with the same problem and approached it in fundamentally the same way, though with significant variations of detail, through its Planning, Budgeting and Programming System. These new methods of presentation have undoubtedly given a better overall view of the trends of the defence budget. But they have probably not been proportionately as useful in aiding decisions involving switches of resources. One main reason is that a functional programme is at its most usable when the strategic task which it costs is clearly separable and can be carried out *in toto* by one Service or another. The strategic nuclear deterrent is an excellent example where the programme costs are largely self-contained and bring out clearly the financial implications of selecting a submarine-launched, air-launched or land-based system, though even here, quite obviously, other factors, political or tactical, may dominate the decision. But the functional programme costing becomes less complete in its validity when individual components of a programme (e.g. early-warning aircraft) can contribute at different times and in different proportions to different functional programmes which are concerned with maritime warfare or the air defence of the UK or the European theatre. In such flexible use of forces, allocation of costs to particular programme elements becomes arbitrary rather than a useful tool of budget management.

The second consideration is the source of the data. Costs of a function have to be built up from a variety of sources, including the military units themselves, the works expenditure input from the Property Services Agency and the future equipment costs from the Procurement Executive. But the primary source of an informed view on their internal consistency and comprehensiveness remains the Service Department, given its continuing role of the executive management of a Service as a totality. Therefore any significant change of assumptions, and consequently of the likely costs, needs to be validated by dialogue between the policy staffs and the executive authorities. While models may be improving in flexibility and complexity and while computer simulation may be increasing its range of possible permutations, the stage has not been reached when the effects of programme changes can be responsibly assessed in central isolation, without careful user consultation.

The third consideration is the ability of a central body of staff to coordinate, interpret and take informed decisions on the basis of such data. The staff need to have a deep professional understanding of the military implications of the military programmes; hence the need for single-Service representation. The military staff also need an understanding of the wider strategic and international scene as a whole; hence the importance of joint-Service staff training. They need to have their own corpus of political and financial advice; hence

the creation of central defence secretariat and budget staffs. They
need to have their own independent analytical capacity; hence the
presence of scientific staffs. The precise way in which these elements
are organised is a secondary question. The most recent emanation
is the twin structure of the Defence Staff and the Office of Management and Budget. But, as has been recognised in the statements
associated with the creation of these bodies and as is supported by
the arguments in the preceding paragraphs, these staffs, as currently
structured, will not be adequate in themselves to validate their
thinking, which can be as radical as they wish, without detailed
consultation with the executive Departments involved inside or
outside the Ministry of Defence. To go further and centralise all the
staff in the centre would invalidate any management capability in
the Service Department. Furthermore, when the policy decisions
have been taken and the resources allocated in principle there is a
large vitally important and continuing task of monitoring the progress
of the expenditure, evaluating its cost-effectiveness when in operational conditions and completing the circle by drawing lessons for
the future. This work must lie with those with executive responsibility
for the programmes to be carried out in military and other units.

   This brief selective survey is not intended to be even the outline
of a review of the system of financial control, which is a major
study in its own right. But it can nevertheless point to certain broad
organisational conclusions. The total spectrum of the Ministry's
activities from the initial gleam in the researcher's eye to the day-
to-day running of an operational unit all have financial consequences,
but that does not mean that they need identical financial structures.
It does mean that there must be overall control and the ability to
review and change a system. A part of the Ministry must be responsible for the efficiency and compatibility of all the many localised
financial systems. This task rests squarely on the PUS as the
Accounting Officer responsible for the working of the Ministry. With
the changes in the 1980s he has now within his staff and particularly in
the central DUS (Finance) and the Director General of Management
Audit the wherewithal to control and review the financial systems.
Another part of the Ministry must be responsible for information
and advice on programme costs as an essential prerequisite for the
major decisions on resource allocation. The creation of the Office of
Management and Budget with its lines into the Service Departments
should meet this need.

   The framework of an adequate central financial system would

seem to have been established and to have a sensible compatibility with the continued existence and role of the Service Departments, provided that adequate advice is made available to the single-Service Chiefs of Staff. Its degree of efficacy gives rise to a separate range of issues which are not primarily ones of organisation. Techniques will continue to be improved and reviewed. The responsibility budget system is one recent example. Renewed attention is being paid to the control methods operated by the Procurement Executive. There are both internal and external systems for monitoring; in the latter case notably the National Audit Office. To make judgements about the higher visibility area of resource allocation is more difficult and more elusive. If major problems arise in the future over the defence budget, as they are bound to do at some time, they do not necessarily mean that the system has failed. They could arise from major shifts in the Government's priorities or economic policies, or from international developments. The test should be whether the organisation can then produce timely comprehensive financial advice to ministers and the Chiefs of Staff.

(3) SIZE OF THE MINISTRY

Size is an important and very visible aspect of the organisation of the Ministry, as it is of the organisation and therefore the functions of any major headquarters whether in the public or private sectors. For the Ministry of Defence, size has four main consequences. First, there is the question of its direct cost. Headquarters staff, often of senior rank and therefore proportionately more costly in themselves, need proportionately more clerical and other support, expensive communications facilities, and accommodation which is in itself more expensive if they are located in the London area. Notwithstanding the major evacuation in the Second World War to Bath, where large parts of the Admiralty still are, much of the Ministry is still located in a hotch-potch of buildings in the London area. Plans in the 1970s to bring about major dispersal of the Ministry either to Milton Keynes or to Cardiff and Glasgow were not carried through. These factors tend to give added prominence to the direct costs of the Headquarters of the Ministry in London and elsewhere which amounted in 1986/7 to £273m.

Second, it adds to the burden of senior management if, in addition to their primary policy responsibilities, many large and multifarious groups are their direct day-to-day responsibility because they are organisationally a part of the Headquarters. This is a special factor for Ministers who then have to account in rather more detail to Parliament for the workings of these staffs. It becomes a still greater burden at a time when the managerial responsibilities of Ministers are being increasingly stressed.

Third, the very size of a Headquarters can add to inefficiency. This is particularly so if, because of a combination of the previous two factors, there is much detailed executive work to be controlled and that control task is also made more difficult because the absence of central accommodation results in time-consuming physical separation, not only between separate line-management areas which need to work closely together but also between the individual staffs and their own superior line-managers. In many cases senior staff have been concentrated in Whitehall away from their staffs, because of political requirements of rapid accessibility to Ministers and the presentational and psychological desire to bring together the senior officers of the three Services.

Fourth, there is a political dimension to the size itself. A very large Ministry attracts, almost automatically, charges of unnecessary bureaucracy. The Ministry of Defence, as the largest Department in Whitehall since the unifications of 1964 and 1972, has been specially vulnerable to such criticism, particularly when there have been major political campaigns to reduce the size of the Civil Service. There is a second reason for such vulnerability. The field of defence tempts, often rightly, the contrast between the 'teeth' of the front line and the 'tail' of the Headquarters structures, and within them of the Ministry rather more than the Command Headquarters. Such criticism leads to pressure, wholly legitimate as an aspiration, for the transfer of resources, flowing from economies, from the 'tail' to the 'teeth'.

Unification in 1964 inevitably concentrated attention on the statistics of the size of this new Ministry. The associated policy of wanting to co-locate in Whitehall as many key senior staff as possible illustrated graphically how limited the results could be even in a building containing 3000 staff, and how much inefficiency was caused by separation between senior staff and their divisions and directorates. In the following decades there has been continuous pressure to reduce numbers. Sometimes it was an element of major organisational studies which had to examine as part of their task whether all the many roles identified in Chapter 1 were essential to the

Ministry itself. Sometimes the pressure came from straightforward economy exercises, which were themselves on occasions more selectively directed at the number of the high-visibility senior posts.

The table at Appendix G shows that over the years very significant reductions have been made. Even though totally valid comparisons cannot be made because of accompanying reclassifications of posts as between Headquarters and outstations, it would seem that the Ministry has reduced proportionately more in size than the Armed Forces; a commendable achievement, not easy to bring about.

The straightforward elimination of work and posts by inspection and other techniques has led directly to worthwhile savings. In addition, there have been savings in numbers by changing the status of groupings (e.g. the privatisation of the Royal Ordnance Factories) or by transferring work to Commands or other formations. Such changes have not necessarily just been presentational devices. They have had real organisational benefits by reducing the burden on senior managers and by increasing the efficiency of the transferred area of work. At the same time there cannot be the easy assumption that all reductions are automatically advantageous and that all additions are to be deplored. A new, well-directed and influential policy staff may lead to economies and increases in efficiency across the defence programme as a whole, far greater than its direct extra costs. For example, the Rayner Report saw the possibility of benefits from increasing resources on certain policy and personnel aspects of procurement. The expansion of the Headquarters effort on operational analysis was considered to be able to increase the more cost-effective allocation of resources.

The interplay between the search for economy and the overall shape of the Ministry has taken several forms. In some cases they have contributed to altering the relative balance between major parts of the Ministry. In others the residual organisation was not affected although there were gains in simplification and economy.

One major line of approach was the search for areas for unification. Such a search had always to be balanced against the continuation of the three Services and the extent to which each Service had to be given its own dedicated specialist support. Understandably, unification was much easier to justify and bring about in the civilian areas. The chronological account in the opening chapters lists a series of fields that were tackled over the two decades following 1964, covering functional areas such as contracts, accounts, information, security, management audit and civilian personnel management. The benefits, the extent of the savings and the organisational and other consequences have varied from area to area. A few examples may be helpful. The unification of the personnel management of civilian personnel led to considerable savings. Major groups of staff (e.g. all the executive grades and all the industrial staff) could each be managed by one division instead of by the four there used to be at the time of the separate Service Ministries and a Supply Ministry. But a more radical consequence was that the change facilitated the development of a personnel policy under which staff could be trained and posted more by professional skills (e.g. finance, logistics) than by single-Service affiliations. The resultant objectivity was highly relevant in such areas as resource allocation and financial control.

Another area which particularly calls for identification and application of best management practices is that of management audit. The Service Ministries had their own organisations to control bids for manpower and to apply such emerging techniques as O and M, Management by Objectives and internal audit. The development, over a number of stages, of a unified Directorate General of Management Audit resulted in a central structure with a greater degree of independence, authority and professionalism, which was most notably used as a key tool in Mr Heseltine's application of the MINIS system to the reshaping of the Ministry.

The Information Staffs illustrate a variety of pressures. Politically and across Government as a whole, they were subject to repeated challenges both of principle (Why have them at all as they are merely unnecessary intermediaries?) and of their size (Why have these staffs become such a growth area in post-Whitehall history?). In the Ministry of Defence there was the extra dimension of the balance between the presentation of overall defence policy, single-Service lobbying and the legitimate flow of information about single-Service activities. Several major studies took place even after the initial creation in 1964 of a central Chief of Public Relations. Although the numbers were not large in relation to the Ministry as a whole, the arguments were fiercely joined because the area symbolised the issue of the right balance between the centre and the Service Departments. The general trend, which encompassed economies, was to reduce both in numbers and rank levels the single-Service staffs within the unified structure but not to eliminate them altogether. At the same time, fully functional sections were built up for such tasks as films, the press desk and facilities. The net result was a significant reduction.

Within the military staff areas, moves towards unification of divisions carrying out related work were more contentious and as a result much more spasmodic. There was effectively none in the P & L areas where work was most obviously in support of single-Service activities. Small central staffs were created but they were to supplement rather than replace single-Service divisions. Their roles were to coordinate (e.g. on pay policy) or to stimulate (e.g. the creation of a Director General of Standardisation and Codification). An exception which proves the rule is the organisational handling of the Medical Services. After numerous studies, a central organisation was set up in 1985 under a single top post, entitled Surgeon General, and it was decided that such facilities as hospitals should be subject to central unified direction of policy. But the accompanying announcement underlined the continuance of three separate Medical Branches each with its own head. The unified directorate-general still provides the consequential element of headquarters single-Service administration.

In the areas of the Naval, General and Air Staffs the contentiousness was at its highest. While the fields of intelligence and certain aspects of signals were unified in the 1960s, the unified bodies still included single-Service groupings. A similar pattern occurred as recently as 1985 when the Operational Requirements staffs were brought together, but still subdivided by Sea, Land and Air Systems. This change was just one, but a very important element in the creation of the new Defence Staff. The driving force was not so much one of economy as of the principle of finding a 'defence' solution. Economies were being sought, but their extent was eroded by the acceptance of another principle by which the single-Service Chiefs of Staff were permitted to have policy staffs of their own under their own direct control as well as to draw on the resources of the new Defence Staff.

A second line of approach to the search for economy has been the elimination of detail. By contrast, this approach is of little significance organisationally. It generally means the excision of posts mostly at the lower levels. It is a thesis to which all have no difficulty in subscribing in theory. In practice it is constrained much more in a Government Department than in the private sector, by the special requirements of the accountability of Ministers to Parliament and of the financial controls flowing from the presentation of Estimates and the role of the Public Accounts Committee and the National Audit Office.

A third line of approach, and one which in theory overcomes the problems mentioned in the preceding paragraphs, is to hive off the activity outside Government. Policies since 1979 have resulted in a sustained thrust in this direction, mostly taking the form of privatisation. Decisions on the ROFs eliminated 18 000 posts and on the Dockyards will eliminate 16 000, in both cases including some Headquarters staff. Further suitable areas will similarly tend to be large self-contained areas of executive work, such as repair of equipment, contract cleaning and catering, printing, rather than policy work in the Ministry. Even if, for example, there was to be a major move to go further in placing research and development work in the private sector rather than in the R & D Establishments, there would still need to be a policy staff in the Procurement Executive to decide upon the scale and allocation of the work, to interface with the Armed Forces and to carry out the necessary monitoring. But there remain some anomalies within the Ministry itself. For historical reasons, which may or may not still be valid, there is far more ship design work carried out within the staffs of the Controller of the Navy than there is aircraft design within the Controllerate of Aircraft.

A fourth approach to economy is delegation, particularly to Command Headquarters which already have staffs working in the same area. This possibility has been made much more realisable with the concentration of the military Command Headquarters in the UK into one or at most two for each Service, and with the withdrawal from most of the overseas theatres. Major UK Commands are now in a much better position to take on management functions for the whole Service. Delegation can cover many areas of the work of a Service Department. Detailed control of naval movements can be carried out at C-in-C Fleet's Headquarters. Much work earlier done in the Air Force Department on aircraft engineering has been passed to RAF Strike Command. The Army Department have created a Logistic Executive which has brought together and rationalised a range of Ordnance and Engineering work.

Notwithstanding these various approaches to economy in posts the Ministry still remains a very large organisation. This is not wrong in itself. In its management activities there are major areas where it remains economical in overall resource terms to carry out a task within the Ministry. Its centralised handling of staff both uniformed and civilian is a good example. In its policy activities the roles described in Chapter 1 are many and complex, and call for close integration for their successful discharge. But the drive for economy has resulted in valuable savings and would seem to have been generally beneficial. While it is not possible wholly to isolate changes brought about by pressure on the size from changes brought about for wider considerations, the pressure on the size has lent support to three important organisational trends. It has encouraged the elimination of duplication between the Service Departments and their Command Headquarters, finding the answer mostly in greater delegation. Second, it has achieved significant savings in the PUS's staff mostly by unification of staffs. As a consequence the centralised staff have had a greater all-embracing role and the self-contained independence of the Service Departments has been weakened. This shift of emphasis is clearly exemplified in the progressive elimination of senior civilian posts in the Service Departments: initially the creation of Second PUSs, then the reduction of the full-time civilian Board Member to Deputy Under-Secretary, and most recently the disestablishment of the three Deputy Under-Secretaries and the three Staff Assistant Under-Secretaries. This shift reflects not only the unification of civilian management but also the centralisation of the financial responsibilities both for the longer-term budgetary allocation and the block Estimates in the Office of Management and Budget. That the process has not gone still further reflects, as has been discussed earlier, the impracticability as yet of finding any way of constructing the financial programme other than from basically single-Service elements for which the Service Departments need size-able finance staffs. Third, similar pressures have led to a similar trend away from the Naval, General and Air Staffs to the Defence Staff, but the checks and balances have been greater here. Conversely, in the P & L field the strength of the argument for unity built round the single Service has been dominant. This is exemplified in the contrast between the present unified civilian personnel management and the three single-Service authorities.

The pressure for economy can be expected to continue and it is healthy that it should. The organisational changes in 1985 which led to the creation of the Defence Staff and the Office of Management and Budget were major in terms both of principle and of upheaval. They were less significant in the size of the resultant savings. In the near future the most promising areas for reductions in the size of the Ministry would seem to lie in delegation to Commands, and in the transfer of tasks, particularly in the procurement and logistics fields, to the private sector, rather than from internal reorganisation within the Ministry.

(4) THE POLITICO-MILITARY BALANCE

Later chapters will discuss the roles of Ministers and the roles of the Chiefs of Staff. Good working relationships are very important. But the balance of the relationship can vary for a number of reasons: political concepts; public perception of the status of the Armed Forces; the international scene itself. Before looking at the separate groupings it is desirable to consider whether there has been any major shift in the balance between the political and military hierarchies.

There is, in fact, little or no evidence of any such shift or indeed of any groundswell of perception of the need for such a shift. This very absence is of itself important. Certainly during the last two decades there have been resignations, but they have involved both political and military figures, sometimes acting in concert. They have been motivated by disagreements on policy issues, notably on the question of resource priorities, for a particular Service, rather than on questions of personal relationships and respective power.

None of the major organisational changes described in Part II would appear to have affected certain basis principles about the relationships between the politicians and the military. Firstly and most obviously there is the primacy of the political control of the Armed Forces and of the associated defence policy, achieved by means of a Cabinet system working through one or several Departments of State. Secondly there is the recognition that the running of the Armed Forces in the field is a professional matter, to be carried out by professional officers through a Command chain but with the ultimate responsibility carried by the political head of the Department. For carrying out this task the senior officers are not only given their policy tasks and allocated their resources by central government but they are also required to conform to wider national policies, for example of a social, education or juridical nature, to whatever extent the executive may determine that these policies should be applied to the Armed Forces. Ethnic monitoring of recruits is a current and politically controversial example. Certain of these policies are reviewed specifically by Parliament in the course of the quinquennial renewal of legislation specifically applying to the Armed Forces. In order to achieve a sensible balance in these related fields of policies, resources and wider national practices, it has for long been regarded as essential that the higher defence organisation provides for an adequate dialogue between the different interests that should contribute to the ultimate decisions. This dialogue has been both symbolised and made real in the composition and use of the Service Boards with their mixture of political, military, administrative and scientific membership. At the parliamentary level there has been an increasing dialogue between Members of Parliament and uniformed personnel as a consequence of the developments within the Select Committee systems. Away from Whitehall, at the formation and unit level, this understanding has been facilitated by the practice of frequent visits by Ministers and exchanges of views with all ranks of Service personnel.

Briefing of the media is a particularly sensitive aspect of this relationship. The biggest proportion is concerned with day-by-day single-Service events and is wholly legitimate. So too are the expressions of disagreement with Government defence policies when expounded by retired officers. Occasionally there may be indiscretions or misguided attempts by serving officers to influence policy usually in favour of one of the Services in its struggle for resources. While this has never amounted to a sustained serious challenge to the politico-military balance, there has on occasion been an undesirable encouragement of leakings and private briefings in the hope of influencing public opinion to modify proposed economies.

The internal developments within the Ministry of Defence in creating a unified Public Relations Staff, usually headed by a professional civilian Information Officer, have played their part in controlling any such problem areas. It is noteworthy that in the last major reorganisation of 1985 the Chief of Public Relations was, for the first time, shown as reporting directly and jointly to the PUS, to whom he had previously reported, and this time also to the CDS. This dual line symbolises the importance both of political control on behalf of the Secretary of State and of the dissemination of information about the Services as an important factor in their well-being and the public perception of their work.

Nor have the organisational changes within the ministerial structure and within the Chiefs of Staff hierarchy, both of which will be analysed in the next part, affected fundamentally the relationships between the two groups. The ministerial reorganisation has been directed at giving greater assistance to the Secretary of State within the Department and in its relations with Parliament rather than at relationships with the Services. Ministers still belong to the Service Boards and can thus still be directly involved in management as well as policy. They are expected – and all the evidence suggests that they remain keen – to visit the Services in the field and thereby to foster reciprocal understanding. On the military side, the greater authority of the post of CDS does not imply any desire to reduce the standing of the Services as an entity. Rather it recognises the continued need for professional advice at the highest level and is no more than a modified way of providing this advice. Therefore it is directed at better coordination of the professional military input rather than its emasculation. Indeed it could be argued that in 1964 and subsequent changes it was the PUS that gained most in power because he was best situated to overview the whole range of the Department's policy and managerial responsibilities. A pursuance of this line of argument would suggest that the recent changes in the responsibilities of Ministers and in the position of the CDS would help to put them in a comparable position.

Taken overall, the changes in the ministerial and Chiefs of Staff structures and their consequent interrelationships have been directed primarily at increasing the efficiency of each rather than bringing about any significant shift in the power balance. But there remains a question-mark as to whether the influence of the single-Service Chief of Staff or the single-Service itself has been unduly weakened. Such a weakening could show itself in two ways. In the fields of strategy and resource allocation policy, ministers could tend to concentrate on CDS and the Defence Staff for their source of advice, and might thereby still fail to be presented with the options for which they have called over the years. In the fields of management, Ministers might prefer not to be involved in the regular use of Service Boards but rather to pick and choose individual areas of functional interest on which to concentrate. They might thereby lose an overall picture of the health and efficiency of the individual Service.

One other aspect is also vital. The Services in the field must feel satisfied that their own standpoints are adequately represented. Therefore, irrespective of what precise machinery is used within the Defence Staff and the Chiefs of Staff Committee or by the Secretary of State to arrive at policy decisions – and the precise arcane workings of Whitehall do not interest unduly the Services in the field – they will still want to be satisfied that, somehow, their Head of Service has a fair, not necessarily a disproportionate say.

(5) RELATIONSHIPS WITH OTHER GOVERNMENT DEPARTMENTS AND WITHIN THE CENTRAL MACHINERY OF GOVERNMENT

The introductory chapter stressed both the high degree of the involvement of the Ministry of Defence with a surprisingly large number of other Departments on a wide range of discrete topics, and also the critical place of defence within the Government policy as a whole.

There is, inevitably, a degree of overlap between these two aspects of inter-departmental relationships. In particular, the relationships with the Foreign and Commonwealth Office, the Treasury, the Cabinet Office and to a lesser but still significant extent the Home Office and the Department of Trade and Industry, span both the particular and the general. But the organisational issues, to the extent that they arise in any significant form, are different and also much simpler in respect of the many discrete topics. Indeed it is not so much an organisational problem as a question of identifying the Department or Departments that need to be involved and despatching the necessary business. What is needed within the Ministry of Defence is a recognised procedure, which in turns builds up a bank of experience for handling the consultation. The normal practice has been to place the prime responsibility on the civilian secretariat or finance divisions. Such a practice is one of long standing going back to the Service Ministries and continued under the various restructurings of the individual divisions since the 1964 unification. The wide, random and erratic spread of such consultations has meant that the Ministry of Defence has throughout preferred such direct consultation rather than the creation of cells of staff from other Ministries 'bedded out' within the Ministry of Defence. This principle has applied even to legal matters (leaving on one side the special circumstances of military law) where, unlike several Ministries, the Ministry of Defence has not got its own Solicitor's Department – though possible changes are being considered here. Conversely, the Foreign and Commonwealth Office and the Treasury have created specific defence cells within their ministries to serve as the primary point of contact with the Ministry of Defence and to act in a coordinating role on defence matters within their own Departments, though that does not preclude a great deal of direct contact between staffs of the two departments – for example, between the Ministry of

Defence secretariats and the various geographical desks in the Foreign and Commonwealth Office.

Hundreds of bilateral negotiations between the Ministry of Defence and other Government Departments will undoubtedly be going on at any one time. Their level is dictated by the importance and political sensitivity of the individual subject. If ministerial consideration is needed this can be carried out either bilaterally or through the appropriate Cabinet Sub-Committee (not necessarily the Defence and Oversea Policy Committee, as the subject could more appropriately fall to whatever structure the Government of the day has set up to handle economic, industrial, regional or social issues) or, exceptionally, the full Cabinet. Ministers and senior officials have worked this system for decades and there is no evidence of any pressure for organisational change within the Ministry of Defence directed at different methods of handling such issues.

On the wider issue of the machinery for the central handling of major defence policy issues, which should be taken to include general questions of procurement policy and the nature of the UK's defence industrial base, there have been one or two landmarks in the earlier decades. Pre-war, in the absence of a Defence Minister and with the three Service Ministers all in the Cabinet, major policy issues tended to go to the Cabinet itself for resolution. The creation in 1947 of a post of Minister of Defence and of a Defence Committee under the Chairmanship of the Prime Minister started a process of greater emphasis on the role of the Defence Committee. The 1964 reorganisation concentrated power and responsibility more clearly in the hands of the Secretary of State for Defence. At the same time it spelt out the role of the retitled Committee on Defence and Oversea Policy as the normal ministerial organisation, subject to the supreme authority of the Cabinet and the Prime Minister, for the collective discharge of responsibility for defence policy. It confirmed the attendance of the Chiefs of Staff as the nature of business required. It also formalised the support of the Committee by a Committee of senior officials which has operated at Permanent Secretary level. The only significant change since then flowed from the creation of the Procurement Executive which gave the Secretary of State for Defence very powerful practical influence over certain major industries, given the high proportion of the defence spent on, for example, the aircraft, electronic and shipbuilding industries, even though the Department of Trade and Industry (in its various incarnations) had the responsibility for the sponsorship of such industries in their totality.

Looked at from the point of view of the determination of Government policies, this increased concentration of power in the hands of one Cabinet Minister made it increasingly important that those other Ministries who were directly and primarily involved in the formulation of defence policies should be adequately in touch with defence thinking, both to make their own inputs and to be able to brief their own Ministers effectively and in good time. This requirement called for good organisational links at the official levels supplemented by ministerial relationships either on a bilateral or a formalised Committee basis. At the official level these tasks fell primarily to the defence sub-departments of the Foreign and Commonwealth Office and the Treasury, with coordinating and secretarial support from the Cabinet Office. Specifically there was senior FCO representation on the Chiefs of Staff Committee (though the frequency of use of this piece of machinery has declined considerably contrasted with the 1960s) and similar Treasury representation on the Equipment Policy Committee in its various forms. But this was only the formal tip of the iceberg in that both Departments had many and continuous direct contacts with the Ministry of Defence, though this was not supplemented by much exchange of staff between these Departments. These three major Ministries together with the Cabinet Office effectively controlled the reference of issues to the Cabinet Sub-Committee.

Whether this machinery is the best that can be devised to ensure that the Government reaches its decisions in the light of a proper balance of diplomatic, economic, industrial and strategic considerations, may be the subject of differing views. What is clear is that in the last two decades the adequacy of these organisational links has not been substantively discussed in public. The Management Review Report of October 1976, even though it contained in its membership a representative of the Civil Service Department, which had at that time the central responsibility for the machinery of Government, made no reference to inter-departmental relationships. The 1981/2 Report from the House of Commons Defence Committee on the Ministry of Defence Organisation and Procurement raised only the one question of the case for the appointment of a Ministerial Aerospace Board in order to achieve closer high-level coordination between the Ministry of Defence and the Department of Industry, a proposal which was rejected. The White Paper of 1984 on the

Central Organisation for Defence simply states, almost *en passant*, that major questions of defence policy will continue to be dealt with by the Defence and Oversea Policy Committee of the Cabinet. The subsequent Report of the House of Commons Defence Committee raises no general points other than to record that the Chiefs of Staff retain their right to access to the Prime Minister. The continued silence is deafening.

IMPLICATIONS FOR THE ORGANISATION

The three main roles of the Ministry were set out in the opening chapter, which went on to stress the scale and complexity of its activities. It suggested that this very scale and complexity calls for the maximum unity of purpose and simplicity of organisation that are practicable. The proviso is as important as the principle. The subsequent four chapters relate how the achievement of unification within a single Ministry led to complexity within that Ministry. Much effort after 1964 had been directed at searching for ways of simplifying that complexity.

These searches were affected by a variety of factors. Five of them have been discussed in the earlier part of this chapter. They make uneasy bedfellows. To some extent they have contradictory influences. This is not surprising and serves to illustrate the difficulty of the organisational problem. But these factors are among those which permeate the working of the Ministry as a whole. They have affected not only the individual functional areas but also the total scene. Certain very broad conclusions can be drawn.

First, the defence roles which HMG retains throughout the world, and the difficult problems of resource allocation and financial control which flow from the scale, nature and cost of these roles, continue to combine to exert pressure in the direction of needing large staffs with a wide variety of functions. The provision of forces to discharge all the different military capabilities needed to support the range of firm commitments or general interests has called for much staff effort in all the main departments of the Ministry. It has so far invalidated any prospect of a simple structure along the lines of a small policy staff and straightforward executive Service Departments. Nor have the hopes that have been expressed of finding a magic formula which would simplify the production of financial data and the subsequent decisions on resource allocation resulted in radical success. The basic

building-blocks still remain stubbornly rooted in the Service Departments with close links between them and the Procurement Executive
and the Property Services Agency, thus calling for intricate cross-
over arrangements with the central military and financial staffs.
There have been worthwhile improvements but of refinement rather
than of revolution.

Second, the resultant large Ministry has, by the very fact of its
size, set off pressures for major reductions. While one often-repeated
pressure has been for arbitrary percentage cuts within the existing
framework, other pressures have been directed at economies from
organisational change. One approach took the direction of unification, if not of the Services themselves at least of their headquarters
staffs. Another approach has been for delegation or hiving-off. Both
approaches have had some successes, but partial and erratic. What
has been a common thread is the continuous state of pressure leading
to a continued high degree of turbulence, though some areas have
been more subject to turbulence than others. The individual consequences are discussed in the next part.

Third, the relationship between Ministers and the senior military
staff underlines the need for the involvement of both groups in all
parts of the Ministry. There is not a purely political or a purely
military field. The managerial roles of the Service Departments still
call for political guidance and an awareness of political sensitivities.
Decisions of major international relationships must take account of
military considerations and vice versa. Whatever form of organisation is adopted in the individual departments of the Ministry there
must be, either inherent in the structure itself or established by well
publicised and clearly laid-down reporting lines, the provision for
consultation which will lead to the final decision-taking by ministers
on an informed basis. This provision can take the form of the use
of the Defence Council or the chairmanship of the Service Boards
by ministers or direct reporting lines in accordance with ministers'
functional responsibilities, or a combination of all three. What is
vital in a complex Ministry, where many staff are serving short
tours and are not experienced in the ways of Whitehall, is that the
organisational systems that are adopted are both clearly understood
and regularly and systematically used.

Finally, inter-departmental relationships have remained remarkably stable in so far as their machinery for negotiation and consultation are concerned. They have had no significant effect on organisational changes, and can therefore be largely disregarded in respect

of the consideration of the developments in individual functional areas. Even in the field of procurement where the only major inter-departmental change has occurred, the machinery set up in 1972 for a policy cell in the Procurement Executive to handle international and industrial uses and to liaise with the Department of Trade and Industry has continued basically unchanged.

Part IV

Functional Areas

7 Ministers, Councils and Boards

EARLY PRACTICES

Control over the Armed Forces by ministers, and associated with them though sometimes in jealous opposition to them, by Parliament, has had a long tradition in the United Kingdom. During the nineteenth century, the prestigious offices of First Lord of the Admiralty and Secretary of State for War together with the posts of Foreign Secretary, Colonial Secretary and Secretary of State for India, not to mention the Prime Minister, meant that a significant proportionate effort of the Cabinet was directly involved in defence or overseas defence-related questions.

During the first half of the twentieth century, different, and to some extent opposing, influences were brought to bear on this representation. Social and economic interests were playing a steadily increasing part in the Government's business, and led to pressures for representation and possibly an increase in the size of the Cabinet and a consequent questioning of the scale of the defence presence. Moreover the creation of the Royal Air Force and then of the Air Ministry under its own Secretary of State added to the numbers in Cabinet. On the other hand two world wars gave a vital role to the Armed Forces and to the national effort to support them. Each war saw the creation of special supply departments: the Ministry of Munitions in the First World War, and the Ministry of Aircraft Production and then the Ministry of Supply in the Second World War. Both wars also saw the setting-up of small key ministerial committees: a War Cabinet was formed in 1916 and was re-established in 1939 to be followed by a modified structure under Mr Winston Churchill's administration. In 1940 a Defence Committee (Operations) was formed consisting of the Prime Minister (who also became Minister of Defence on the abandonment of the 1936 post of Minister for Coordination of Defence), the Deputy Prime

111

Minister, the Foreign Secretary, the Minister of Production and the three Service Ministers, with the Chiefs of Staff in attendance. A parallel body, the Defence Committee (Supply), handled the production programmes. The Service Departments exercised their continuing responsibility for day-to-day administration of their Services through their well-established Boards or Councils.

The first major modification of the ministerial structure occurred in 1946 with the creation of the Ministry of Defence under its own Minister. One important consequence was that he became the sole full member of the Cabinet representing defence interests. The Service Ministers could thereafter attend only on invitation for specially relevant items, and it was a privilege more often sought after than achieved. They did, however, retain their responsibility to Parliament for the administration of their Services, in accordance with Cabinet policy and within the resources allocated to them. They were made members of the Defence Committee which was formally set up to operate in peacetime under the Prime Minister's chairmanship and with the Minister of Defence as its Deputy Chairman. Once again the Chiefs of Staff were to be in attendance. The 1946 White Paper specifically provided that though the Chiefs of Staff would normally discuss major strategic issues with the Minister of Defence before submission to the Defence Committee, the Chiefs of Staff could go direct and the Minister would not be acting as their mouthpiece at the meeting.

With the aim of providing ministerial coordination for handling administrative matters of common interest to the three Services, the Minister of Defence established a Standing Committee of the three Service Ministers meeting under his chairmanship and supported by the appropriate military Board members. A parallel Committee was set up to handle supply matters in the form of a Ministerial Production Committee, again under the Minister of Defence's chairmanship and including the Service Ministers, the Minister of Supply and the Minister of Labour. Neither was very effective.

The period from 1946 to 1963 which saw the moves towards a unitary Ministry of Defence was an uneasy time for ministerial relationships. For the Service Ministers there was a gradual erosion of their position although they still remained heads of their own, separate departments. The anomaly was clearly perceived by Mr Macmillan in 1957 when he commented that although his directive had given his Minister of Defence power to give decisions on all matters of policy, at the same time the Secretaries of State and the

First Lord could plead their constitutional authority and responsibility. Once again, procedural steps were taken to try to overcome this dilemma. In 1958 the Service Ministers were instructed that they could make submissions on matters of policy only through the Minister of Defence.

It was also an uneasy time for the relationship between the Chiefs of Staff and their Service Ministers. While the Service Minister presided over his Board and the Chief of Staff advanced his proposals in that single-Service medium, on which the representation came entirely from within the Department, the Chief of Staff was increasingly conscious that political power lay elsewhere – and increasingly so from 1957 onwards – further down Whitehall in Storey's Gate, the location of the small central Ministry. In turn this put the Service Minister in an exposed position, squeezed between the Chief of Staff, who sought his support to win his case with the Minister of Defence, and the Minister of Defence himself, who was hoping for support for his policies via the Service Ministers as colleagues in the Government and the Party.

THE CHANGES IN 1964–81

1964 saw the first major attempt to resolve this problem as part of a much wider solution. The creation of the unified Ministry involved the abolition of the offices of the First Lord of the Admiralty and the Secretaries of State for War and Air. At the same time, the title and composition of the Cabinet Committee was changed. It became a Committee on Defence and Overseas Policy with the new Secretary of State for Defence now the sole defence ministerial member, though he continued to be accompanied by the four Chiefs of Staff as the business required. Within the Ministry the Secretary of State was to be supported by three Ministers of State and three Parliamentary Under-Secretaries of State, who were given as their primary functions single-Service responsibilities. While this allocation probably reflected pragmatic political realities it was certainly the view of Mr Macmillan, when he launched in December 1962 the initiative which led to the reorganisation, that the new central minister should not have to account to Parliament for such matters as pay, recruitment, training and discipline. The load would in his view be too onerous. He envisaged at that time a Minister of State for each of the Services and in addition a Minister of State for Logistics and a Minister for Weapons Development.

Internally, the 1964 actions included the establishment under the Secretary of State of a Defence Council. This was a legal necessity. It would formally exercise the powers of command and administrative control previously exercised by the Board of the Admiralty and by the Army and Air Councils. The Council was comprised of the four senior ministers, the four Chiefs of Staff, the Chief Scientific Adviser and the Permanent Under-Secretary of State. The membership probably seemed at the time to nominate itself, but there is no evidence that much thought was given to whether it would be an effective instrument for contentious decisions, given the preponderance of single-Service affinities. The former Board of the Admiralty and the Army and Air Councils became subsidiary Boards of the Defence Council. While the Secretary of State was formally the Chairman of each Board, the appropriate Minister of State would normally be asked to act for him. The balance of their composition remained basically the same, with the new single-Service Second Permanent Under-Secretaries fulfilling the traditional role of the senior administrator.

Mr Denis Healey, who had inherited this new system, tried to make the structure work with the one very tentative modification of giving the Ministers of State some purely advisory across-the-board functional tasks. He also, in his initial years, called fairly regular meetings of the Defence Council, though his own style was for smaller *ad hoc* meetings. Experience gained in his initial defence review, coupled with the resignation of his Minister (RN), led him to modify the three Ministers of State to two functional Ministers, but leaving the three Parliamentary Secretaries with their single-Service responsibilities, which would now include the routine chairmanship of the Service Boards. It was not easy for the functional ministers to find initially a satisfactory and effective method of working. In the first place the devised division between 'Administration' and 'Equipment' was not simple, and was made more complicated by the existence of the Ministry of Technology which had recently been formed and which had its own concept of equipment policies. In the second place there was an absence of direct central support for the two Ministers, though this was gradually remedied by a series of reorganisations of both the scientific and administrative senior staff.

Notwithstanding these measures it was inherently unsatisfactory for Ministers of State to have, at their level, a less comprehensive oversight of the Services than the Parliamentary Secretaries and Chiefs of Staff enjoyed on an individual basis. It was therefore not surprising that the Labour Government proposed and the Conservative Government implemented in 1970 the combining of the two posts into one Minister of State. This arrangement lasted for a decade, with only a short interregnum of eighteen months in 1971/2 when a Minister of State (Procurement) was created to oversee the launching of the new Procurement Executive. After this settling-down period the work was absorbed by the Minister of State. Contrary, however, to the provisional views of the 1970 Labour Government, the succeeding Conservative Government did not functionalise the Parliamentary Secretaries, nor did the Labour Government when it returned to power in 1974.

Thus the 1970s were a period of stability in respect of the ministerial structure. The Service Boards, too, continued to operate on a regular basis. The Defence Council was more problematical. It had hardly met at the end of the 1960s. The Headquarters Organisation Committee, seeing the need for some visible but smaller top-level body, proposed a Defence Policy Executive of the two senior Ministers, the CDS and the PUS. This was not accepted, but neither did the Defence Council meet under Lord Carrington. The Management Review also saw such a need; indeed it had in their view become stronger because the range of business on which the Service Boards could take final decisions had contracted, in part because of the creation of the Procurement Executive which had removed the direct responsibility for procurement from the Navy and Army Boards, and in part because major policy and resource issues fell to be decided by bodies which crossed single-Service boundaries. The Review team, while they still saw the need for a top-level mechanism for the management of each Service within the agreed policy framework, concluded that there would be advantage in having a recognised and visible focus at the top of the Ministry. They went on to attempt a definition of the range of subjects such a body should consider: 'the future objectives of the Ministry; resource allocation; major investment decisions; the research programme; our approach to collaboration and other industrial issues; dispersal, manpower and other across-the-board issues that might arise from time to time, e.g. the use of the Defence estate'.

The size of the Defence Council made the Management Review team question, as had the Headquarters Organisation Committee, whether it was in its existing composition the ideal body. They too favoured a reduction but not to as small a number as four. They proposed a revised Defence Council of nine: the two senior Ministers only, together with the four Chiefs of Staff, the Chief of Defence Procurement, the Chief Scientific Adviser and the Permanent Under-Secretary of State. Once again, as befell the earlier recommendation, this one was not accepted. One obvious reason could have been that it would have been very difficult for a Parliamentary Secretary to chair a Service Board when his Chief of Staff had been at a relevant Defence Council meeting and he had not. But the message about the need for visible collective leadership was taken and the Defence Council in its fuller form met quite frequently for the rest of the life of that Labour Government.

FUNCTIONALISATION

Mr Francis Pym made no changes in his eighteen months in office. Mr John Nott was immediately faced with the need for major cuts but found himself with, in his view, inadequate uncommitted sources of staff advice. His problem was exacerbated when his Parliamentary Secretary for the Royal Navy felt that he had to lend his support to the Navy's opposition to proposed cuts. Accordingly Mr Nott introduced in May 1981 a fully functional ministerial structure with a Minister of State for the Armed Forces and a Minister of State for Defence Procurement, each assisted by one Parliamentary Secretary. There can be no doubt that this split had a far greater logic than the one attempted in 1967. The existence within the Ministry of Defence of the Procurement Executive which allowed the Minister for Defence Procurement to handle the whole span of a piece of equipment from its operational requirement, through development, to production, was a great improvement. The only failure in this logic was that supply management and repair lay with his colleague although they could be regarded as integral parts of the life-cycle of equipment. There were some other infelicities brought about essentially by loading problems. The Armed Forces side was effectively being reduced from three to two Ministers and yet there remained a very large amount of case-work, much of it involving correspondence with Members of Parliament, which still had to be handled. Therefore all matters affecting civilian personnel were allocated to the Defence Procurement Minister even though civilians were an integral part of the personnel package of the Services. Again, the formal separation of operational analysis and operational requirements from the size and shape and the strategy responsibilities of the Armed Forces Minister was of dubious logic.

In explaining the reasons for the restructuring, the Secretary of State went, interestingly, back to the 1963 White Paper and quoted three objectives. The 1963 Paper saw a need for the Secretary of State to be able to delegate much of his authority. Over the previous ten years Secretaries of State had been able to delegate to the one Minister of State, but the new structure of four functional Ministers enabled him to do more and go further. Second, restructuring would strengthen the political direction available to the department and thus accountability to Parliament. This assertion is less clearly measurable. If it is referring to the trend towards a greater managerial role on the part of the Ministers, then there is no doubt that functional Ministers are by definition less tied to an individual Service and can therefore more easily give directions for change. Conversely, they could be less in touch with Service sensitivities. Third, the 1963 Paper asserted the preservation of the separate identity of the Services, and the need to provide their individual Boards with political direction. Now, it was asserted that the political direction available to the individual Services would be enhanced through the presence of a Minister of State (i.e. for the Armed Forces) in the chair. This would certainly be valid just so long as the load on the Minister of State for the Armed Forces, supported as he was by only one Parliamentary Secretary, would permit him regularly to attend Board meetings. But there was the risk that, in a desire to preserve his objectivity, he would not want to participate in their discussions of their perception of key contentious size and shape issues.

Mr Nott informed the House of Commons Defence Committee in November 1981 of his reasons for the change. He added that he regretted losing the representational role which the former single-Service Parliamentary Secretaries performed, and that he expected that the Services themselves regretted it also, but he was sure that the wider need to have a functional organisation was right. At the Committee's request he reported further to them in May 1982, during the South Atlantic campaign. He confirmed that the new structure had proved helpful in increasing ministerial control both over the forward equipment programmes and in enabling the management of the Armed Forces to be looked at in a comprehensive defence as well as single-Service way by having the two Armed Forces Ministers as members of all three Service Boards. He also underlined the value to him that this system afforded through his greater ability to delegate. The bulk of his time in the previous weeks had been taken up with the management of the South Atlantic crisis.

Satisfaction with the top structure was reaffirmed in the 1984 White Paper on the Central Organisation for Defence. There were no changes either in the Defence and Oversea Policy Committee of the Cabinet or in the ministerial structure of the Department. The formal position of the Defence Council was confirmed, but its size was increased to fourteen by the addition of the Vice-Chief of the Defence Staff (who in practice replaced the abolished VCDS (P&L) and the Second Permanent Under-Secretary of State. These additions symbolised the importance of the two key blocks they controlled under the reorganisation: the Defence Staff and the Office of Management and Budget. The position of the Service Boards was unchanged, although their membership declined with the abolition of the Vice Chiefs and the single-Service Deputy Under-Secretaries. The Paper, however, laid more stress on the Service Executive Committees than on the Service Boards, seeing the executive Committees as being the bodies through which the single-Service Chiefs of Staff would exercise the detailed management of the Services.

CONCLUSIONS

Looking at the series of changes from 1946 to 1986, a clear pattern of evolution, with some minor temporary hiccups, stands out.

At the Cabinet and Cabinet Sub-Committee level the need for a special grouping has remained constant. Its membership, for the most part, appoints itself. Its efficacy is not really a question of organisation but of the extent of the use made of it. The need for effective regular consultation between ministers on defence topics has, if anything, increased. The resource demands of defence, still continuing at a very high level forty years after the end of the Second World War, have major effects on the Chancellor of the Exchequer's policies. The continuous tensions in international relations and the large political dimensions of NATO are key issues for the Foreign Secretary. The industrial implications of major procurement choices affect regional as well as industrial and economic ministers. Formally, the regular links between the Cabinet Office, the Ministry of

Defence's central military and Secretariat staff, as described in Part III, should ensure that the Secretariat of the Defence and Oversea Policy Committee (DOPC) are aware of issues of major political significance and can prepare the way for timely meetings. But, such are the demands on the time of ministers collectively that the DOPC by itself in formal session cannot be expected to meet frequently enough to provide adequate political guidance. Efficiency could be increased if, in addition, there were regular bilateral contacts between the Secretary of State for Defence and his key colleagues. Such meetings can have value not only in respect of their immediate agenda but in setting the tone for close inter-departmental contact at the official level. In practice the performance has been erratic, and on occasions unduly hindered by clashes of personality.

At the departmental level the position of the Secretary of State has been firmly and clearly established. The major problem for years was one of loading. The combination of duties is formidable and in some ways unique within the Cabinet. The spending demands have been consistently high over the forty years, notwithstanding the series of reviews and adjustments of policy. But the Secretary of State, much more so than the heads of most other major spending Departments, is directly responsible for the management of the money. He also has major international obligations, involving frequent visits both at the governmental level and to see British forces abroad. At home, too, he is drawn into the affairs of many other Departments. The role of the Forces in Northern Ireland; the place of defence equipment requirements in determining the future policy for British industry (e.g. the recent case of Westlands); the use of the Forces as aid to the civil power: these are just three recent issues that exemplify the continuing broad span of involvement. This combination of duties points inexorably to the importance of effective delegation. For that reason alone, quite apart from the need for a 'defence' look at many internal management issues as well as the thorny problem of resource allocation, the case for functional ministers seems strong and durable.

There has been no comparable progress in the acceptance of the Defence Council as a working mechanism, as opposed to a formal authority. The reluctance of Secretaries of State to try to use it as a policy body was understandable just so long as there was a fear of an embarrassing alliance between single-Service Ministers and single-Service Chiefs of Staff. Even so, some Secretaries of State seemed to overcome or avoid this possible risk. But the 1981 functionalisation of the ministers has removed this disadvantage. Yet the 1984 Paper with its stress on CDS and PUS as the principal official advisers, suggests that a smaller *ad hoc* grouping is likely to be the practical method of reaching most decisions. One argument in favour of the use of the Defence Council, which extends obviously to its subordinate Service Boards, is to have a visible corporate body at the head of what is still a very large, physically scattered and inevitably amorphous body of staff. There is an important aspect of leadership and motivation, as well as a mechanism of letting the middle and even the more senior staff (there are hundreds at the two-star level) see the thinking at the top of the Ministry. But there is the other equally important aspect, as has been discussed earlier, of ensuring a regular dialogue between the politicians and the military. A potentially serious gap could develop if, in addition to the very limited use of the Defence Council, the Service Executive Committee rather than the Service Board becomes more and more the main body of decision-taking for the individual Service. Both the military and the politicians could then lose. Ministers are in touch with the public and with external attitudes. They are elected. It is essential that the military should be aware of the wider non-professional thinking and realise the practicability or otherwise of possible future directions they may wish to follow. Equally, it is important that Ministers, when they operate functionally, should not be too selective over the areas in which they decide to concentrate. The Services have to be understood in the round; not just, for example, as targets for rationalisation in selected areas.

Broadly similar considerations apply to the administrative and scientific representation on the Service Boards, which is now provided by the Second Permanent Under-Secretary (no longer helped by the single-Service Deputy Secretaries since their abolition in 1984) and the Controller Research and Development Establishments, Research and Nuclear (CERN). Indeed the practical problem of regular attendance is greater for them in that they are members of both the Board and the Executive Committee of each Service Department. Yet their central positions should allow them to play a valuable part in the linkage between policy-making and management, more than ever important with the increased polarisation of the Ministry between the central Defence Staff and the Office of Management and Budget on the one hand, and the single-Service Departments on the other.

8 The Chiefs of Staff

THEIR NATIONAL STATUS

Of all the major parts of the Ministry there can be no doubt that the one surrounding the Chiefs of Staff has commanded, and still commands, most public and political interest and scrutiny whenever changes are mooted. A ministerial reorganisation may produce a temporary political ripple and some discussion almost academic in tone by commentators, but it pales into insignificance when contrasted with the degree of interest in any issue concerning the Chiefs of Staff. In such a context the generic term 'Chiefs of Staff' should be taken to cover the spectrum from the concept of any form of tri-Service adviser or 'Supremo' – be he a Chief Staff Officer, a Chairman of the Chiefs of Staff Committee or a Chief of Defence Staff – through the three single-Service Chiefs of Staff, to the range of policy staffs primarily in the planning, operational, intelligence and operational requirements fields who work directly for one, or three, or all four of the members of the Chiefs of Staff Committee.

Why is there such a keen interest? Its primary cause must be the special position of the single-Service Chiefs of Staff. Traditionally the holder of such an appointment is regarded as the head of his Service. (It is interesting to note that this is so even if the Chief of Defence Staff who is his senior comes from his own Service.) As the head of his Service he is more than its executive leader. He is genuinely accountable to the Service. He is regarded publicly as the symbol of the Service and, as such, a preserver of its heritage and a custodian of its future. The shades of his predecessors, dead and living – and if living, often very vocal – are watching how he discharges those responsibilities. And, more widely, the nation too is conscious of the very special place the Armed Forces do or may occupy in preserving the way of life of the nation and indeed their own individual lives.

This sense of the continuum places the Chief of Staff, or more accurately tends to force him, willingly or unwillingly, into a corner in the ring where he may be regarded as being somewhat apart from politics or at least the Government of the day. Governments may come and go and obviously have the right and duty to impose their own defence policy. But the country, so the argument may run, will always need the Armed Forces and may sometimes have to call on them unexpectedly and notwithstanding all the endeavours of the Government. Therefore the Chief of Staff has an obligation to watch the interests and well-being of his Service over a longer time-scale and in a somewhat different framework from that of his political masters.

This is a difficult and possibly a dangerous line of argument. It could be explored in much greater depth through constitutional arguments spreading over into the prerogative and the position of the monarch. But for these purposes it is sufficient to note that the pressures are there. It is therefore a significant factor influencing and introducing an element of uneasiness into the relationship which exists between defence ministers and the Chiefs of Staff. It accounts in part for the real and symbolic importance attached to the right of direct access of the Chiefs of Staff to the Prime Minister. Such access reflects not only the Prime Minister's ultimate responsibility for defence but also the special position of the Armed Forces in the national structure, and is regarded by senior officers as being a significant symbol.

THE POLITICO-MILITARY RELATIONSHIPS

In formulating their policies ministers are faced with a degree of tension in their relationships with the Chiefs of Staff. If the defence capabilities of the country are to be exploited to the full, ministers need to have confidence in the heads of the Services whom they appoint. They are their senior professional advisers. That they disagree from time to time is normal and healthy, and there is no absence of documentation of lively exchanges between people who are necessarily strong-willed in their respective professions. But if ministers do not accept, or, worse still, do not respect, and basically distrust, the professional advice they are given, a potentially serious gap and crisis of confidence will arise. There were signs of this in 1957–8, and again in 1981. The degree of seriousness varies with the nature of the subject. It is at its most acute in operational matters. It is probably least important if it concerns what might be termed social standards, where the Services tend to have a self-perpetuating military society with a degree of isolationism from the wider movements within society at large, and where ministers and Parliament operate on a wider canvas and can speak for public opinion. It is at its most difficult and ambiguous in such areas as resource allocation and the levels of military capability to be provided. Here each Service is fighting its own corner and using every possible professional argument to advance its cause. The professional views must be heard and given respect, but in the end it is ministers who should and must take the decisions.

Clearly ministers must have the right to reject or modify particular pieces of advice. On what basis do they do this and what effect does it have on the relationship? The problem was more acute for ministers when they were Service ministers, because they were directly and visibly associated with the Service (e.g. all the overtones of the title of First Lord of the Admiralty), they were surrounded by its atmosphere, and were its spokesman round the Cabinet table. However, even with the creation of an overall Secretary of State and the subsequent introductions of functional ministers, there has remained the problem of the source of alternative professional advice. The search for this has led to the creation of a Chief of Defence Staff (CDS), which in turn introduced a new range of relationships and cross-currents between the CDS and the single-Service Chiefs of Staff. But it was not logically inevitable to go to another source to get a range of options. Theoretically, at least – and indeed in practice on many occasions since the formation in 1924 of the Chiefs of Staff Committee – the Chiefs of Staff in their corporate capacity could give ministers alternative courses of action to consider, even if at the same time they expressed a clear preference.

Running through the many arguments over the precise powers and responsibilities of any fourth appointment was the dominant issue of the corporate responsibility of the Chiefs of Staff. The argument in favour derives from the axiom that advice and responsibility should go hand in hand. Military commanders are in a unique position because of the degree of their direct responsibility for the lives of their personnel. If, therefore, those who initiate the major executive orders have not been a direct party to the decision, it is questionable, so the argument runs, whether there will be the essential total response of acceptance. An extension of this argument would recognise that the spirit of corporate responsibility could still be preserved if that responsibility was in some way shared with a fourth member round the collective table. But the breaking-point is seen by some as likely to arise when the fourth member is not only *primus inter pares* but has ultimate responsibility which does not have to be shared, and when he is supported in the formulation of his advice by staff who are separate from and independent of the policy staffs of the individual Services.

It must also be remembered that the position of a single-Service Chief of Staff is by no means as clear-cut as the apparent simplicity of the term 'head of Service' suggests. His previous appointment will probably have been that of a senior Commander-in-Chief. He will have had executive powers and a staff exclusively dedicated to assist him in his task; and if there were shortages in resources it will have been tempting to say that they (Whitehall) were to blame. The move to Whitehall changes a clear struggle for a much more amorphous and fluid one. He is no longer so directly in charge. It is a world which he might not like; indeed might not know. There have been sad examples of ineffective if not disastrous tours of duty by Chiefs of Staff who had either had little or no earlier experience of Whitehall, or who were temperamentally unsuited notwithstanding a fine record in the field. The personal qualities have to be mixed in a different way. Of the several major elements the most difficult and the most elusive is probably the relationship with the politician. The different nuances can be seen from two interesting comments. Lord Harding summed up the task of a Chief of Staff as 'doing the best you can in the interests of the Army *vis-à-vis* the politicians. You must stand up to them but always remember they have the last word.' Lord Attlee's approach was, 'A good CIGS must be a good Committee man, able to reconcile conflicting points of view, cooperate with men whom he does not necessarily regard as superior or even equal, and while securing the trust of his soldiers be able to relate their wishes, advice and needs to those of the body politic.'

But if there are uncertainties about the position of a Chief of Staff he is at least the head of his Service. If he then goes on to become Chief of the Defence Staff the uncertainties become if anything greater. While his status may be one of great eminence, it is not easy to see how he defines it. He is not an operational Supremo. In any case, the opportunity for exercising any clear operational role has declined greatly from the days of the overseas integrated national Headquarters to the subordination within the NATO Command structures of today. He can play a valuable role in discussions within

NATO but this role is a complex mixture of strategist, politician and diplomat. But the primary duty of being the chief military adviser to the Secretary of State, unless there is also total executive subordination of the Services under his control, raises difficult questions of tact and judgement about the degree of detailed involvement he seeks, the extent to which he by-passes formal staff channels, and the way in which he challenges other sources of advice.

These are some of the broader considerations which need to be borne in mind when considering the evolution of the Chiefs of Staff general area over the last two decades. But, in order to understand the particularly sensitive reactions to change, it is necessary to look back considerably further in time to a period when the creation of a Chiefs of Staff Committee long antedated any collective ministerial or departmental structure.

EARLY DAYS

The starting-point, which has remained the basic keystone in all future developments, was the creation in 1924 of the Chiefs of Staff Committee. This step reflected the political recognition of the need for greater coordination. Its absence in the First World War had been noticed particularly in such combined operations as the Dardanelles. The need had been further underlined by the creation of a third Service, the Royal Air Force, when it soon became clear that the air was an essential element of land and sea operations. The Chanak incident of 1922 was a typical example which led to instructions from the Prime Minister to the three Service Chiefs to draw up joint plans for operations. The 1923 Report of the Sub-Committee of the Committee of Imperial Defence on National and Imperial Defence went further, in recommending that the three Chiefs of Staff form a Committee with an 'individual and collective responsibility for advising on defence policy as a whole, the three constituting as it were a super chief of the War Staff in commission'. Here was the first explicit formulation of the concept of collective responsibility, which has remained the most strongly held and debated principle ever since.

At the time of its creation, the Chiefs of Staff Committee had no Ministry of Defence to provide support and no Minister of Defence as the responsible minister. The Committee's line of reporting was to the Committee of Imperial Defence and therefore formally and indeed in reality to the Prime Minister. Gradually the staffs of the three Chiefs of Staff formalised their joint working arrangements. From 1927, the Directors of Plans of the three Services sat together as a Joint Planning Committee. From 1938, the Directors of Intelligence, supported in this case by a Foreign Office representative, formed a Joint Intelligence Committee as a sub-committee of the Chiefs of Staff Committee.

This system, austere in its small staff resources and relying on the Service Ministries both for inputs and for subsequent executive action, provided strategic and operational advice and direction throughout the Second World War. It can be argued that its basically unchanged continuance reflected not so much organisational perfection as the personality of the Prime Minister, who had also taken the portfolio of the Minister of Defence and took the chair at the Committee whenever he wished. Complete continuity for him was provided in the person of his own military representative in the guise of his staff officer, General Ismay, who sat permanently on the Committee. But it is interesting that such a very different personality as Mr Attlee, who as Deputy Prime Minister was also Deputy Chairman of the Defence Committee, was impressed with the workings of the machinery, and paid tribute to Mr Churchill's success in solving what he termed 'the deadly problems of civilians versus generals in wartime'. It is also noteworthy that soon after their involvement in hostilities the United States Government created a Joint Chiefs on British lines, and that a little later in 1942 the two Committees came together as a Combined Chiefs of Staff Committee and exercised a profound effect on the conduct of operations.

It was therefore not surprising that while Mr Attlee had favoured from as far back as the early 1930s greater coordination and the creation of a Ministry of Defence, his own wartime experiences and the apprehensions about any German type of OKW pointed to the continuance of the Chiefs of Staff Committee system under the new organisational plans of the post-war Labour Government. Its secretariat was now formally embedded in the new Ministry but, for the rest, the 1946 White Paper came out strongly in favour of the continuance of the collective role and in support of direct and personal presentation to the Defence Committee by the Chiefs of Staff of their strategic plans. One of their primary tasks would be to advise the Cabinet Defence Committee on an annual basis of their strategic requirements, which would form the basis for a negotiation of the detailed proposals for the apportioning of resources. This resounding reaffirmation tended to cut the Service Ministers out of the direct policy line and to place greater stress on their role as responsible to Parliament for the maintenance and administration of the Services. This unsatisfactory arrangement, at least for the Ministers, was probably eased by the continuing high political involvement in all the problems of national service.

THE MOVES IN FAVOUR OF CREATING A CDS

This system lasted for ten years. Even within the Chiefs of Staff there were divided views. Field Marshal Lord Montgomery, though it is widely recognised that he was not at his best as a Chief of Staff, favoured a move towards an overall Supremo Chief of Staff, making a doubtfully valid analogy between the Minister and his Chief of Staff with his own position as a Commander in Chief when he favoured a Chief of Staff (used in the other military sense) working to him. On the other hand, Marshal of the Royal Air Force Sir John Slessor wrote in support of the corporate responsibility of the three Chiefs of Staff, basing his arguments on the axiom that 'the man who gives advice to the Cabinet must be the same man who has the ultimate responsibility for putting it into effect'. At the same time he favoured the continuance of some form of Chief Staff Officer as a fourth member, seeing such a post as being invaluable both as a day-to-day link with the Minister and as the main point of contact with international organisations such as the emerging NATO structure.

An earlier chapter has described the hectic flurry of activity from 1955 to 1958, which saw a series of changes from a Chairman of the Chiefs of Staff Committee via a Chairman and Chief Staff Officer, to a Chief of the Defence Staff. Emotions ran high and there were many confrontations between ministers, including the Prime Minister and the three single-Service Chiefs of Staff. But the latter still retained very powerful positions for several reasons. The Chief of the Defence Staff had no real body of staff of his own. The formal source of advice to the Government on military matters remained the collective forum of the Chiefs of Staff Committee. Yet, the very existence of a Chief of the Defence Staff added a major new dimension. By definition he would be an eminent senior officer: indeed from that time right up to the present, one who had invariably been the Chief of Staff of his own Service. He would be accommodated very close to the Secretary of State within the Whitehall building and thus highly accessible to ministers. They could easily seek his advice, and the Chief of the Defence Staff could, if he so chose, offer informal views in contradiction of his single-Service colleagues. But there were counterbalancing pressures. He had to live with his colleagues. Collectively they represented the Armed Forces. When it came to formal advice the whole elaborate and highly competent staff machinery of the Chiefs of Staff Secretariat would swing into play, following agreed procedures of circulation and clearance of papers, which led back into the Naval, General and Air Staffs in the Service Ministries and later the Service Departments of the Ministry of Defence. These staffs remained greatly influenced by their loyalties to their own Chief of Staff.

Even so, 1958, with the creation of the Chief of the Defence Staff (CDS), is a very significant landmark. It had become the starting-point for whatever direction would be followed in the future. The following twenty-five years span many reviews of the total defence staff area. In these reviews three key aspects and their interplay were dominant: the powers and resources of the CDS himself; the collective position of the Chiefs of Staff Committee; the development of central military staffs and their lines of reporting.

From 1958 to 1963, when Admiral of the Fleet Lord Mountbatten was CDS (he finally left the post in 1965, a length of tour which was never repeated; see Appendix E), further changes were limited to the appointment of a permanent central chairman of the Joint Planning Staff and to the provision of a personal military briefing staff. The major reorganisation of 1963/4 is significant in this area almost more by omission than by commission. With major changes in many parts there was no change in the Chiefs of Staff Committee or its role. The Chief of the Defence Staff was still limited to tendering his own advice only when there was a divergence of views among his single-Service colleagues. The creation of the Defence Staff was a major psychological attempt to bring together the three military staffs, but the weight of staff effort and the executive power still rested back in the Naval, General and Air Staffs, even though some limited steps were taken to build up an autonomous central capability.

THE CENTRAL DEFENCE STAFFS

The roles and powers of the new central staffs varied appreciably. The Defence Operational Executive and the associated Defence Operational Centre were essentially bodies for rapid access to information as detailed operational instructions continued to issue from the Service Departments. The Defence Operational Requirements Staff formed a small military element, operating alongside the central scientific and administrative staffs, who together would probe the requirements initiated by the single-Service Operational Requirements staffs to prevent duplication of effort. They would look at longer-term concepts and give advice about research and development programmes. But the initiative for and the progressing of new requirements lay with the Service Department staffs. It was in the strategic signals and intelligence fields that integration and executive authority went further. The logic of such a move in these two areas was powerful. Yet, even here, the level at which advice was organised within the directorates on a single-Service or functional basis was hotly disputed. It was not until the 1966 Defence White Paper that the change-over to a functional structure, and then at the higher levels only, was introduced into the intelligence field.

The next few years saw a series of measures essentially aimed at upgrading the level and quality of the military resources of the centre. Turning the head of the central Operational Requirements Staff from a two-star to a three-star officer is an obvious example. The reorganisation of the long-established Joint Planning Staff into two separate directorates for plans and for operations was a gain in efficiency rather than a change in power, as all these staff and their programmes of work were ultimately directed by the Chiefs of Staff collectively. Absence of agreement could therefore result in stalemate, about which a CDS, however frustrated he personally might feel, was powerless to do anything. It was not until 1970, following the first interim report of the Headquarters Organisation Committee, that the CDS was given the authority to initiate work in his own right. All the evidence suggests that this right was used sparingly in the next decade, so sparingly as to be astonishing. Why this was so can be only a matter for speculation. One view could be that the latent power might have been the catalyst for a less rigid approach by CDS's colleagues. A different view could be that the four Chiefs of Staff saw themselves primarily as a 'collective' to defend the Services against all comers.

The next major review of the whole defence structure carried out by the Management Review in 1975/6 and of which the Chief of the Defence Staff, the Master General of the Ordnance, the Air Member for Personnel and the Vice-Chief of the Naval Staff were the military members (an interesting and carefully balanced straddling of Services and functions), saw no grounds for change in this area. Indeed, when discussing the case for a smaller top management group for the Ministry, they saw the Chief of the Defence Staff and the three single-Service Chiefs of Staff as all being core members. Furthermore, when discussing the role of such a group they expressed the view that it should not affect the role of the Chiefs of Staff Committee in providing military advice to the Government, nor the role of the Defence Policy Staff which should continue to be tasked by the Chief of the Defence Staff both as Chairman of the Chiefs of Staff Committee and as CDS in his own right.

The Management Review Report recognised and discussed the continuing fundamental problem of resource allocation, including the need for flexibility to transfer resources between parts of the defence budget, and the need to develop broader operational concepts against which individual projects could be judged. They saw the first issue as solvable if the existing posts of Assistant Chief of Defence Staff (Policy) and his administrative counterpart were to be empowered to introduce alternative assumptions for the Long Term Costings to those produced by the Service Departments. As for broader operational concepts, they looked to a closer partnership between the central staffs and those in the Service Departments, and welcomed recent changes introduced by the Chiefs of Staff into the terms of reference of the Sea/Air and Land/Air Warfare Committees.

This generally clean bill of health may have derived credibility from the measures agreed in the previous year which involved major reductions in the role, size and equipment of all three Services. These changes seem to have been secured and negotiated through the Department and the Chiefs of Staff Committee without unacceptable opposition or procrastination. Perhaps it was the even-handedness and economic inevitability of the cuts which facilitated their passage.

1981–5: THE INCREASE IN POWER OF THE CDS AND THE EXPANSION OF THE DEFENCE STAFF

What is starkly clear about 1980/1 is that there was no comparable satisfaction on the part of Ministers with the performance of the military staffs including the Chiefs of Staff Committee. An earlier chapter has described Mr Nott's vividly expressed dissatisfaction and his decision to lay down his own assumptions for the review of the defence programme, which in turn led to his determination to strengthen the position of the central military staffs, including that of the CDS. There was at this time a greater willingness to permit senior military staff to speak and write publicly on current organisational issues. Some of those who were in central positions at or about that time have commented adversely on the absence of timely and decisive military judgement on defence priorities, and have deplored the tardiness of the military staffs as contrasted with the speed of response of administrative and scientific senior staffs. But there is one unresolved point. It is not clear why, if there had been deadlock, advantage was not taken of the powers conferred in 1970 on the CDS to offer his own advice.

Be that as it may, changes were soon set in hand after personal consultation between Mr Nott and his CDS. There is a strange ambivalence of view about their significance. The outcome itself was that the Chiefs of Staff, still acting collectively, were to give advice on strategy and the military implications of defence policy. The Chiefs of Staff Committee was still to be the body where CDS sought the views of his colleagues. The CDS was then to be empowered to offer independent military advice as well as a proper reflection of the views of his colleagues. Admiral of the Fleet Lord Lewin subsequently described the change as the biggest since 1964. Mr Nott summed up the changes as being 'largely a matter of emphasis – placing greater stress on CDS's own advice and the machinery needed to formulate it'. A cynic could say it was little more than semantics. A realist could say that it gave greater encouragement to a CDS, if he so wished to do, to flap his wings, and greater leverage for the Secretary of State to encourage him to do so.

The South Atlantic campaign intervened between the announcement in principle of the changes and the promulgation of the subordinate staff organisation within CDS's area, which was redesigned to support them. But it is doubtful if the campaign is relevant in any major way to the making of a judgement on the value of the changes. It has been said that it proved their value in that CDS was the sole regular military adviser to the Government and that this arrangement worked well and expeditiously. But the campaign involved operations rather than the more difficult and contentious problem of resource allocation. And, by chance, the CDS was an ex First Sea Lord so he could speak with authority on the key aspects of the campaign. A CDS of another cloth might have felt the need to be accompanied to key meetings by some of his colleagues. Moreover there was by then general acceptance, irrespective of the recent changes, that the CDS had a special responsibility for operations overseas which were not being conducted within the framework of NATO. In any case the South Atlantic campaign was not central to the type of likely future tasks. Taken in the round, the major threats to and the dominant proportion of the UK forces are deployed in the NATO area.

The autumn of 1982 saw the foreshadowed restructuring of the central staff under CDS. The primary aim was a tighter organisation, under a new post of DCDS who would bring together the previous separate direct reporting lines to the CDS of DCDS (Operational Requirements), ACDS (Policy), ACDS (Operations) and ACDS (Signals). The new titles of ACDS (Commitments) and ACDS (Command, Control, Communications and Information Systems) involved functions very similar to those previously carried out by ACDS (Operations) and ACDS (Signals), though now banding together alongside ACDS (Programmes) under the new DCDS. The more significant change was to concentrate in ACDS (Programmes) responsibilities for defence policy and strategy, operational requirements, programmes and resource allocation. The logic is impeccable but it may seem a tall order: little less than the delegation to one two-star officer of the spadework on the fundamental problems that had bedevilled British defence policy for twenty years or more. Furthermore, as the Naval, General and Air Staffs remained unchanged, ACDS (Programmes) and his staff would be in a difficult position of producing independent advice to CDS and drawing on the deep professional knowledge of these three single-Service staffs over the whole range of these subjects.

In the event, the organisation was given little opportunity to show if it could work effectively. When Mr Heseltine became Secretary of State three months later he set in hand his studies which, as have already been described, resulted in the following year in a further major reorganisation. The resultant new shape was based on a

concept of two principal advisers to the Secretary of State – the CDS
and the PUS – to whom an expanded and integrated Defence Staff
would report, with an Office of Management and Budget in a
relationship of constructive tension, and the Service Departments
headed by their single-Service Chiefs of Staff concentrating almost
exclusively on the management of their Services.

IMPLICATIONS OF THE 1985 CHANGES

Three points are worthy of recapitulation here about the reciprocal
relationships of the CDS, the single-Service Chiefs of Staff, the
restructured Defence Staff and the residual Service Departments in
the context of the new concept and structure. First, the July 1984
White Paper on the Central Organisation for Defence avoids,
presumably with deliberation, any explicit statement of the 'collective
responsibility' of the Chiefs of Staff Committee. CDS is now to be
responsible for tendering advice on 'strategy, forward policy, overall
priorities in resource allocation, programmes, current commitments
and operations'. In tendering his advice, CDS 'will take into account
the views of the Chiefs of Staff'. Thus, at this level, smooth future
working will continue to depend on good personal relationships
between the four Chiefs of Staff.

As for the single-Service Chiefs of Staff, they 'will continue as the
professional heads of their Services, and as such as "senior advisers
to CDS" '. They would also remain responsible for fighting effectiveness and overall efficiency as well as management and morale. In
order to coordinate effectively these various responsibilities and to
ensure the necessary linkage between policy-making and management, there were two specific provisions. The first was one of liaison;
the single-Service Chiefs of Staff were to have access to the Defence
Staff which, for its part, was to be responsive to their needs. The
second was that each Chief of Staff was to have sufficient staff to
enable him to direct the work of his Service.

As a consequence there was a further redistribution of the former
Naval, General and Air Staffs as between the Defence Staff and
the Service Departments. The outcome can be exemplified by the
arrangements made in the Air Force Department where, under a
two-star Assistant Chief of Air Staff, there were to be directors in
charge of air support, air offence and air defence together with a
director of briefing and coordination. This group of staff would be

working closely with all the main parts of the Defence Staff, sometimes with an identifiable RAF cell, sometimes with wholly integrated staff. In the case of the Defence Programmes Staff there was to be at the one-star level a Director Air Force Plans and Programmes; in the case of the Systems Staff there was to be a two-star ACDS (Operational Requirements) (Air Systems). On the other hand in the Commitments Staff tri-Service integration was to go down further, but here, as can be seen from the size of the operational staffs left in the Service Department, the concentration would be on broad aspects of operations rather than executive detail. Similar structures, but reflecting their special needs, were set up in the Navy and Army Departments. Here, therefore, as at the Chiefs of Staff level, much would depend on the staff in the Defence Staff, on the one hand, and the single-Service Departments, on the other, establishing good working practices.

The White Paper said that a major task of the new organisation would be to clarify responsibilities. Certainly the initial press comment brought out the potential ambiguity. *The Times* reported the next day that the Service Chiefs had said that the new organisation could work well and that the Chiefs of Staff had received certain assurances and adequate safeguards. But in its comment *The Times* referred to the annihilation of the Chiefs of Staff's policy-making functions. This is certainly too melodramatic a picture. But at the end of all these changes, which became increasingly hectic in the 1980s, certain conclusions can be drawn.

CONCLUSIONS

First, there has been general acceptance, contrasted with the 1950s, of the need for a Chief of the Defence Staff. Ministers want a personal military adviser, and they want him to have authority. Most other countries have such a post, with variations in powers and terms of reference. A CDS is also essential for the many inter-governmental and high military level talks, notably in NATO. There is also advantage in having an independent rather than a rotational Chairman of the Chiefs of Staff Committee.

Second, there is acceptance of the need for some integration of military staff into a central structure. Intelligence, communications, the balance of weapons systems, as well as plans, the broad framework of operations and overall defence policies have all now proved to be areas where it can be achieved successfully.

Third, there is acceptance that there is the need for a Head of Service and that such a head should chair some form of executive and policy-making body comprising his military colleagues with administrative and scientific support. Furthermore, if this body is to give effective direction to the Service Commands, its work cannot be limited to the personnel and logistics areas. It must also take operating and training factors into account, as well as the arrangements for and timing of the introduction of new weapons systems. It also needs, in a rapidly changing technical world and with a developing threat, to give thought to the contribution the individual Service can make to the overall strategy and capability and to the consequences of changes to the working arrangements between the Services. But there is a residual issue of the relationship between the executive body and the Service Board with Ministers in attendance.

What question marks remain? Certain key points can be identified. Possible organisational developments will be discussed in a final chapter. First, there is the extent of the CDS's authority and his power – leaving on one side the question of wisdom – for overruling or ignoring his single-Service Chiefs of Staff colleagues. Second, up to what level is there a need for single-Service expertise in the central defence staff areas? The question, put in practical terms, is whether, for example, a Brigadier could command confidence if he were to be put in charge of operational requirements for anti-shipping warfare. If, in some areas at least, it is considered that the basic structure will have to be single-Service elements headed by one or more senior coordinating officers, there is a further question of whether integration by itself has led to staff economies or whether economies have been achieved simply by imposing arbitrary cuts simultaneously with a change to a more unified arrangement. Third – and in a way this is a mirror-image of the second question – will the single-Service Chief of Staff consider that from the combined provisions of right of access to the Defence Staff and the provision of a residual capability within the Service Department he has adequate resources to discharge his responsibilities for fighting effectiveness and efficiency?

9   Personnel and Logistics

THE PERSONNEL AND LOGISTIC FUNCTIONS AND
THEIR PLACE IN THE SINGLE-SERVICE ENVIRONMENT

Personnel and logistics (the P & L area as it has become known) are not in some ways obvious bedfellows. Logistics is in itself a comparatively new term. The top official military committee covering the main elements which comprise logistics – supply, maintenance, repair, storage, movements and accommodation – is still known as the Principal Administrative Officers Committee (PAOs). Two of the major elements of the logistics spectrum group themselves much more naturally with other organisational areas rather than with the personnel field; in-service supply, maintenance and repair have close affinities with the Procurement Executive's functions; accommodation issues link directly with the Property Service Agency's responsibilities for the construction and maintenance of all defence buildings. The responsibilities of the Principal Personnel Officers (PPOs) for the Serviceman and Servicewoman have a greater internal coherence, covering as they do all aspects of recruitment, basic training, postings and promotions, and all the supporting services, such as medical, dental, chaplaincy, pay and physical fitness, needed to keep the personnel effective. Admittedly the PPOs look to the PAOs to provide them with the material essentials such as food, clothing, accommodation and equipment. But the policy connections are not great.

At the same time there are two basic common factors. In terms of the end-product of the fighting man the two Board Members in each Service have traditionally been responsible for providing their Naval, General and Air Staffs with the wherewithal to produce effective units. In organisational terms there is perhaps a slightly negative but still valid reason for this P & L area having been a stable centre within the Board structure of each of the Services. In wartime, procurement functions have been removed to other specially created Ministries. As to the Naval, General and Air Staffs, they

136

have for long been caught up in the wider issues of joint planning and operations and of conflicting claims on resource allocation, all pointing to a centralisation in a defence staff. But the PPOs and the PAOs have been subject only very rarely to external pulls. There have been minor different practices of demarcation over training – though, even there, the essential logic has been to transfer training to the Naval, General and Air Staffs the closer it came to operational, as opposed to basic or trade, training. The one major amputation was the loss of works services to the Ministry of Public Building and Works, later converted to the Property Services Agency.

The organisational pattern which results in each Service having its own PPO and PAO heading a self-contained supporting structure, in turn working its way down through Command Headquarters and subordinate formations to the individual unit, is based essentially on the self-contained nature of each Service. This total Service environment has a long tradition, exemplified by the maxim that an army marches on its stomach. Expanded somewhat it is the line of argument that if a man is to risk his life and fight effectively, he must be confident that his superiors will look after him. Looking after him covers personal, physical and material needs. It includes maintaining his equipment to ensure that it is safe, and repairing it as quickly as possible; it includes medical support. The argument extends to sub-specialisations in most areas of his support; it requires different skills to repair a tank and a destroyer; the medical effects of high-speed aviation are very different from exposure to prolonged conditions of heat or cold on land. Bringing these various considerations together, the argument runs that it is not just enough to have these specific specialised skills at unit or formation level in the field. The whole purpose of the Headquarters staff is to put together an effective fighting package. That needs staff officers who understand the environment of the individual Service. If a Chief of Staff is to be held responsible for the efficiency of his Service, he must have at his direct disposal specialists in the whole range of the support fields who command his confidence.

On the other hand, the critic, while accepting the case for sub-specialisation, particularly so the closer one moves towards the operational unit, will point to the many common factors. He will also point to the benefits of scale, in particular in the savings of resources by bulk purchase and distribution. He will suggest that centralised purchasing does not necessarily invalidate specialised skills in handling the purchases. He will question whether there is any difference in the basic training of a cook, or a driver or a helicopter pilot. He will see that there are benefits of flexibility, as well as economies in overheads and an improvement in the public image of the Services, that come from having one Pay Corps or one Provost Arm or one Chaplaincy Service.

The spectrum is wide. It affects the Services in the field at least as much as the Headquarters organisation. Different solutions may be possible.

There is nothing novel in this brief, highly selective analysis. The separate structures and the issues behind closer working between them have been known for decades. What has happened is that since the Second World War, when there was a marked growth in inter-Service cooperation, they have gained greater prominence because of the budgetary pressures, because of continuing probing on the part of Select Committees and because of the mounting ministerial interest and involvement in managerial issues.

POSSIBLE LINES OF APPROACH TOWARDS CHANGES

The theoretical solutions have also been on the table for a long time. There is the one-Service solution, which would presumably have a series of unified Corps (Medical, Pay, Engineering, etc.) supported by unified schools and support establishments but still with sub-specialisations in skills. Sub-specialisation might also extend to unit structures (e.g. single-Service repair units) where the distinct front-line organisation of Army and RAF formations, as in West Germany, called for it. At the centre there would be one Principal Personnel and one Principal Administrative Officer. This approach has never got very far in this country.

Within the fundamental assumption of the retention of three separate Services, there is a range of possibilities not necessarily mutually exclusive. There is limited unification in certain areas: e.g. a Defence Supply Agency on American lines handling the most common items for all three Services but in association with special-ised single-Service supply branches; or a unified medical corps; or a unified chaplaincy service. There is the major-user principle, where one Service undertakes a particular task for all three. There is a joint system whereby individual Services come together *ad hoc* to share and run together a common facility. Or there is an internal drive within each Service to seek economy and efficiency by broadening, over related areas, the duties of specialised corps. Pay staff, for example, can move into automatic data processing (ADP) work study, accounting and internal audit, as has been the commercial trend in the private sector.

Such changes can either be imposed as an arbitrary act or they can first be evaluated and tested. This latter process has to be carried out against two basic principles. The first is, to some extent at least, measurable: will it be more cost-effective? The second is unquantifiable: will it improve efficiency and morale?

There are two organisational aspects to this question of change or stability in the P & L area. There is the need for the formal provision of some mechanism which could take initiatives, could test and evaluate against the two basic principles, and could subsequently give directions. Second, there is the organisation needed to keep the show on the road and, where required, to implement change.

The need to study change was recognised in the 1946 White Paper. The newly created Minister of Defence was given, as one of his three functions, responsibility for the settlement of questions of general administration on which a common policy for the three Services would be desirable. No targets were set. To carry out this work the Minister was given a Standing Committee of the three Service Ministers under his Chairmanship, to be served by the PPOs and the Principal Supply Officers as the PAOs were then called.

Nothing major resulted from this machinery. In 1957 Mr Duncan Sandys' comprehensive terms of reference included authority to give decisions over a total range of areas including the 'organisation' of the Armed Forces. But this clearly and understandably came low down in his order of priorities and there were no major developments in his time or in the immediately following years. None the less, Mr Macmillan continued to feel that there was scope for worthwhile change. When launching in December 1962 his new initiative on the organisation, he commented that there were a number of activities that the Services could easily share.

The 1963 White Paper consequently went somewhat further in asserting a general belief in the desirability of some change. It commented that economy and efficiency might be improved by removing different practices in the field of administration. It cited the possibility in some fields of a common defence approach and in others of the extension of the procedure whereby one Service would undertake a task on behalf of all three. While it stressed the focal role of the individual Service Board in the management of the Service it proposed two steps to enable management problems to be dealt with on a defence basis. Policy staffs who operated in identical management fields for each of the Services should be accommodated as close together in Whitehall as possible. The organisation of the PPOs and the PAOs should be strengthened by the appointment of a Deputy Chief of Defence Staff (P & L), who together with the Second Permanent Under-Secretary of State (Defence Secretariat) would be responsible for the closer coordination of management policies and procedures in respect of both the internal organisation of the Ministry and the practical arrangements in the Services out in the field. When Mr Healey took office he reinforced this structure by charging his Deputy Secretary of State with the task of studying this whole subject.

1965 and 1966 saw a simultaneous assault on two different lines. A series of investigations were made, particularly on the supply side, into ranges of equipment such as accommodation stores, clothing, motor transport and food. In some cases a single management authority was appointed. In others unified direction of policy was the solution. On the personnel side a Committee – the first of many as it proved to be – was set up to consider the scope for some integration of the medical services. Closer cooperation between the three recruiting organisations was considered. This approach, on an area-by-area basis, was in fact to extend over the next two decades, with annual White Papers reporting progress.

At the same time, the Geraghty Report, while acknowledging the risks and imponderables of major change and while assuming the continuation of three separate Services, recommended integration rather than a continuation of the process of rationalisation. They saw such a radical change as offering a greater prospect of savings in staff, of standardisation, common servicing and larger orders with economies of scale. Such an integration would be achieved from the top by setting up functional Controllers of Personnel and Supply who would report to each of the Chiefs of Staff.

This report marked the high point in the possibility of a totally functional solution. It was not accepted. But their message of the scope for further economies was recognised to have validity. Ministers therefore decided to proceed by giving greater impetus to the studies of individual areas. At the top level this was to be achieved by the ministerial reorganisation which created a Minister (Administration), and by the appointment in early 1967 of a Chief Adviser Personnel and Logistics who was to act as the principal adviser to the Secretary of State on P & L matters, subject to the overriding authority of the CDS. He was also to be the permanent chairman of the PPOs and the PAOs. In effect this appointment was a significant upgrading of the DCDS (P & L) of the 1964 creation.

The next three years produced further measures of rationalisation. But the Headquarters Organisation Committee was not satisfied that even a four-star Chief Adviser of Personnel and Logistics had sufficient authority. Their recommendation, which was implemented in 1970, was to give him the power to initiate and coordinate action on matters affecting all three Services: additional authority very comparable to the changes they had recommended on the position of CDS. The outward sign of this change was the retitling of the post to that of Chief of Personnel and Logistics. On the other hand, the Committee, after studying in detail over the following twelve months the way in which work was carried out in the Ministry in the P & L area, saw no need for any major changes in the structure in the Ministry. They saw greater scope for savings by means of delegation to Commands. Nor did the other major report of that period, the Rayner Report into Defence Procurement, affect, as it might have done, the supply and repair responsibilities of the PAOs. It could have analysed the effect of the principle of whole-life responsibility for an item of equipment on the existing division of functions between the PAO and the proposed Systems Controller. However, other than stating that users should be encouraged to discuss their in-service problems with suppliers – something of a statement of the obvious – it concluded that to look beyond this to the differing ways in which in-service support and the supply of spares were carried out would require a further major study.

On the personnel side these years had seen the creation and first results of the work of two major outside bodies: the Armed Forces Pay Review Body and the Top Salaries Review Board. Their existence, coupled with the consequences of the introduction of the military salary, gave a very considerable impetus to the role of CPL, together with his small cell of central military pay staffs and the central defence secretariats operating under a Deputy Under-Secretary (P & L), on pay and pension matters. The outside bodies expected a 'defence' view on pay. They recognised that each Service had its own specialised cases – flying pay, submarine pay, parachuting pay – but they expected and got a high degree of coordination through the CPL machinery working in turn through the PPOs Committee.

Even if the central staffs had established a useful role on the pay front, the Defence and External Affairs Sub-Committee of the House of Commons Expenditure Committee was not impressed in their 1974/5 first report by what they saw as the very limited degree of coordination and direction provided by the Central Staffs. The Sub-Committee had studied two particular areas – Service training and the RAF manpower economy project. Their general conclusion was that the Services still enjoyed too great a degree of autonomy in their management and organisation. On training specifically, they recommended a reconstitution and strengthening of the Defence Training Committee's working party so as to include a full and critical study of the operational and environmental reasons for differences in training objectives. More generally they wanted to see a strengthening of the role of the central staffs to achieve better control of the use of resources, more active cooperation and greater harmonisation of administrative organisations.

The Ministry of Defence's initial response was to leave the wider issue to the Management Review which had just been set in hand, and to appoint an outside expert to inquire into the extent to which the Ministry could make use of joint training. His report confirmed the Ministry's view that the scope for joint training was necessarily limited and that only in relatively few areas was further progress feasible. While the Ministry and the House of Commons Sub-Committee agreed on this point, the Sub-Committee was disappointed that the Ministry did not accept a recommendation to set up a central organisation to stimulate the development of joint training and to create an overall policy, but preferred to rely on supervision of the existing Defence Training Committee both by the PPOs and by the Minister of State. The Ministry and the Sub-Committee clashed even more sharply over a recommendation by the Management Review that the post on CPL should lapse and that coordination on P & L matters should be transferred to the Vice-Chief of the Defence Staff, who would be at three-star level. The Sub-Committee regarded this as weakening rather than enhancing, as they wished, central supervision of key areas of Service administration, training and logistic support. After a series of exchanges a compromise was reached which saw the two posts still being combined into one, but one with some shift of emphasis as implied in the new title of Vice-Chief of the Defence Staff (P & L). Moreover, the post was to stay at four-star level and would have added authority by virtue of membership of the Defence Council.

The next few years saw a series of studies into the most cost-effective arrangements for individual parts of the P & L areas of each of the Services. The Royal Dockyards were the subject of almost constant review. The advent of the Conservative Government saw the use of the Rayner-style study which in the Ministry of Defence included the system of provisioning of food. To assist the renewed search for savings there was the drive for privatisation. All this activity was carried out either collectively through the existing PPO and PAO central machinery or by the individual Board members on a single-Service basis. No new organisational arrangements were introduced. Nor did the change of ministerial structure in 1981 fundamentally affect relationships. A working arrangement developed whereby the Parliamentary Secretary for the Armed Forces tended to take a special interest in tri-Service questions in the P & L areas, dealing normally with the VCDS (P & L) and the Second PUS as his key advisers.

The much bigger 1984 reorganisation took what might appear to be a somewhat surprising turn in this field. The combined effect of the need to provide strong support for CDS and PUS in the running of the new, enlarged Defence Staff and the desire to make savings in top posts, resulted in the VCDS (P&L) losing his P & L label and concentrating on defence policy issues. Within his subordinate structure it is true that the DCDS Programmes had Personnel also added to his title and was charged with the central coordination of Service personnel matters including, specifically, the medical services, which, as the result of yet another study, were to have an integrated tri-Service Ministry organisation managing three single-Service medical branches in the field. But it must be doubtful whether, when there are acute pressures on the determination of strategic and budgetary priorities and resources, the DCDS (Programmes and Personnel) will be able to provide the time for personnel matters which the VCDS (P&L) had been able to afford in the previous years.

Moreover there would no longer be the linkage of a common chairman of the PPOs and the PAOs. For the PPOs there still would be a central chairman, the DCDS (Programmes and Personnel), even though as a three-star officer he might be outranked by individual PPOs. On the logistics side the DCDS (Commitments) was to include in his tasks a strengthening of the capability for central logistics and movement planning. But the emphasis here will be on the operational rather than the managerial aspects of logistics. Nor will he be chairman of the PAOs: this will fall to the senior of the single-service PAOs.

The White Paper restated the Government's intention to pursue opportunities for rationalisation but provided no senior military focal point to follow up this aim. The initiative for this would now seem to lie principally with Ministers personally, supported by their civilian staffs, notably the Deputy Under-Secretary (P&L). Subsequent annual Defence White Papers have not discussed the organisational aspects of rationalisation but have limited themselves to reporting progress in specific areas.

HIGHER APPOINTMENTS

There remains one highly sensitive and important aspect of personnel management which has not come under the executive direction of the PPOs, but which can conveniently be discussed here as it exemplifies in heightened form the tug-of-war between central and single-Service control. This is the field of higher appointments, traditionally handled by the Naval, Military and Air Secretaries working usually under the personal direction of their Chief of Staff and with a fair degree of involvement on the part of all the Service Board members.

The possibility of changing this practice was mooted by Lord Ismay and Sir Ian Jacob, who recommended the creation of a 'purple' list of all officers of two-star rank and above. This concept of a single list could, it was held, result in objective advice being given to the Secretary of State. It could also, in the longer term, help to lead to the creation of a single Service.

The proposal was not accepted, but the 1963 White Paper laid down that proposals for the promotion and appointment of senior officers should be referred to the Secretary of State. It also announced the creation of a new post, at three-star level, of a Defence Services Secretary who would be the sole future channel of communication between the Sovereign and the Secretary of State. With a post of this seniority there must also have been the embryonic thought that it could become a source of independent advice on higher appointments. But this was not to be. The single-Service Chiefs of Staff jealously preserved their powers of appointment. Senior tri-Service posts in the Ministry of Defence and in international headquarters were filled according to a general principle of strict rotation, and the CDS's part even in the appointments to international posts was limited. The Defence Services Secretary was soon to be downgraded to a two-star level, primarily dealing with the Palace. From time to time there might be rumbles of discontent from Ministers about the tightness of the straitjacket in which they were being placed. But even, for example, in 1977, when the RAF incumbent of the post of CDS died within a few months of assuming office, there was an interregnum of only six months during which the post was filled from another Service until an RAF officer could succeed and thus, as it were, complete the RAF's turn.

It was only in 1982 that a real change became possible. As part of the package intended to strengthen the position of the CDS, a Senior Appointments Committee was formed, consisting of the CDS and the Chiefs of Staff, to oversee the promotion and appointment of all three- and four-star officers, and of two-star officers in certain key posts. Admiral of the Fleet Sir Terence Lewin considered it to be of vital importance. It gave the CDS an opportunity to break away from maintaining a strict balance between the Services which had in effect greatly reduced any practical choice in the past. It also afforded a safeguard over the future of an officer who had served outstandingly in a central post. The value of this new arrangement can be judged only with time. But if one of its intentions is to provide a range of choices for the top posts, it will need to go back some way into the career pattern of individual officers if it is to be effective. This would in turn mean a greater restriction of the autonomy of the Naval, Military and Air Secretaries.

REVIEW

The P & L areas have therefore seen two decades of sustained scrutiny and much change of practice. The high costs of defence and the need, within the constrained defence budget, to transfer resources as far as possible to equipping the front line, have driven the Services to look themselves at their own systems and structures. In addition, mostly led by Ministers and the centre, the Services have looked at a wide range of possibilities of integration and rationalisation. The changes have been significant, even if not outwardly so, because they have, for the most part, been effected within the framework of existing single-Service structure. This would not have been a foregone conclusion twenty years ago when possibilities of radical unification and functionalisation were in the air. But, once it was decided to proceed more pragmatically within the framework of the existing basic single-Service structure, the organisational issue became predominantly one of devising a central machinery which would provide an impetus for the examination and evaluation of change but would leave the work essentially with the single Services for execution and subsequent management. This machinery took the form by the late 1960s of direct ministerial involvement, supported by a central very senior military officer who was in turn supported by comparatively small numbers of military and administrative staff. This central body had neither the resources nor the expertise to carry out detailed studies in what were often highly specialised and very professional fields. The work was commissioned from a variety of sources: internal tri-Service committees; outside experts from the private sector; mixed high-level bodies. Not all the studies were uniformly successful, and their quality varied. But even though the pace of change may be questioned, the result in many fields is a streamlined system, with a far greater degree of inter-Service interdependence. Certainly each of the PAOs now has major responsibilities on behalf of all three Services. And on the PPOs side there have been some significant moves in the training field, even though, understandably, there is still much sensitivity about the vital need to instil the spirit of the individual Service into the volunteer who, in the absence of conscription, is the only source of manning.

The most recent changes suggest that though the search for further rationalisations across the Services will continue, the feeling is that all the easy and fruitful pickings have taken place. The major thrust must accordingly now be within the management of the single Service, spearheaded by the PPO and the PAO in his single-Service capacity to increase cost-effectiveness and reduce overheads.

An analysis of the incidence of costs, particularly in the logistic fields, suggests that this is the most profitable approach. The big costs lie in provisioning and stock-holding practices. Decisions as between repair or replacement of equipment likewise have major financial implications. Rationalisation as such has little effect on these policies. Pressure on the single-Service budget is a much more effective force at the central level, and it should be increasingly helped at the unit level by the introduction of responsibility budgets. At the same time it remains important to have a central post, such as there was in the time of a VCDS (P&L), to act as a catalyst for independent studies and to watch that the various specialist branches in each of the Services do not erect undesirable protective walls round their policies and their career structures.

On the personnel side the central role is a subtler one. Each Service has built up and jealously guards its own style of life, traditions and corps structures, and the reasons should not be dismissed lightly. Ministers, Parliamentary Committees and bodies such as the Armed Forces Pay Review Board look at these from their various standpoints and make comparisons, criticisms and judgements. There is value in having a senior officer as an interlocutor, a role which the VCDS (P&L) played to bring about compromise in the recent changes in the top management arrangements governing the three medical corps. Functional Ministers are likely to continue to ask questions in these areas and, with other pressures on the DCDS (Programmes and Personnel) on top of his personnel responsibilities, they may turn increasingly to civilian administrative support from within the Office of Management and Budget.

10 The Place of Scientific Staff in the Defence Organisation

GENERAL SCENE

For some decades, defence weapons systems have been operating at the frontiers of the latest technologies. The accelerating rate of the new scientific breakthroughs has led, almost inexorably, to design complexities, big increases in costs and growing uncertainties about the length of effective life of the weapons in operational service. The resultant tactical and sometimes strategic problems have exposed ministers and senior Service officers to difficult decisions in fields where they cannot be expected to have much expert knowledge.

These developments have heightened the demand for technically qualified staff in Government, as well as in manufacturing industry and university research, both to devise and control the associated research and development programmes and to interpret and analyse the military consequences of these programmes. How relevant, for example, were such breakthroughs as nuclear fission or the laser beam or space technology going to be to defence and how could they best be exploited? Over the years a number of identifiable tasks have become the primary responsibility of staff qualified in these fields. There is the semi-strategic role of operational analysis, modelling possible battlefield scenarios for which a technical intelligence appreciation of the military and scientific potentialities of possible hostile powers has also to be supplied. There is the very large investment put into research and development, carried out both inside Government and out in industry and the universities. There is the work alongside the Services either in the Ministry or in operational Commands advising them on such matters as the potentiality and best tactical use of weapons systems. Some of these roles call for specific, more or less self-contained groupings of experts. In other

148

cases the scientifically qualified staff find themselves as part of larger teams where they might be integrated with military staff, an increasing number of whom have become technically qualified in recent years.

This chapter is therefore deliberately entitled 'the place of scientific staff in the defence organisation' rather than simply 'the scientific organisation', because scientists are widely deployed throughout the Ministry and in Commands, and are not concentrated only in those areas which are directly controlled by senior scientific staff. Two such major areas have emerged during the organisational changes described in the earlier chapters; one under the Chief Scientific Adviser (CSA), with its main thrust in the field of operational analysis and broad research objectives; the second under the Controller Research and Development Establishments, Research and Nuclear (CERN), with its efforts directed to the allocation of resources and policy control of work in these fields. But other scientists have important roles to play in other parts of the Ministry: in the recently reconstructed Defence Staff; in the Service Systems Controllerates of the Procurement Executive; with the operational, training and logistic staffs of the Services in the Service Departments.

While these organisational arrangements emerged as part of the successive organisational changes, there were two wider considerations also at work which influenced some of the arrangements. The demands for scientifically qualified manpower became very large. In order to recruit and retain sufficient people of talent, an acceptably attractive pyramid of career and promotion opportunities had to be created. There was a growing political and public perception that not only were such staff needed as key practitioners in the defence fields, but that there should be representation at the very highest levels so that an authoritative scientific voice could play its part in the major policy deliberations.

Before going into more detail on the emergence of the two main scientific structures, a few words should be said on the staff themselves.

THE SCIENTIFIC CLASS

The phrase 'scientific staff', as generally understood in the Ministry, refers to a class structure which was itself created as a part of the evolution of the Civil Service itself. Major groupings have been brought about over the years, notably as a result of the Fulton Report in 1968. These larger groupings, which gathered together smaller packets of staff working in related areas in different ministries or even in different parts of the same ministry, were considered to have a number of advantages. They simplified pay and grading. They facilitated the movement of staff from area to area. They paved the way for the formation of an open structure at the higher level which embraced and theoretically created openings at the top for all classes. The outcome for the Ministry of Defence was to concentrate the vast majority of its staff into three groups: Administration; Science; Professional and Technology (P & T). This last group was basically orientated towards engineering. The differences between the Science and the Professional and Technology Groups were not wholly clear-cut. The P & T Group tended to dominate the manning of such areas as the Royal Corps of Naval Constructors used in the Ship Department and the Royal Dockyards, the Royal Ordnance Factories and the RAF signals specialisms. But there was also a place for scientists in these areas. And, within the Science Group which tended to dominate in the R & D Establishments, a significant proportion of its members had originally joined with engineering degrees. The scale of these skilled resources can be seen from the fact that there are over 8000 scientists in the Ministry of Defence (about two-thirds of the Scientific Class in the whole Civil Service) and over 17 000 engineers and supporting technical grades, the large majority of whom are concentrated in the Navy Department's ship-design and dockyard fields. There are those who argue that this balance is not right, particularly at the higher levels, and that greater emphasis on practical engineering experience, especially in industry, would be a valuable asset and discipline in the handling of expensive procurement programmes.

THE ROLE OF THE SCIENTIFIC STAFF

The defence roles, which were identified as most calling for scientific skills, gained in importance as modern technologies transformed the Armed Forces from the 1930s onwards. Scientific breakthroughs, such as radar, the gas turbine engine, semiconductors, nuclear propulsion and nuclear weapons, had fundamental effects on weapons systems and, consequently, on strategy and the resultant allocation of resources. The growing scale, complexity and lethality of weapons systems called for greater analysis of comparative effectiveness. An early example is the use made by Mr Churchill in the Second World War of Sir Henry Tizard and Professor Lindemann (later Lord Cherwell). The use of scientists also extended steadily to the personnel side, where, for example, the costs of the training of pilots called for the devising of more scientifically based methods of selection and of the use of the more economical simulator.

These broad trends led not only to the identification of specific areas of work where it was considered that scientific skills were particularly relevant, but to organisational groupings around these skills with a hierarchy of their own. One area became defined as operational analysis: the use of mathematical modelling to evaluate the performance and comparative effectiveness of individual weapons systems, and to go on from that to the even more difficult evaluation of the capabilities of opposing forces on the likely major fronts. A second area, and by far the largest in terms of staff and money, was the whole area of defence research and development. The requirements of national security, and the doubtful availability of funds in the private sector for medium-term research, led to the practice, even before 1939, of much of this work being carried out in Government Establishments rather than in industry, and Establishments such as RAE Farnborough and RRE Malvern (now RSRE) acquired international status. The intra-mural practice continued after the war and extended into the particularly demanding and secret field of nuclear weapons with its centre at AWRE Aldermaston. Such establishments required very substantial resources for their wide range of tasks spanning feasibility studies, project development, specification for contract purposes, technical monitoring and acceptance testing. To bring together the work in the R & D Establishments and also the work carried out extra-murally by the universities and industry, there had to be a sizeable headquarters effort responsible for the determination of policies, the allocation of resources and the interrelationships with the policy staffs of the Services.

A third area was directed at the best application of the new weapons when they came into operational service. Scientific staffs were deployed alongside the Services not only in the Naval, General and Air Staffs in the Ministries but also in the operational Commands. This work extended from the tactical to the logistic and personnel fields.

A more general, perhaps more nebulous but potentially influential area of work was that of the informed, independent, scientifically 'numerate' adviser. There was a perceived risk that new technologies might not be objectively weighed by understandably partisan supporters of a particular tactical approach or weapon system. There was also a wider, still less specific fear that major errors of judgement might be made because so few of the policy-makers, whether ministerial, administrative or even military had an adequately deep understanding of the potential consequences of technological change. To produce a new all-round generation of leaders with sufficient breadth of understanding in these fields would by definition take time and massive changes in our educational system and social perceptions. Therefore the immediate solution was to give the scientist, *per se*, a seat at the top table.

THE SERVICE AND 'SUPPLY' MINISTRIES

The 1940s and 1950s saw these various roles being performed predominantly in the separate Ministries of the time and by staff whose careers were to a large extent self-contained within the Ministries. There was, for example, a Royal Naval Scientific Service and comparable bodies of staff in the other two Service Ministries. During these two decades each Service Ministry had a Chief Scientist or Scientific Adviser with a place on its Board or Council. One key function was to provide a link with the activities of the R & D Establishments. The policy and management of the large majority of the R & D Establishments remained under the Ministry of Supply in its various guises. But, in addition, the 1946 White Paper recognised the need to integrate military and scientific thought, and to see that in planning defence research account was taken of the wider scientific effort in the country as a whole. Its organisational solution was a Committee on Defence Research Policy, based in the new Ministry of Defence and bringing together all those involved operationally and scientifically in the Service Departments and the Ministry of Supply. Their operational line of advice would be to the Chiefs of Staff; their wider considerations would go to the ministerial Defence Committee. The Chairman of the Committee was to be a scientist of high standing who would be appointed for a period of years and would be, alongside the Permanent Secretary, the Chief Staff Officer and the Chairman of the Joint War Production Staff, one of the principal advisers of the new post of the Minister of Defence.

THE CONSEQUENCES OF THE 1963/4 UNIFICATION

The 1963 White Paper contained an appraisal of the place and role of science within the unified Ministry. It confirmed the post of Chief Scientific Adviser (CSA), at that time Sir Solly Zuckermann, who had assumed that title as well as being Chairman of the Defence Research Policy Committee when he joined the Ministry in 1960. It established the status of 'science' by making the CSA a member of the Defence Council and stating that he was one of the three principal advisers (i.e. alongside the PUS and the CDS) of the Secretary of State. To enable the CSA to play a full part in the formulation and control of the defence research and development programme, the Paper announced a series of organisational changes. The former Defence Research Policy Committee would be split into two new Committees, each under the CSA's chairmanship. The first, the Defence Research Committee, would have mainly scientific members, including outside independent scientists. It would be overseeing all military research that did not directly support approved weapons systems. The second committee, the Weapons Development Committee, would be advising on the major projects to be included in the development programme, and relating them to resources, defence policy and operational requirements. Its membership would need to be more widely based and to include military and administrative staff. Both committees would need to have representatives from the Ministry of Aviation as it then was.

The White Paper also considered the organisation of the scientific staff. As part of the creation of a unified Ministry it saw the need for a central capability of scientists, small in number, to work alongside the new central Defence Operational Requirements Staff. More generally and symbolically it set up a Defence Scientific Staff, to which would belong not only the central scientists but also the scientists of the Service Departments whenever they were engaged on problems of a defence rather than of a single-Service character. This duality was reflected in the position of the three single-Service Chief Scientists, whose posts were still to continue and who were to remain members of their Service Boards. They now also had a direct line of reporting to the CSA as did his two immediate deputies, the

Deputy Chief Scientific Adviser (Projects) and the Deputy Chief Scientific Adviser (Studies).

In the subsequent hectic period of studies into a wide range of capabilities and individual weapons systems which were initiated by Mr Healey, individual members of the defence scientific staff were greatly used on an *ad hoc* basis as members and sometimes chairmen of multi-disciplinary working parties. But the lack of a formalised, permanent capability was felt, and the 1965 Defence White Paper announced the formation of a Defence Operational Analysis Establishment at West Byfleet which would be directed by one of CSA's staff. Nevertheless there were those who thought the scientific organisation was still too diffuse. The Geraghty Report commented that it was too widely dispersed among the three single-Service Chief Scientists' areas and that the Defence Operational Analysis Establishment was the only integrated element.

The next change may seem, in retrospect, a regression. It did not become a permanent feature and was primarily brought about on grounds of personality, though explained on an organisational basis in the 1967 Defence White Paper. When Sir Solly Zuckerman left the Ministry of Defence in 1966, his post was divided into two. His two previous Deputies, whose posts were abolished, became respectively Chief Adviser (Projects) and Chief Adviser (Studies). The former, Sir William Cook, who was *primus inter pares* in that he was made a member of the Defence Council and professional head of the scientific staff in the Ministry of Defence, was designated as the adviser to the recently created functional Minister of Defence for Equipment in the project field. The latter, Professor Cottrell, had as his primary duties to undertake studies in the field of defence policy and systems analysis and, in that capacity, to chair the Defence Research Committee and the Operational Analysis Committee.

Valuable though the individual contributions undoubtedly were, the division of the CSA post and the consequent loss of some status weakened formally the standing of this source of independent opinion, particularly on broad policy. The ground could be made up by personal influence but this has always been an uphill struggle in a department as hierarchical as the Ministry of Defence. This split structure lapsed in 1971 when Sir Hermann Bondi was appointed to the revived post of Chief Scientific Adviser.

THE EFFECTS OF THE FORMATION OF THE PROCUREMENT EXECUTIVE

Conveniently, the report of the Rayner Committee on the organisation for defence procurement was received almost simultaneously with the arrival of the new CSA. The Rayner Report, by creating a Procurement Executive within the Ministry of Defence which was to include a Controllerate with responsibility for the administration of all the military Research and Development Establishments, brought into the Ministry from a separate Department thousands of members of the Scientific Group. New allocations of responsibility had to be laid down between the CSA and the Controller Research and Development Establishments and Research (CER) as he was then called (his relationships with his fellow Systems Controllers in the Procurement Executive are better considered in the chapter on procurement). The division followed very closely the recommendations of the Report 'A Framework for Government R & D' (Cmnd 4814) under the chairmanship of Lord Rothschild, which proposed that departmental structures should be based on two distinct functions, with a Chief Scientific Adviser concerned with policy and requirements and a Controller of Research executively concerned with programmes and resources. CER fulfilled the latter function. As the line manager of the vast proportion of the scientists in the Ministry he was made professional head of the scientific staff throughout the whole Ministry. In the research field he was to be responsible for the overall programme of applied research carried out both intra- and extra-murally on behalf of his customers, which included both defence and the linked field of civil aviation. It was for the CSA to formulate the broad objectives which had to be met by this research activity. CSA also retained his responsibilities for studies and operational research and, more generally, for advice to the Secretary of State on the scientific aspects of defence policy, operations, logistics and force structures and, still more generally, for the potential impact of scientific advance on future weapons.

The next few years saw a gradual tidying-up of some of the loose ends and awkward interfaces flowing from this major absorption. One strongly recommended but incomplete action in the Rayner Report was the transfer of the Atomic Weapons Research Establishment from the Atomic Energy Authority to the Ministry of Defence. Legislation was required. The transfer took place in 1972/3. Both the CSA and the CER were affected. Unlike the non-nuclear R & D

Establishments where CER had responsibility for both the programme and the provision of resources, he looked after only the resources in the nuclear case. Control of the nuclear programme went to CSA, including responsibility for the important links with the USA. These changes took time to settle down, as did the development of lateral links between AWRE and other R & D Establishments. Another uncertain boundary area was the position of the single-Service Chief Scientists. Apart from their work directly alongside the operational requirements and operational staffs of each Service Department, one of their major roles had been to provide a linkage between their military colleagues and the activities of the Research and Development Establishments when located in a separate Ministry. The creation of the Procurement Executive offered a more economical solution, by way of giving to each of the CER's three deputies – who were themselves grouped on a systems basis closely analogous to the three Services – a second role as Chief Scientist to the relevant Service Board.

The next major stocktaking of the scientific structure, and in particular of the relationships between CSA and CER, took place as part of the 1976 Management Review. The Review saw a need for each Service Department to have available to it scientific advice given by a staff which understood its operating environment and at the same time had a close involvement with the work in the R & D Establishments and in CER's headquarters. The Review saw a reciprocal need for CSA to have a good flow of information about Service Departments' forward thinking in order to help him formulate the objectives of the defence research programme. But the Review considered that both objectives could be met by a more economical structure under CER, and they saw a need for a further look at how the single-Service Scientific Advisory Groups, as the scientific staff in these Departments had been entitled, should be headed. The atmosphere at that time and since has been very much directed at achieving a reduction in the number of senior posts in the Civil Service as a whole, the growth of which had become a sensitive political issue. The size and prominence of the Ministry of Defence required it to make at least a proportionate contribution. In the following years various adjustments were made. The organisation under CER, who in 1982 became CERN to reflect his nuclear responsibilities, was put on a more economical, functional basis but with the penalty of an untidy degree of cross-reporting. In order to provide the Service Boards with scientific representation at a level of rank which would be on a par with the uniformed members, and which could no longer be provided from within the scientific staff left within the Service Departments who were under a two-star Chief Scientist, CERN became the scientific member of each Service Board. In this way his position on the Board resembled closely that of the Second Permanent Under-Secretary. During this period there were only minor shifts of emphasis under CSA, which post continued to be filled at about five-yearly intervals by distinguished academics brought in from universities. This practice both continued the tradition of supplying an overtly independent point of view and facilitated links with the universities, thus easing the position of the CSA on the Defence Research and Intramural Resources Committee (DRIRC) which had replaced the Defence Research Committee in 1978.

THE CONSEQUENCES OF THE 1984 REORGANISATION FOR THE ANALYTICAL CAPABILITIES

The most recent stocktaking can be found in the 1984 White Paper on the Central Organisation for Defence. It is, in this scientific area, a somewhat ambiguous document. It stressed that in an increasingly technological environment it was essential that the best scientific advice should be available to inform the whole range of defence decisions, and that consequently the scientific staff should be reorganised to make better use of their expertise, to clarify lines of responsibility and to end cross-reporting. But the first measure was to put the Chief Scientific Adviser under the Permanent Under-Secretary in that he was to be responsible through the PUS to the Secretary of State. This decision was viewed with concern by the House of Commons Defence Committee. They were assured in oral evidence by the Secretary of State and the PUS that this change in no way prevented direct access by the CSA and was simply directed at getting an ordered flow of work. Nevertheless they remained of the view that the CSA's status had suffered and they hoped that it would not lead to a loss of influence of scientific advice within the Ministry.

The second and organisationally more fundamental change was to integrate the scientific staff into the Defence Staff, particularly in the area under the Deputy Chief of the Defence Staff (Systems) where the Director Concepts (a military man) would be responsible for tri-Service defence studies and operational analysis. In addition, within the three Sea, Land and Air Systems O.R. areas, scientists would be an integral part of the directorates. To watch the balance of studies right across the board, CSA was given a post at two-star level (in some ways a revival of a 1968 arrangement) to carry out this work independently from the Director of the Defence Operational Analysis Establishment (DOAE). This integration removed scientific staff from the Service Departments, and the post of Chief Scientist (which had already been downgraded to two-star level in earlier economies) in each of them was abolished. The Service Board and its Chief of Staff had therefore no residual direct source of senior scientific advice. One route open to them would be to go to the appropriate Systems area of the Defence Staff with its integrated scientific personnel. Another continuing route would be via CERN who still remained on the three Service Boards but whose direct responsibilities lay in the Procurement Executive.

CONCLUSIONS

1964 and 1971 can therefore be seen as the two major stepping-stones in the evolution of the role of scientists in the Ministry. The creation of the Procurement Executive and the concentration of all the Research and Development Establishments within its management have resulted in a high degree of clarity in the organisational position and roles of the CERN. He receives his requirements from his colleague Systems Controllers or, if the research work is at an earlier and less specific stage, from the centralised research policy machinery. He allocates the work intra- or extra-murally. He thereby establishes the essential links with industry and the universities. As a member of each of the Service Boards he can keep them in touch with potential relevant developments. The post and structure have an air of permanence.

The post of CSA has to combine by its nature – and more so than most senior posts in the Ministry – personal influence and executive authority. Personal influence involves many imponderables. Status can certainly be one, particularly in the effectiveness of contact with outside academics in this country and with defence scientists internationally. There must be a question whether the 1984 change has affected this adversely. Personal influence is also affected in as large a ministry as Defence by the degree of the formal direct involvement. The CSA has been since 1964 a member of the Defence Council, but the non-use of this most senior body has denied him one opening for the expression of policy views. He is not a member of the Chiefs of Staff Committee, nor of the Financial Planning and Management Group, the body set up in 1978 and comprising the CDS, the PUS and the Chiefs of Staff which oversees resource allocation. Regular attendance at these two influential bodies is not available to him. His formal powers therefore derive from his activities in the research and operational analysis areas and from his position as a deliberately selected neutral chairman of the Equipment Policy Committee. His informal power depends greatly on the extent and nature of the use ministers make of him. There are divided views on the post's overall effectiveness, contrasted with its 1964 position as one of the three principal advisers.

The integration of scientific staff into the Defence Staff is an interesting development. It may help to create the objective atmosphere of looking for the maximisation of capabilities, which lay behind Mr Heseltine's thinking, rather than the preservation of single-Service interests. But it may also mean that in each systems area the scientific voice is not heard loudly enough. Equally the removal of the bulk of the scientific effort from the Service Departments (though not from their Commands) is another facet of the intention in the 1984 Paper that there will be a two-way traffic between the Defence Staff with its integrated scientific staff and the Service Departments. Unless that becomes practicable on a regular basis there must be a risk that the Service Departments will lose a valuable dimension to their thinking.

Finally, in the context of the use of scientists as a resource, it is noteworthy that, notwithstanding the Open Structure created in the 1970s, very little use has been made of scientists, or for that matter engineers, outside their specialist areas. Four of the eight Controllers of Defence Procurement were Ministry of Defence scientists, who had served in R & D Establishments. The policy post at Deputy Secretary level within the Procurement Executive which has gone through various guises has been filled once only by a scientist. Apart from these posts no senior scientist has been deployed outside the professional fields to fill a general policy post within the Ministry. Given the significance of technology to all aspects of the defence programme, ranging from military capability, to costs, to industrial ramifications, it must be questionable whether the maximum use is being made in the policy fields of this particularly relevant background of expertise.

11 Procurement

PROCUREMENT: ITS SCALE AND SENSITIVITY

The Chiefs of Staff may hit the headlines from time to time as symbols of the fortunes of their individual Services. But the area of defence procurement is the one which has attracted and still attracts the most sustained attention, sometimes melodramatic exaggeration, in respect of its successes and failures. Defence policy is a complex question; the theory of deterrence has, regrettably, become an arcane almost academic specialisation. By contrast, the big defence equipment projects can be publicly presented in stark terms from a variety of standpoints: their huge cost, especially when they appear to be out of control; their technical risks, particularly in developments in the space and nuclear fields; their alleged operational validity or obsolescence; their export potential; their relevance, if any, to civil developments. Public and parliamentary interest has been sustained at a high level over many years, not surprising when the Ministry of Defence accounts for some 50 per cent of the output of the aerospace industry, some 40 per cent of the ship-building and ship-repairing industry and even 20 per cent of the electronics industry. Nor are the scale and associated problems a purely UK national problem. We may tend to go in for more public self-criticism but the same issues flowing from similar operational and technical demands have affected all the major powers to the east as well as to the west of the Iron Curtain.

DEFENCE PROCUREMENT AND NATIONAL SELF-SUFFICIENCY

The history of defence procurement since the Second World War is a major subject in its own right. It also encapsulates the contentious issue of national self-sufficiency which has underlain many of the shifts of procurement policy over the last forty years. At the end of the Second World War the United Kingdom was still essentially self-sufficient in all key defence equipment requirements. In the following ten years major decisions were based on the continuation of this policy, notably the initiation of a national atomic weapons programme and the development of three types of V-bombers. But the scale of the perceived threats and the speed of advance of technology meant that even the superpowers had to devote massive resources to maintain and modernise their military capabilities. It became more and more difficult and expensive for countries such as France and the United Kingdom to try to stay in the same league. The costs of indigenous research, development and production grew so much that, quite apart from their demands on skilled manpower and technologies, the Armed Forces, even within the high proportion of GNP allocated to defence, could not buy enough volume of equipment to sustain the required size and quality of the front lines. Remorselessly governments were being forced to make compromises over self-sufficiency. In the UK, the first decision of fundamental significance was to cancel Blue Steel and buy the American Thor missile.

Although the technological and financial pressures all seemed to point in the same directions of greater dependence through off-the-shelf foreign purchases or greater interdependence through collaborative projects, subsequent decisions showed erratic and sometimes contradictory trends. There was always the fear, so difficult to quantify, that the loss of indigenous procurement capacity could mean that the ability to fight might be impaired. Supplies could be cut off if the supplying country disagreed strongly enough with the Government's policies. Examples, spanning three decades, such as the Suez and South Atlantic campaigns, are quoted.

Therefore two concepts have continued to be in conflict: the ever-mounting budgetary pressure to reduce costs by these allegedly cheaper sources of supply, as against the desire to retain a national capability in key fields. The outcome has see-sawed from time to time. Changes of policy have led to decisions to re-enter fields such as electronic counter-measures and the heavy-weight torpedo where it had earlier been decided to abandon self-sufficiency. Re-entry tends to be demanding in research effort, costly and late in producing results.

This fundamental theme has run strongly through the post-war history of procurement. It has placed great political question-marks against procurement policies. The inherent difficulty of the decisions themselves have placed great demands on headquarters staffs. Ministries themselves have come and gone as part of the effort to find the best organisation to resolve the problems. But there have also been other major issues affecting procurement policies which have had important organisational consequences notably the system for formulating operational requirements, the interrelationship of defence and non-defence technologies and the search for greater control over defence equipment costs. Each of these issues needs to be explored at least briefly because of the effects on the central organisation for defence procurement as well as the interfaces of that organisation with the policy staffs of the Armed Forces and with the rest of Whitehall.

THE INITIATION OF THE OPERATIONAL REQUIREMENT

The essential prerequisite, which sparks off all defence procurement activities is the formulation of a new military requirement either to replace existing obsolescent equipment or to combat a new threat or to exploit a new technology. The responsibility for its initiation has always lain with professional military staffs, as it is essential to have user experience of what is tactically feasible and what would be the abilities and human limitations of the serviceman in operating the final weapons system. To relate these practical factors to technical possibilities, the Operational Requirements Staffs were for many years located as an integral part of the single-service Naval, General and Air Staffs alongside their collagues who had operational, tactical and training responsibilities. But considerations other than purely single-Service ones had also to be brought to bear. Intelligence assessments about future potentially hostile capabilities needed to be evaluated. In certain geographical and tactical circumstances there was seen to be a choice not only between different weapons systems, but also between which Service could most effectively discharge the future role – e.g. the competing bids in the 1950s and 1960s to operate surface-to-air guided weapon (SAGW) systems. The growing costs of weapons systems, exacerbated by short production runs, placed increasing emphasis on sales potential and consequently on the scope for adjusting the requirement to facilitate overseas orders. British industry, for its part, wanted to be consulted more and earlier about performance parameters. Conversely, military staffs concentrating on their operational needs and the pressures on the Service budget, might regard an off-the-shelf purchase from abroad as the most cost-effective short-term answer. A number of staff branches in different parts of the Ministry represented these different, often conflicting views. The organisational challenge was how best to group them so as to arrive at a balanced decision making process. But the organisational problem did not end at the operational requirement stage.

THE INCREASING PROBLEMS OF RESEARCH DEVELOPMENT AND PRODUCTION

Once a requirement was established the subsequent decisions over research, development and production became steadily more complex from the 1950s onwards. Notwithstanding the varied world-wide tasks which faced the Services in the 1950s, the pattern at that time was to be almost wholly reliant on the *ab initio* development in the UK of new weapons. Many new projects were started, particularly by an aircraft industry still splintered into several companies. Ambitious technical advances were attempted which later, because of cost escalation and changes of policy, sometimes linked with a change of Government, became the subject of spectacular cancellations such as the TSR 2, the P 1154 and the HS 681. Tank and ship design was likewise nationally based. Supporting these many projects lay a very heavy effort, carried out in government establishments.

The 1960s and 1970s saw a series of policy initiatives, to break out of this very expensive, independent straitjacket. Attempts were made to standardise requirements across NATO members, particularly within Europe. Another approach was the *ad hoc* search for collaboration. This was almost total failure. With the USA it never succeeded, because of the industrial imbalance between the two countries and congressional reactions which could invalidate government-to-government agreements. The best that was achieved was occasional offset sales agreements. Within Europe there was more success, though it was usually achieved on an individual basis, notwithstanding general governmental statements in favour of collaboration in both development and production. Different agreements were reached with different countries: helicopters with France in the 1960s; the Tornado with West Germany and Italy in the 1970s. Gun and tank deals were explored with West Germany, and other, smaller projects with, for example, Norway and the Netherlands. The European Fighter Aircraft (EFA) is the latest example. The fact that its independent French rival project flew at Farnborough in the 1986 SBAC Show is a graphic example of the continuing problem.

This trend towards collaboration fitted in broadly with moves towards industrial rationalisation within the UK. Amalgamations between smaller companies produced groupings which were better placed to undertake collaborative international ventures. These larger groupings were more marked and occurred more rapidly in the airframe, aero-engine, electronics and guided-weapons fields than in those of armoured fighting vehicles and naval vessels. But in all these fields any contribution towards R & D costs from the private sector was slow to emerge.

The high research, development and production costs of defence procurement gave rise to growing political and public debate about the proportion of scarce national scientific and technological resources devoted to the defence sector and the harm it did to our international competitiveness. Attention was also focussed on the adequacy, timeliness and cost-control of production within British industry and of the competence of the Ministry's staff to monitor industrial performance. The first major attempt to introduce comprehensive methods of control was contained in the Gibb/Zuckermann Report of 1961. Within the general debate the issue of the spin-off from defence work to civil exploitation was examined, though the result was at best indeterminate and probably leant towards scepticism about the value of any such spin-off. The debate drew attention to the apparent isolation of the defence R & D Establishments from the civil sector.

COSTS

The financial consequences of these various policies came together in the cumulative effect of defence procurement on the defence budget. More money had to be found for equipment at the expense of personnel, works or other support expenditure. The proportion of the defence budget devoted to defence procurement has gone up significantly during recent years (see Appendix F), and by the 1980s amounted to nearly a half of the budget. Even so it did not meet the needs of the Services in time, quantity or the degree of spares support. The equipment programme was in some ways a major rogue elephant within the budget because of its unpredictability contrasted with manpower requirements and costs. But, at the same time, the very size of the procurement programme had its short-term political and budgetary advantages in that it offered the seemingly easiest way to overcome sudden financial pressures. Changes in the equipment programme, though collaboration was a complicating rigidity, could be less difficult to bring about than the modification of treaty obligations. The rate and degree of obsolescence of a weapons system were not easily quantifiable. Major adjustments to the phasing of defence expenditure could be achieved by postponing or advancing re-equipment programmes.

ORGANISATIONAL CHOICES

These were highly complex and difficult policy issues. They involved a range of government departments and the governments of other countries. They straddled economic and international policies and had major consequences for British industry. In addition there was a huge executive management task. Thousands of projects had to be monitored for their quality, cost and timely delivery. Their consequences for the individual Services were immense. There were direct links throughout the whole process of research, development and production between the sponsoring Service and the project management team. To support all this work a large research and development effort was needed; some of it directly related to the individual projects, some of it more generally based.

The question repeatedly asked was how all this wide range of work was to be handled within Government? This question could only be answered when four issues of principle were resolved. First, was there in reality an entity called defence procurement round which an organisation should be structured, or was there nothing more than the individual needs of the Services? Second, should the policy for procurement be no more than one element, albeit an important one, of the Government's economic, trade and industrial policies? A third and highly contentious issue was how, within the fields of concepts and operational requirements, the varied and sometimes competing claims of the single Services should be harmonised. Finally, when all the parts of the programmes were being assembled for financial coordination and control, it was unclear whether the aggregation of the bill for all defence procurement or the aggregation of each Service programme in its totality comprising procurement as well as personnel and logistic costs offered the more logical and cohesive discipline.

Solutions to these issues were made more difficult by the disparate organisational starting-points. The management of the Services had developed from the very similar basic organisations of the three Service Ministries which had survived the Second World War fundamentally unchanged. But defence procurement, because of the scale and urgency of wartime demands, had seen the creation of separate ministries such as the Ministry of Aircraft Production and the Ministry of Supply, controlling most (naval vessels were one major exception) of the military procurement. The 1946 White Paper did not debate the issue of separate ministries. It recognised the need for coordination, which it sought to solve by the creation of a Ministerial Production Committee consisting of the Service Ministers, the Minister of Supply and the Minister of Labour under the chairmanship of the newly created Minister of Defence. Working for this Committee was to be a Joint War Production Staff under a permanent chairman who was to be in the new Ministry of Defence. Over the following years in accordance with the continuing policy of self-sufficiency the Ministry of Supply set up its own Controllerates for atomic and guided weapons. The organisational struggles of 1955 and 1958, described in Chapter 2, did not pay much attention to procurement. The time was still not considered ripe to contemplate any merger of the supply tasks. But the Minister of Supply was put on the same somewhat subordinate footing as the Service Ministers in that he was required in the 1958 White Paper to put proposals of policy to the Minister of Defence.

1959 saw the return of the Master General of the Ordnance and his staff from the Ministry of Supply to the War Office, though the Army's increasing needs for electronics and guided weapons remained a responsibility of what was retitled the Ministry of Aviation. Its separate existence emphasised the links between military and civil aviation and the rapid growth of the importance and complexity of guided weapons. The following years saw frequent criticism of this restructured ministry, directed at least as much at its managerial systems and competence (e.g. the Gibb/Zuckermann Report) as at its separate existence. Indeed the 1963 White Paper reiterated the indivisibility of civil and military research and development and the importance of the role of sponsorship of the aircraft industry as a whole. This White Paper concluded that it would be undesirable to place such a heavy additional load, much of it outside the defence sphere, on the proposed unitary Ministry of Defence. The approach was to ensure the necessary coordination both by giving the new Ministry a central role in laying down the programmes of research, development and production which the Ministry of Aviation was to carry out, and by accommodating the senior staff concerned with defence projects in the same building as the Ministry of Defence's relevant policy staffs.

The next few years saw the responses to the three key procurement organisational questions – the self-contained entity of defence procurement, the consideration of the operational requirement, and the handling of procurement costs within the total defence budget – moving in somewhat different directions.

The Labour Government created, on coming into office, two major new Ministries: the Department of Economic Affairs and the Ministry of Technology. The Ministry of Technology was set up to become a ministry for the major industries and to speed the application of new scientific methods to industrial production. For some industries, notably the computer industry, the responsibility was assumed forthwith. For others, such as the engineering and shipbuilding industries and the aircraft production section of the Ministry of Aviation, it was recognised that such transfers would take time to prepare. It was not until January 1967 that their incorporation into the Ministry of Technology took place. This separate arrangement tended to increase the gulf between defence needs and the preferred industrial solutions.

The responses to the second and third questions could be handled within the organisational framework of the Ministry of Defence. The second concerned operational requirements. Measures aimed at broadening the framework within which operational requirements were examined have been described in Chapters 8 and 10. The creation of an Operational Requirements Committee and a permanent central OR staff was able in its early days to bring about greater harmonisation in the radar and guided-weapons fields. The formation of a scientific-led Defence Operational Analysis Establishment by the amalgamation of erstwhile single-Service groups offered a more objective capability. The strengthening of the commercial sales input into the formulation of the operational requirement followed the creation of a special post, to be filled by a senior industrialist, of a Head of Defence Sales. But these various measures did not convince the Select Committee on Science and Technology. Their 1969 Report

(Cmnd 4236) still saw a fundamental weakness in the system, in that operational analysis confined too much of its effort to producing quantitative answers to specific weapons studies and too little to thinking ahead so as to help in the formulation of overall policies at an early enough stage.

As to the third area of the financial structure, the reorganisation in 1967 which resulted in the appointment of a Minister of Defence (Equipment), supported by central administrators headed eventually by a Second Permanent Under-Secretary of State (Equipment) seemed to be supporting the concept of looking at defence equipment within the Ministry as an entity in its own right rather than as an integral part of the programme of each Service. But their authority was limited. The separate existence of a Minister of Technology weakened the position of the Minister of Defence (Equipment). Though the Second Permanent Under-Secretary of State (Equipment) had been made an accounting officer, he was working on a repayment basis with the Ministry of Technology. Therefore for a high proportion of the expenditure on the equipment votes he was an agent rather than a final arbiter. The separate organisational hierarchies led to unsatisfactory policy divisions, and much time-consuming negotiation.

THE RAYNER REPORT AND THE RECOGNITION OF AN ORGANISATIONAL ENTITY

The Rayner Report of 1971 and its swift implementation marks an organisational watershed. For the first time there was to be a coherent pattern across all the elements of defence procurement. They were now united to form a sub-department of the Ministry of Defence, analogous in some ways to the three Service Departments though somewhat more self-contained in its supporting services. Within this unified Procurement Executive (the PE) the thrust was towards value for money. The method of achievement was to be by the creation of fully accountable units of management, with the project manager being given full responsibility and being supported by the necessary range of specialists. A high degree of profession-alism among the staff was an essential part of the approach.

This approach led to certain key organisational relationships. First, there was the customer/supplier relationship between the Services and the PE. It was to be close and yet clear in its demarcations.

Another part of the Ministry under the ultimate control of the Chiefs of Staff Committee and operating usually through the Operational Requirements machinery was responsible for the statement of military needs. The role of the Procurement Executive was to be to provide a clear picture of what they could provide for the funds which might be made available. The final outcome of defence budget allocations was usually achieved only after many permutations of equipment delivery patterns with their differing industrial, budgetary and operational consequences. Once development and production were under way the continuing close dialogue between the supplier and the user would be carried out through the umbrella provided by the position of the three Systems Controllers who were members both of the Procurement Executive Management Board and of the Board of their own Service. The match was not perfect, as the Controller of Aircraft, for example, had responsibilities for the supply of equipment to all three Services, but mixed uniformed manning of the Controllerates helped to build the necessary confidence as well as provide the specialist user background.

Second, there was the relationship between the Procurement Executive and British industry: another customer/supplier relationship but with the PE as the customer this time. This operated at several levels. There was the individual project, with the direct interface between the project management team and the manufacturers. There was the relationship which was developed gradually between the major companies and the Procurement Executive Management Board as a whole when wider horizons were reviewed, including the overall performance and resources of the company and the matching of the size and structure of British industry to the aspirations of the Services. There were the still wider questions of the size of the national industrial base, policies towards British industry as a whole, and the possibilities for collaboration or foreign purchase. The responsibility for the sponsorship of the major industries partially involved in defence – aerospace, electronics and shipbuilding – had been allocated to the Department of Trade and Industry. Most decisions on the industrial base were carried out bilaterally with that Ministry but, given the scale and implications of the largest defence projects, final decisions were occasionally referred to Ministers collectively. The new organisation allocated to the Systems Controllers the primary responsibility for individual projects. For the wider questions such as the UK industrial base and collaboration the Chief Executive, the Secretary and the Controller Policy (as three of the top posts were initially entitled and which were placed within the centre of the PE, outwith the individual Controllerates) took the lead. Their task was to handle the broad strategy, so as to relieve, quite deliberately, the Service Systems Controllers of the responsibility of thinking through procurement policies, procedures and methods. The Chief Executive was not intended to involve himself in the detailed management activities of the Systems Controllers on their projects, and for that reason the Systems Controllers were made Accounting Officers in their own right.

By far the largest body of staff and valuable physical resources which were transferred from the Ministry of Aviation Supply to the PE were the Aviation Research and Development Establishments. The form of their incorporation into the management concepts lying behind the PE raised difficulties. The work of these Establishments spanned pure research, applied research and development. Within those fields the work was not only for defence needs and defence customers but also for other Ministries and other outside users. The organisational solution was to bring all the Establishments under one Controller. Their tasking would still come from a variety of sources: from the Systems Controllers themselves, for work related to specific projects; far broader research objectives from a group covering various interests and which would include the Chief Scientific Adviser in his new guise, the DCDS (Operational Requirements) and the Department of Trade and Industry. But the management of the research programme, and in particular its sub-allocations between the Establishments themselves, the universities and industry, would be for the new Controller.

The twin concepts of the indivisibility of defence procurement and the primary role of executive project management, were brought together in the top organisational grouping established within the Procurement Executive, entitled the Procurement Executive Management Board (the PEMB). In addition to the Systems Controllers and the Controller R & D Establishments, the PEMB consisted of the Secretary, the Controllers Policy, Personnel and Finance and the Head of Defence Sales under the chairmanship of the Chief Executive who in turn reported to the Secretary of State. Unlike the Service Boards, the PEMB was not chaired by a Minister. This variation was possibly explainable by a desire to stress the managerial nature of the Board's work, but it was at the same time recognised that there would need to be close contact with whichever minister to whom the Secretary of State delegated a primary interest in procurement matters. The role of the PEMB of providing a focal point of leadership and direction to the staff brought together within the PE was highly desirable. Management practices had varied between the Controllerates when they were in separate ministries, and staff morale had been harmed by the many earlier changes.

The power and influence of the Board varied from area to area. On individual projects, little would be gained from collective discussion of the details but there would be mutual benefits from the identification of common problems and best management practices. On the personnel front, the Board could follow up the thrust for greater professionalism and the creation of a career within the procurement area. On finance, the significance of a central Board role depended greatly on the precise subject. The elements within the defence budget that were directly at the disposal of the PE were small: essentially its staff and their infrastructure and a small element of the costs of the R & D Establishments. For the vast bulk of the PE expenditure which went on project development and production costs, the programme responsibility lay with the Centre in conjunction with the Service Departments. The role of the PE was to give advice on the industrial implications and the relative financial penalties of alternative major changes in programme that might be contemplated. Taken overall, the PEMB brought together a spread of responsibilities and a breadth of expertise that put it in a position of being able both to make a contribution to defence policies and to give a coherence to the new sub-Department.

The years 1972–6 were very much a settling-in period for the PE. Certain changes were made in the top structure, but without changing the overall tasks. The Chief Executive was retitled Chief of Defence Procurement (CDP). The Controller of Guided Weapons and Electronics was abolished, as had been foreseen, and his work divided up between the three Service Systems Controllers. Within the responsibilities of the Controller of R & D Establishments, much rationalisation took place, including the absorption of the Atomic Weapons Research Establishment. Project management practices were reviewed. The arrangements for decision-making on projects, particularly at the requirements stage, were also examined in the light of criticisms made by the Defence and External Affairs Sub-Committee of the House of Commons Expenditure Committee, when they paid particular attention to the procurement of guided weapons in their 1975/6 session. But the first fundamental review of the Procurement Executive as a whole and its relationships with other parts of the Ministry of Defence was contained in the Management Review Report of October 1976.

THE STOCKTAKING OF THE PROCUREMENT EXECUTIVE BY THE MANAGEMENT REVIEW

This report expressed clear endorsement of the basic organisation. Bringing together all defence procurement under the Secretary of State for Defence was seen as a major organisational improvement. So, too, in their judgement, was the unification of defence procurement under its own management in a discrete part of the Ministry, and the consequent treatment of procurement as a specialised task. Such a structure offered valuable benefits in enabling the Ministry to speak with one voice to UK industry and to foreign collaborative partners. Given the successful way that the organisation and the staff had settled down, it was thought to be timely to look at internal relationships between the PE and the rest of the Ministry and at certain sub-structures and allocations within the PE itself.

On the handling of Operational Requirements the Report saw no need for any basic change. There was, in their view, still a clear case for the split symbolised by the roles of the two central committees. The Operational Requirements Committee dealt essentially with basic military requirements. The Defence Equipment Policy Committee looked at broader issues affecting all parts of the Ministry, including the PE, when it reviewed what was the best way to meet the requirement in the light of such considerations as cost, possible foreign exchange demands, the effect on UK industry, sales potential and scope for collaboration.

In certain other areas the report considered that now that the PE had been satisfactorily established there could be benefits of efficiency and economy from eliminating some of the rigid separation between the PE and the rest of the Ministry. Civilian staff could be better managed as an entity. Such a practice need not undermine the thrust for procurement expertise. General financial policies, as opposed to the financial and contractual control of individual projects, would also be better handled centrally, enabling the Ministry to speak with one voice to, for example, the Treasury and the Public Accounts Committee. The two central Deputy Under-Secretaries for Civilian Management and Finance and Budget who took on these responsibilities from the PE Controllers were made members of the PEMB, in this way ensuring that they were directly aware of the special needs and problems of the PE. Another linkage between the PE and the rest of the Ministry was introduced through the scientific staff. Members of the CER's staff were double-hatted as Deputy Chief Scientists in the Service Departments, to help reconcile Service aspirations with technical possibilities and to enable the R & D Establishments to understand the military priorities.

Finally, the report itself and other contemporary developments strengthened the overall position of the CDP. He was made Accounting Officer for all expenditure instead of the previous sub-divisions between the four individual Systems Controllers. At the same time, it was recognised that there should be, if anything, more delegation within the project management field. The two measures were not incompatible. The formal position of Accounting Officer gave CDP a stronger hand to initiate procedural changes. The individual projects which came before the Public Accounts Committee, although few in number, were usually major and complex and thus both served as samples of the efficiency of his organisation and highlighted problem areas. Separately the revival of the Defence Council as a working body – at least for a few years – and the creation of the Financial Management Planning Group, of which CDP became a member, helped to strengthen his position as one of the key central advisers in the ministry as a whole.

THE 1980s

Mr Nott's reorganisation of 1981, which was directed primarily at strengthening the defence rather than the single-Service orientation of the Ministry, also had the effect of providing a greater direct ministerial input into procurement matters. Instead of having part of the attention of one Minister of State, there were now effectively two Ministers full-time operating in this field. Apart from internal advantages, this change gave British industry greater accessibility to ministers, and increased the resources which could be devoted at the key ministerial level to sales efforts and to discussions with allies on collaborative ventures. It also provided a capacity for handling in Parliament major new initiatives such as the change in status of the Royal Ordnance Factories.

This reorganisation was welcomed by the House of Commons Defence Committee in their 1981/2 session. But much of the very extensive evidence taken in this session was devoted to defence procurement practice, and to taking views from British industry on their perceptions of the Procurement Executive, sparked off by the cash-flow problems that had been experienced by the imposition of a moratorium in 1980/1. Most of their recommendations and the Ministry's responses to them (Cmnd 8678 of October 1982) concerned management practices and procedures such as delegations to project managers, prime contractorship, the profit formula, quality assurance, contractor selection and project monitoring which did not have organisational consequences. But the Committee did raise two points of organisational significance.

First, they favoured the amalgamation of the two major equipment-orientated committees, the ORC and the DEPC, which had been recently recommended by an internal Ministry report. The Ministry in their response merely commented that the proposal was still being considered. Second, they were concerned at the degree of high-level coordination between the Ministry of Defence and the Department of Industry. They regretted that the Rayner recommendation for the appointment of a ministerial Aerospace Board had never been implemented. To this point the Government responded that there was well-established formal and informal liaison at all levels between the two Ministries, and that, in addition, Ministers from the two Departments had been meeting together to discuss defence industrial subjects and the future prospects of the aerospace industry. The creation of such a Board as proposed was therefore considered unnecessary.

The major initiatives set in hand by Mr Heseltine on the organisation of the Ministry concentrated initially on the central issues of defence policy formulation and resource allocation, together with the thrust towards responsibility budgets, which, within the PE, concerned only the R & D Establishments. Consequently his initial policy statement to the House of Commons on 12 March 1984 made no reference to procurement as such, though, in reply to a question, he stated that the review would be covering that area and that he had already asked the National Defence Industries Council to help him by looking at the interface between the PE and the arms manufacturing industries.

This statement was followed up by the fuller White Paper (Cmnd 9315 of July 1984) which expressed the view that the centralised procurement structure of 1972 remained basically sound. The White Paper went on to put the emphasis on better value for money, to be achieved by greater competition, by retaining only essential activities within Government and by permitting industry to contribute more positively to the design of new equipment. The theme of professionalism was reiterated once again with a new emphasis on exchanges of personnel with industry. The boundary between procurement and the support organisations of the Services was mentioned as a subject for further study. More specifically the Paper indicated that with the centralisation of the Operational Requirements staff in the enlarged Defence Staff there was no further need for the Operational Requirements Committee. There would now be one broader Equipment Policy Committee which would advise Ministers and the Chiefs of Staff on the balance of the whole equipment programme. The Report stated that the CDS and the PUS were to be the two principal advisers to the Secretary of State, but its attached organisation chart showed the CDP as formally reporting through the PUS though, unlike the similar change in the status of the CSA, there was no reference or explanation in the text itself.

The 1985 Defence White Paper (Cmnd 9430), which presumably reflected the views the industry members of the National Defence Industrial Council (NDIC) had given to the Secretary of State as well as the advice he had received from Mr Levene in his capacity of personal adviser, reiterated the basic soundness of the structure. It stated that Ministers would be involved at an earlier stage in equipment decisions and project strategy, particularly with an eye to increasing international collaboration. In order to give added weight at the official level to collaboration, the post of CDP had already been split into two in December 1984 when Mr Levene took over as CDP and the previous CDP filled a new post at Permanent Secretary level of Chief of Defence Equipment Collaboration.

Further progress along the recently defined lines was reported in the 1986 Defence White Paper (Cmnd 9763). The Paper also announced revised procedures for the PEMB, directed at its ability to consider the progress of major projects and to act more along the lines of a commercial company. The particular commercial practices were not identified. The procurement field continued to be one of high political visibility with the December 1986 decisions on the future AEW aircraft. The Ministry has announced that it has set up a committee to look into aspects of the history of this project, but it is not clear whether attention will be wholly concentrated on policy and managerial aspects, or whether any organisational points will arise.

REVIEW

Looking back over this whole period, there can be no doubt about the dominant significance of the Rayner Report and the 1972 reorganisation. The outcome was a structure which is organisationally capable of controlling equipment projects in a professional way, and of working closely and effectively with those other staffs in the Ministry of Defence who are involved in the concepts for, financing of and operating the resultant weapons systems. It has also been of great benefit that the PE has had reasonable internal stability for fifteen years. There was plenty to be done in a very difficult and demanding field to raise morale and improve efficiency. At the end of the day the PE cannot and is not expected to deliver the goods solely by its own endeavours, though it can do much to improve the performance of industry where the primary responsibility lies. But there does seem to be general agreement that this period has seen worthwhile improvements in the efficiency of the organisation and also, thanks to considerable efforts on both sides, in its relations with industry.

Changes elsewhere in the Ministry, especially recent ones following the 1984 reorganisation, may have effects on the relations between the PE and the rest of the Department. The ministerial structure probably gives the PE more clout. The greater concentration in the new Defence Staff reduces the importance of the links with the Service Departments that were achieved through the membership of the appropriate Systems Controller and CERN of each Service Board. New links will have to be fostered with the centre, in order to ensure that industrial and technological implications are given due weight.

At the very top the advantages of the present structure are debatable. A CDP, formally coequal with PUS, had both symbolic and organisational merits. Now there are three top posts involved but their relationships may well cause duplication of work within the Ministry and confusion in industry and abroad. CDP and PUS will be brought into discussions on all major projects. Yet, for his part, the Chief of Defence Equipment Collaboration needs to be accepted by other countries as being of top weight if his voice is to count. Much will depend on personal relations. The top structure has a transitory air.

Another topical issue is the relationship with the Department of Trade and Industry, highlighted, once again, in the post-mortem on the Westland affair. As an organisational issue it would seem to be overplayed. It is surely healthy that there should be differing viewpoints. Where the balance is to be struck between the interests of the defence budget and longer-term national potential is a complex question worthy of debate. The issues should be exposed and argued out, preferably in a Cabinet Sub-Committee, where all the factors can be deployed, rather than in a two-man Ministerial Aerospace Board. There is no evidence that the central policy cell within the PE is inadequately structured to present a rounded defence viewpoint. What is more debatable is whether the Government collectively have a clear, fully considered policy.

The scope and need for further organisational changes will be discussed in the last chapter. If further changes are made, it should be with clear recognition that the present organisation represents much progress in recent years.

12 The Permanent Under-Secretary of State and His Department

The standard and well-established practice in most major Government Departments has been for a Minister or Secretary of State to have as his senior official a Permanent Secretary (or Permanent Under-Secretary of State – PUS – when the minister is a Secretary of State). Two main roles were traditionally associated with a PUS: in policy matters he was the principal adviser to his minister; in administrative matters his duties included the wide financial responsibilities which flowed from being the Accounting Officer. In recent decades there has been a certain loosening of the excesses of centralisation in these two roles, flowing from the increasing load and complexity of work in the big Departments. Ministers have received, and have usually liked to receive, advice direct from the senior and even middle-rank administrative members of the PUS's staff, as well as from the increasing numbers of specialist staff – doctors, architects, engineers – who have joined Government Departments. There has, by contrast, been less flexibility of practice on the part of Service officers where the hierarchical tradition tends to concentrate the source of advice in the most senior officers. In the area of the Accounting Officer, too, there has been a degree of delegation, often associated with the creation of self-contained areas of executive work within a policy department.

THE ROLE OF A PUS IN A SERVICE MINISTRY

The pattern within the defence area was set originally in the Service Ministries. Each had its Permanent Secretary who was also Accounting Officer. But there were two fundamental differences between Service Ministries and civil Departments. On the military aspects of the policy for the individual Service the advice to the minister came from the head of the Service, the Chief of Staff, who coordinated the views of his military senior colleagues. Within the executive roles of the department the dominant task of the running of the individual Service was carried out down a military chain of command and organisation. Certainly, there might be large numbers of civilians working with the individual Service. An extreme example is the Royal Navy Supply and Transport Service, which provides a wholly civilian-manned organisation in its shore-based units but is still part of a Naval Command structure which reports ultimately to the Chief of Fleet Support, a uniformed member of the Admiralty Board.

Organisationally, this shared responsibility was reflected in the structure of the Service Boards, with their common features of a ministerial chairman, a preponderance of military members and the Permanent Secretary. In terms of work-load, the pattern developed that the Permanent Secretary's activities concentrated on four main areas. As Accounting Officer he was responsible for all the expenditure of the Department, from the preparation of Estimates, through the placing of contracts to the final accounting and audit. This work required large numbers of staff, some working closely alongside their military colleagues, particularly at the planning and conceptual stages, others more deliberately detached when it came to scrutiny and audit. Second, he was responsible for organising and carrying out the conduct of business with other Government Departments and with Parliament. Third, he was responsible for the management of all the civilian staff. Fourth, he was available as a source of advice and independent counsel both to ministers and to his military board colleagues. This last role extended down through his hierarchy to comparable relations between the administrative desk officer and his military colleague. At its best it could supply valuable advice to Service Officers who might have just arrived in Whitehall and sought an understanding of Government policy or the way to get things done in Whitehall. It could also supply an intellectual challenge to military views. At worst it could be seen as frustrating duplication and procrastination.

The 1946 reorganisation had no effect on the roles of the PUS in each of the Service Ministries. But in creating a Ministry of Defence with the emphasis on its role of coordination of policies the White Paper was allocating roles to the Permanent Secretary very different in their balance from those of the Service Ministry PUSs. While he was an Accounting Officer it was only for the small staff of the new Ministry itself and the few inter-Service units the Ministry controlled directly; e.g. the Imperial Defence College. He was not responsible for the big blocks of defence expenditure. Nor did he have large areas of executive work being carried out by civil servants. The emphasis was much more on coordination, on providing a secretariat service and on being a personal adviser to a very isolated minister – indeed, until the creation of the post of CDS, probably the principal adviser.

THE EXTENSION OF THE PUS ROLE IN THE UNIFIED MINISTRY

By contrast, the 1964 reorganisation had very major effects. First and foremost, the PUS in the unified Ministry was at the top of an organisation which combined the financial and management roles of the PUSs of the former Service Ministries with the policy and advisory role of the Storey's Gate Ministry of Defence. In addition, he was placed in a position which gave him new and important responsibilities in respect of the whole complex area of resource allocation and the thrust for greater efficiency and economy by means of rationalisation, integration or whatever methods were considered most appropriate. He was formally stated to be one of the three principal advisers to the Secretary of State, together with the CDS and the CSA, but he was also made responsible for coordinating their views and establishing the means for doing so. This latter responsibility was a very major and influential one, as it called for a sensitive yet determined combination of making the new structure work from the start and at the same time maintaining the political desire and thrust towards a still tighter, more across-the-board structure.

The art of the practical can be seen in the shape of the initial top structure under the PUS, to which Mr Macmillan had attached considerable importance in the working-up period of the summer of 1963. Realising the unifying potential of a unitary civil service structure among the three Armed Services, he had commented to Mr Thorneycroft that there must be one Permanent Secretary and not four, and one Accounting Officer. His first point was met in that while the initial structure was very much on a federal basis, the senior civil servant in each of the Service Departments became a

Second Permanent Under-Secretary and therefore expressly assisting
and subordinate to the PUS. A fourth such post was created to
head the new grouping of defence secretariats with responsibility for
advising on the defence programme and budget and other matters
of major policy, and also for identifying fields in which the administration might with advantage be placed on a defence rather than a
single-Service basis. However, the formal Accounting Officer
responsibilities for each of the Services stayed initially with the
Second PUSs rather than being centralised, primarily for practical
reasons over the way in which the finance and accounting work was
organised.

This essentially federal structure with a new, superimposed central
policy element evolved steadily over the following twenty years. The
changes were greater and faster than on the military side. This is
neither surprising nor wrong. The majority of the Ministry's military
staffs were and still are concerned with directing their Services out
in the field, and their organisation was responsive to the Command
structures and tasks. By extension, the civil service divisions in the
Service Departments of the Ministry which are closely associated
with Service management have also changed least in terms of fundamental structures and relationships, though there have been economies of scale and a greater degree of cooperation and agency work
has developed across the three civilian staffs flowing from changes
on administrative policy. But those civilian staff who were perfor-
ming more general Whitehall-type functions could respond and adapt
their organisation more easily than could a tri-Service military staff
to the policy requirements of ministers wishing to be given a 'defence'
service whether in budgetary fields, or on foreign relations or industrial policy matters.

The changes in the roles of the PUS himself, as well as in the
organisation of his Department, show direct responses to the major
stages of evolution which have been described earlier: the rejection
in 1967 of a one-Service solution and the subsequent thrust for a
combination of functional and single-Service management; the
creation in 1971 of the Procurement Executive and its subsequent
closer integration in 1977 into the Ministry; the creation in 1985 of
two central power blocks in the form of a Defence Staff and an
Office of Management and Budget. These changes affected different
parts of the PUS's Department at different times and in different
ways. What follows is an analysis by major function.

THE FINANCIAL ORGANISATION

The central areas spanning the various aspects of finance and budgeting have seen the most adjustment, reflecting in large part the basic problems described in Chapter 6 of the interrelationships between single-Service building-blocks and broad allocation of resources, and between strategic objectives and budgetary availabilities.

At the Accounting Officer level the initial arrangement left the primary responsibility with the single-Service Departments in the hands of their Second PUSs. Following the change to a functional structure at the Minister of State level, the three single-Service Second PUSs were replaced by two functional Second PUSs (for Administration and Equipment respectively) who had to operate initially with single-Service votes until a new Vote Structure of seven essentially functional Votes was introduced in 1970. Under this arrangement the PUS himself became responsible for just one Vote; that which dealt with the pay of civilians. This structure was also short-lived because the introduction of the Procurement Executive in 1971 necessarily led to the abolition of a Second PUS (Equipment), when the new Chief Executive and his Systems Controllers became Accounting Officers. So too did the Managing Director Royal Ordnance Factories and the Chief of Fleet Support who controlled the Royal Dockyards, in these two cases because of the separate policy thrust to make their two organisations more like commercial trading businesses. (Their subsequent history, which has resulted in the Royal Ordnance Factories (ROFs) being hived off as an independent public corporation and the Royal Dockyards about to be put under private sector management, has at least borne out the special circumstances surrounding their operating practices.) Therefore, ignoring the ROFs and the Royal Dockyards, there were now six Accounting Officers.

The 1976 Management Review analysed this division. It saw sound doctrinal arguments for having only one Accounting Officer, who would in this way underline the essential unity of the Ministry's expenditure spanning the conceptual stage, through the procurement of equipment and the efficiency of that process, to the in-Service management of men and material. But the scale and complexity seemed too great, and for pragmatic reasons the Report recommended a concentration on two Accounting Officers – the PUS and the CDP. In the difficult area of equipment, the Management

Review saw a rational split between the PUS, who had to be responsible for the scrutiny of requirements and their acceptance as a charge of the defence budget, and the CDP, who had to account for their efficient procurement. These recommendations were accepted. They underline both important principles of organisational divisions of work and the interdependence of the two areas united in the Ministry. They also strengthened formally the position of the PUS and, perhaps even more so, that of the CDP who now took over the final financial responsibility for all major equipments from the single-Service orientated Systems Controllers. The 1985 reorganisation did not change the concept of two Accounting Officers, while defining the PUS as the principal Accounting Officer, and formally showing CDP's reporting line to the Secretary of State as passing through the PUS.

At the level of Deputy Secretary in the central defence policy and budget areas, the organisational problems of creating an effective centre and still providing an efficient dialogue with the Service Departments, and later also with the Procurement Executive, showed themselves in the number of adjustments that were made after the initial start in 1964, though, it should be stressed, the original broad concept proved to be sound. Over the two decades the central blocks of work covering the areas of defence policy, programmes, allocation of resources, budgeting, the financial Estimates for the year ahead, the final outturn and its audit, were combined in a number of permutations. A pattern gradually emerged in the centre whereby the policy and programmes work was brought together under one Deputy Secretary, who also had a policy line into the single-Service Departments through the Assistant Under-Secretaries attached to the Naval, General and Air Staffs. These latter Under-Secretaries also reported to the single-Service Deputy Secretaries who would present to their Service Boards the totality of the single-Service share of the defence budget. A second, more financially orientated grouping was built up which initially concentrated on the Estimates year and financial procedures but its remit was gradually extended. The post assumed responsibility for the budget (i.e. the longer-term costings) as well as for the following year's Estimates. A recommendation of the 1976 Management Review abolished a separate central finance hierarchy within the Procurement Executive, and this post (by then entitled Deputy Secretary (Finance and Budget)) became the Principal Finance

Officer for the Ministry as a whole, including the control of the now unified accounts and internal audit staffs.

These various arrangements, all directed at ensuring the most cost-effective use of resources, were supported by improvements in working procedures. The Long Term Costing cycle of ten years gained in importance as a planning tool. Better machinery was developed whereby the central defence secretariat staffs worked more closely with the central military staffs under the Assistant Chief of the Defence Staff (Policy), to lay down policy assumptions and options and thus to help to break away from a programme which was essentially initiated from three single-Service building blocks. The outcome of all this work was, from 1977 onwards, reviewed by a new high-level committee, the Financial Planning and Management Group, which was chaired by the PUS, with CDS, the three single-Service Chiefs of Staff and the CDP as members, and which advised the Secretary of State on main resource allocation decisions. This Group filled a gap in the central machinery. The task was not one which fitted neatly or easily into the machinery of the Chiefs of Staff Committee. Nor was it a task which the Defence Council in formal session had ever discharged, even though it could be argued that as the supreme body with all the component strands represented – political, military, administrative, scientific, procurement – it was a task for which it was suited.

Notwithstanding these arrangements, criticisms continued to be levelled against both the organisational arrangements and the tools of the trade. Two internal studies in 1980 and 1981 drew attention to weaknesses in the budgeting system and the subsequent financial management. There was alleged to be a lack of adequate machinery to prepare the detailed work on the basis of which advice on resource allocation could be formulated. Furthermore, when it came to monitoring and forecasting the trends of approved expenditure, either in the form of the outturn of annual estimates or the effectiveness of contracts for major projects, criticism was levied against the system of block adjustments and contract procedures. The Defence Committee of the House of Commons in its June 1982 Report considered that although there might be what they termed 'the rudiments of a system of procurement . . . in the Financial Planning and Management Group and the Long Term Costing Exercise', there was still no adequate mechanism for the allocation of resources. In particular they deplored the absence of a clear role for operational analysis and the attitude still to be found on occasions in the Services that resources should be allocated by a combination of separately determined Service priorities rather than according to defence priorities.

Both Mr Nott and Mr Heseltine shared these concerns. The former looked for change and improvement through the functionalisation of ministers and the increased authority of the CDS. The latter, while confirming these steps, went also for a major change in the deployment of the civilian resources across the Ministry. The central posts of the DUS (F & B) and the DUS (Policy and Programmes) were restructured, a third central post was created, and the three Deputy Secretary posts in the Service Departments were abolished. A Deputy Secretary (Policy) was created as one of the four pillars of the new Defence Staff, but the post no longer had a responsibility for programme work. Within the new concept of the Office of Management and Budget, a Deputy Secretary (Resources and Programmes) was created supported by three Under-Secretaries whose areas of work were organised functionally under the headings of systems, programmes and resources. They had taken over, *inter alia*, the work of the three Under-Secretaries (Naval Staff, General Staff and Air Staff) and programmes were looked at in single-Service budget terms only under their central direction and then only up to the one-star (Assistant Secretary) level. It will be noted that, notwithstanding the 'defence-orientated' superstructure, the building-blocks were still based on the three single-Service programmes. The third Deputy Secretary, also in the Office of Management and Budget, had now become the DUS (Finance). While he had lost his budgetary responsibilities he was now in charge of the extensive programme for the introduction of responsibility budgets into the large proportion of Service and civilian units and establishments for which this system was considered to be practicable.

This reorganisation, apart from pointing up constructive tension between the Defence Staff, with its emphasis on policy and concepts, and the Office of Management and Budget, with its emphasis on financial planning and cost-consciousness, represents a marked shift of the senior civilian staff away from the Service Departments to the centre. Within the Service Departments and their associated Boards and Executive Committees, the single-Service Deputy Secretaries and the Staff Assistant Under-Secretaries (AUS) had played a significant role, not least as interpreters of central policies which they could discharge through their contacts as members of the PUS's staff. All this dedicated source of advice was swept away. The one, but very important, linkage that remained was the Second PUS, who under this reorganisation still continued to be a member of each Service Board (and its executive sub-committee), as well as assuming much wider responsibilities as a result of heading the Office of Management and Budget.

OTHER AREAS OF CENTRALISATION

Other parts of the PUS's department also saw considerable changes in their internal organisation from 1964 onwards. The moves were generally towards a functional or unified structure. While new relationships had to be established and while in some areas the loss of direct single-Service links took time to be accepted, these changes went through, for the most part, without the controversy and questioning that surrounded the policy and budget areas.

The largest single area was that under the DUS (Civilian Management), first established in 1967 and then extended in 1976 to absorb the staff in the Procurement Executive, thus embracing the policy responsibility for at that time over 250 000 civilians – non-industrial, industrial and locally engaged abroad. While the day-to-day management of the vast majority rested with the line management areas, this unification permitted greater attention to be paid to building up specialist skills in such areas as finance, accounts ADP, logistics and contracts. In turn this facilitated postings to be based on skills rather than constrained within a single-Service environment, and in this way to assist in the building-up of a corps of Defence civil servants. At the same time, it was still sensible and efficient – and gave recognition to established loyalties – for civil staff out in the Commons to be attached to one service for most of their career.

The change to a more functional tri-Service grouping was much more marked in the headquarters of PUS's Department, where unified organisations were gradually set up in a wide range of areas including public relations, management audit, quality assurance and a Ministry of Defence civil police force. At the same time, even within the Ministry, there is still a need in the secretariat and finance areas for staff who have a deep understanding of the implications – *vis-à-vis* Parliament, the public, other Government Departments and other countries – of the wide range of problems that arise in the single-Service Departments – problems such as low-flying needs and routes. Army field training ranges, the use of overseas ports and

airfields, the law of the sea, etc. Each Service Department continues
to be organised with blocks of civilian staff working alongside military
colleagues in the PPO and PAO areas.

THE TRENDS OF CHANGE 1964–85

Looking back over the changes in the two last decades, certain
features stand out clearly. The position of the PUS, as defined in
1963, has been confirmed, perhaps enhanced and certainly broad-
ened, in policy terms. In addition, his managerial responsibilities
have greatly increased both because of the centralising effects of
functionalisation and because of the added spread following the
incorporation of the Procurement Executive in the Ministry. Under
the PUS the structure of his Department has evolved to meet ministerial wishes. Greater emphasis and staff resources have been
concentrated on central defence policy and management. There has
been an accompanying effort to increase the professionalism of the
administrative staff, and at the same time to produce a 'defence' civil
servant. This process has been easier to carry out with the civil
servant than with the serving officer. The former belongs to a unitary
service. The latter's main role is still in the operational unit; his
career and expertise are not centred round Whitehall. But this
centralising process has not been carried to extremes. Where
specialist skills and single-Service requirements go hand in hand, as
in the Royal Naval Supply and Transport Service, the functional
strength of the military line-management structure has, rightly, been
the overriding consideration.

The question of the power-balance begs in itself a number of
Three general questions arise from the consequences of these
changes for the working practices and decision-making processes of
the Department. Has the power-balance within the Ministry shifted
undesirably? Is there too much duplication between the military and
the civilian staffs? Has there been a gain in efficiency from the
changes? There is no easy answer to these questions. They are all
unquantifiable and the views must be more than usually subjective.

The question of the power-balance begs in itself a number of
preliminary questions. But it must go back to the ultimate purpose
of the Ministry, wich is to provide effective Armed Forces, and to
the contribution to that task which the Civil Service can play. Nothing
in the last twenty years has altered the position out in the Commands
– that, with the absence of conscription and given the likely scale of

volunteers for the Forces, with the need for a lot of personnel permanently available in static units and given the comparative military and civilian salary scales and overhead costs, it is sensible to have a significant number of civilian staff working alongside their uniformed colleagues. This is not duplication; it is a cost-effective contribution to military capabilities, mostly provided at the junior level. At the Ministry itself there has been no major shift in the allocation of work as between civilian and military staff. The issue, if there is one, is at the policy level, and can be expressed, crudely perhaps, as the power to influence ministers for a particular policy against military advice. Even here, it has always been recognised that budgetary, political and industrial factors have to be weighed against military perceptions of the best solution. The question therefore narrows itself down to unreasonable influence. It has been highlighted by the 1984 reorganisation. By making the PUS and the CDS the two principal advisers, by giving the PUS a joint responsibility for the Defence Staff with one of its four main areas now filled by a Deputy Secretary, and by formally placing the science and procurement areas under the PUS, the cumulative effect of these changes can be argued to represent an undesirable shift in the balance. This question has been expressly addressed by the House of Commons Defence Committee who sought the views of several most senior officers. There were differing shades of opinion but the general conclusion is that no significant change had occurred. This opinion is likely to be supported by the vast majority of the practitioners in the Ministry over recent years who have realised that the complex structure is very dependent, if it is to work successfully, on a recognition of respective roles and on a basis of cooperation rather than oppositon.

The second question of undue duplication arises primarily in the existence of apparent parallel hierarchies in the secretariat and financial areas in the Ministry. There was duplication in the former Service Ministries. Pressures of staff cuts and the creation of the Defence Secretariat, which brought together into central divisions the various activities involved in relations with the Foreign and Commonwealth Office, with NATO and with other Government Departments, have seen a gradual clarification of areas of work. The concentration of all the defence policy work of the Defence Secretariat under the DUS(P) as one of the four major blocks of staff under the VCDS has probably completed the process of clarification of duties and elimination of duplication in this field. In the finance area different factors are at work. The increasing emphasis on systems audit and scrutiny, embodied in the concept of the Office of Management and Budget as the equivalent of the commercial company's finance directorate, calls for a somewhat different type of financial role deliberately set in a separate rather than a parallel or integrated hierarchy. In areas of project management, and in line-management fields in the Services, such as Ordnance and REME, where the growth of costs has led to the development of financial expertise and control systems in the uniformed corps, there is a growing case either for integrated staff or for the professional staff also having the direct financial responsibility. The introduction of responsibility budgets is likely to reinforce this trend. The emphasis in PUS's organisation on the increasing Parliamentary requirements for information about Estimates and outturn and on the deeper scrutiny of systems through management audit processes, is likely to grow, with day-to-day financial control being exercised by the line manager with whatever staff were most appropriate.

The third, still more debatable question is the evidence of any increase in efficiency. There are several positive pointers. The same fundamental tasks are being carried out with significantly less staff in such areas as civilian management. Other ministries and outside bodies such as the Armed Forces Pay Review Board find it not just more convenient but also more efficient to get a coordinated Ministry of Defence view. Staff in areas such as internal audit and manpower control gain from being able to make comparisons across the three Services in line-management practices. In the most visible and controversial area of resource allocation and financial control, the answer can perhaps only be one of 'not proven'. As has been argued in Chapter 6, a shift in the allocation of defence resources from one Service to the other does not prove the efficacy of the Ministry's budgetary systems; it could be the direct effect of major international developments. Equally the absence of a shift does not necessarily prove that the cake is divided up on the same continuing basis without any central policy control. Similarly on annual financial control, the close correspondence of the outturn with the provision in Estimates does not of itself prove cost-effectiveness. What can perhaps be said with some conviction is that there has been a general increase in financial awareness and financial skills and that the restructurings that have taken place have strengthened the lines of control from the centre.

The steady process of centralisation within PUS's Department culminating in the 1984 arrangements has placed very heavy loads on the PUS and the Second PUS. PUS's policy span is probably as wide as that of the CDS. The CDS has many international responsibilities; the PUS's counterbalancing load is his dealings with many other Government Departments. But, in addition, PUS has direct management responsibility not only for the running of the Department but also for the policy aspects of the 200 000 civilians it employs. For the Armed Forces, the single-Service Chiefs of Staff, not CDS, have these tasks. This suggests the need for a high degree of delegation. But his immediate deputy, the Second PUS, has now the direct responsibility for the running of the Office of Management and Budget. He is also now the sole administrative member of the Service Boards and Executive Committees. For the former task the organisation contains within itself the possibility of delegation. The area of the Service Departments does not. It would be an undesirable development if there were to be a weakening in the dialogue between the strengthened centre and the Service Departments. Paradoxically the enhanced powers of the Defence Staff and the Office of Management and Budget are very dependent on a continuing free and reciprocal flow of information between them and the Service Departments if a dangerous gap between policy and execution is not to develop. The adequacy of the staff resources at the senior level to direct and provide this liaison is questionable.

Part V
Summing Up

13 Review of 1964–86 and Its Lessons for the Future

This last chapter is a review or a stocktaking. It cannot point to a conclusion. All organisations, however much or little the rate of change may be, are dynamic. There is no final solution. What has happened over the last two decades reflects both the needs as perceived by Ministers and the wider political environment in which they were operating. These two factors have had a dominant effect on the evolution of the Ministry's organisation over these years which turned out to be ones of intense activity and internal change. Every Government, indeed almost every Secretary of State for Defence, saw a need to review and change some aspect of the Department's organisation. Furthermore, it was a period when there was widespread attention to the structure and machinery of government as a whole, as exemplified by the Fulton Report, the concept of Management Reviews and the 1979 White Paper. Other Ministries also (e.g. the Department of Trade and Industry and the Department of the Environment) went through major surgery. But none was so frequently analysed and altered as the Ministry of Defence, as the chronology in Appendix A illustrates.

THE WIDER WHITEHALL SCENE

The earlier chapters have shown that many of the reviews were extensive and the subequent changes were sometimes major, and often more than cosmetic tinkering. But, somewhat surprisingly, given the extent of the Ministry's involvement with other Ministries on policy issues as opposed to practical questions of day-to-day administration – the Treasury, the Foreign and Commonwealth Office, the Department of Trade and Industry and the Cabinet Office

with its broad coordinating as well as special intelligence responsibilities – the reviews were predominantly introspective, other than
the Rayner study which led to the dismemberment of the Ministry
of Aviation Supply. On the one hand, there was the constant search
for better internal ways of determining the broad parameters of
defence policy. On the other, there was little questioning as to
whether the form of external interaction with these other Departments, and the structure of the defence-related sections of these
Departments, were most conducive to identifying and then contribu-
ting to the judgements which at the end of the day the Cabinet had
to make on Britain's role in the world and the part defence played
in it.

THE INTERNAL PRESSURE FOR CHANGE

What then led to this continuous, sometimes frenzied internal self-
questioning? Cynics might echo the quotation from Petronius, made
in the report by Mr Rayner's Project Team, that 'We tend to meet
any new situation by reorganising, and a wonderful method it can
be for creating the illusion of progress while producing confusion,
inefficiency and demoralisation.' As a generalisation this is unfair.
The problems and the motives were more complex and more difficult.
Three distinct strands can be identified, but they are very different
in their nature. There is the search for an organisation which ministers feel will be responsive to them and give them objective advice.
There is the need to adapt the organisation to handle rapidly
changing international and technological scenes. There is the belief
that, somehow, a better organisation will help to solve the perennial
problems of the size of the defence budget.

First, a Secretary of State may have wanted to make his mark on
the Ministry, by adapting it, and in particular its top structure, to a
form with which he could most comfortably and effectively work.
This is wholly understandable and could be beneficial. The post is a
daunting one and, though important and prestigious, has not proved
to be the best of political stepping-stones. Much of the executive
work with which defence ministers are faced is, or seems to be,
relatively remote from political pressures and experiences. Hitherto,
although the occasional Secretary of State has had the intermittent
assistance of personal advisers, there has been no organised structure, on the lines of the French 'cabinet' system or the American

wide spread of political appointees, to help him by providing advice direct and by forming a counter-balance to what on taking up appointment must seem to be a vast and generally smooth-running machine, set in its ways and views. He is therefore looking either for allies who are in a position of strength within the machine or for procedural methods which will simplify his task and thus help him discharge his responsibilities. So one Secretary of State may have favoured the use of the Defence Council. Another may have concentrated sources of advice and power in a few hands (e.g. the CDS and the PUS) with whom he can establish a close rapport. Yet another may have tried to build some source of alternative advice into or alongside the machine (e.g. the Programme Evaluation Group). 'Le stil c'est l'homme' is probably fairer than Petronius.

This desire to adapt the structure to personal preference leads to frequent change when ministers are moved as often as – with a few exceptions – has happened in the defence field in the last thirty years. (The frequency of ministerial changes in Appendix D contrasts markedly with the position of senior military and civilian posts as shown in Appendix E.) The cumulative effect would seem to be inefficient. There has been too much and too erratic and sudden turbulence. And this frequency of change can be harmful to the solution of the fundamental policy problems. If the changes in the world role of the UK and the economic and industrial situation of the country were going to have major effects on defence policy, the simultaneous imposition of both frequent organisational and frequent ministerial change would seem to be disadvantageous rather than constructive.

Turning to the second strand, these two decades have seen changes in world role and technology affecting the Ministry which were probably greater and were certainly faster, more demanding and more puzzling than in previous periods. In the field the Armed Forces have had to redeploy and regroup frequently to meet the rapidly changing roles. These adjustments have necessarily had an interaction with their superior authorities in Whitehall. Technologically, developments in nuclear power, guided weapons, electronics and computers have posed difficult questions, not just of evaluation and development, but also as to whether the Ministry was best structured to handle the industrial aspects both nationally and internationally.

Third, Governments have faced through this period the dominant budgetary problem of the conflict of tasks and resources. During the early years, solutions could be and were sought down the road of withdrawal from imperial commitments. Difficult though the diplomatic and domestic political repercussions might have been, it is arguable that at least Governments had a degree of greater freedom of manoeuvre than when the primary defence tasks had become concentrated in NATO and when there were the added pressures and rigidities of an Alliance. But, even here, the apparent freedom of manoeuvre sometimes turned out to be illusory, in that the spiralling costs of new equipment, which the public sometimes perceived to be out of control (e.g. from the TSR2 to the AEW replacement), seemed to nullify the efforts to economise by means of the abnegation of overseas commitments. Consequently ministers, when assuming office, were regularly and immediately faced with this fundamental clash of requirements and resources and with the impatient, shrill imperative from their Cabinet colleagues to find a solution. Was the system wrong? Could help be found by making organisational changes? One area which understandably sprang rapidly to mind was that of central policy: surely the staff there should be structured to offer quickly a radical range of policy options. Or another *deus ex machina* might be to tackle equally radically the overheads of the Armed Forces and their associated civilian components. After all, businesses were apparently able to bring about rapid changes from desperate losses to admirable profits, by the sleight of hand of restructurings, radical prunings, new styles of management, incentive schemes. Had not the time come when such highly traditional organisations of the Armed Forces, admirable and essential as many of their customs and loyalties might be, must likewise accept an accelerated rate of change? Such a new approach could not only revitalise the institutions but carry with it major savings in running costs and purchases.

These three general pressures, to which several other secondary concerns could be added, led to the chronology of changes detailed in the preceding chapters, and to the focusing of attention on those areas within the Ministry such as the top structure, procurement and the rationalisation of the personnel and logistic functions which have been analysed in greater depth. Are the changes which have been introduced simply the children of their times or do some or all of them seem to offer a more lasting improvement in efficiency? Management has grown into a respectable science in recent years notwithstanding the excesses of mumbo-jumbo round its edges. Certain principles of the optimum span of control, clarity of delegation, setting of clear targets, feed-back and constructive tension have secured considerable endorsement in a wide range of public and private organisations at home and abroad. Is it possible to look at the changes which have taken place in the Ministry in terms of both efficiency and national constitutional circumstances and classify some as likely to last, some as being more ephemeral and some as incomplete even within their own stated aims? Such a classification is inevitably subjective, but it may help to identify success and failure together with possible areas as targets for attention in the foreseeable future.

THE MINISTERIAL STRUCTURE

After various fits and starts, there is now a fully functional ministerial structure. This affords the Secretary of State the best chance of being able to delegate effectively to his political colleagues, with whom he finds it most natural to speak the same language. It also minimises the risk of clashes of loyalty which have led in the past to politically embarassing resignations and which made the Secretary of State reluctant to use the Defence Council or any adaptation of it. There is little, perhaps no evidence that the absence of a political figurehead, even with such a prestigious title as that of the First Lord of the Admiralty, has in any way affected the morale of the Forces in the field. And there is still ample opportunity in the House of Commons and the House of Lords for the public political representation of single-Service views. This basic ministerial structure on functional lines seems therefore likely to last. Within it there could still be changes at the Parliamentary Secretary level to reflect loading imperatives, but most unlikely to the extent of giving them any single-Service affiliations. But it will require special efforts on the part of ministers to ensure that they have a feel for each Service as a living whole.

THE FOUR CHIEFS OF STAFF AND THE DEFENCE STAFF

The two decades have seen the evolution, jerky but all in the same direction, of the post of the Chief of the Defence Staff, and of the enhanced powers of that post *vis-à-vis* the expanded central military and now also civilian staffs, as well as in relation to the single-Service Chiefs of Staff. While the precise powers of the post and the way in which they are exercised are likely to vary with the style of each Secretary of State and the approach of each Chief of the Defence Staff – and there will be reciprocal influences between the two – it seems probable that Ministers will wish to continue with what in their perception is likely to be the clarity, simplicity and authority that this supremo post offers. All changes in this area are watched by the Armed Forces, both the serving and perhaps even more so the retired, with great sensitivity and much suspicion. The 1984 changes were major. It will take time for them to be assimilated and for new working arrangements to be evolved between the enlarged centre and the rump of the Service Departments. Moreover the new structures have not yet been tested either on the requirements and policy sides by a major defence review, or on the operational and associated logistic sides by any major military task. But they contain within them fundamental compromises which are open to tugs-of-war which could go in either direction.

There is the position of the single-Service Chiefs of Staff. They were not converted in 1984 to what can be termed in shorthand Inspectors General. Indeed, they were left in 1984 with three specific safeguards to preserve their traditional status. They still had the formal right of access to the Prime Minister. There was the obligation on the Chief of the Defence Staff to consult them and represent their views on major policy issues. They had the combined availability of staff advice from two main sources. They were granted a right to use the central military staffs. They were permitted to have a form of policy staff of their own which would both maintain the input into the central staff and provide them with the ability to issue effective policy guidance and executive instructions to their own Services.

The safeguards and staffing arrangements meant that they would in theory suffer no diminution in the range and quality of advice available to them. But this type of compromise could be subject to several pressures. A CDS could find the consultative impositions irksome. A single-Service Chief of Staff could consider that Ministers were not getting clear and authoritative enough advice from the integrated central staffs. A further drive for economies in Whitehall numbers could place under particular scrutiny the apparent dupli-cation of staff effort between the new and avowedly comprehensive central Defence Staff structure and the residual policy and liaison cell left under each single-Service Chief of Staff.

The other area for a tug-of-war is the make-up of the various elements within the expanded central Defence Staff. Some cells have a longer established and more convincing air than others. Unitary staff for intelligence and communications were among the first to be brought together in the 1960s and now have an air of permanence and a basic rationale. So too, in general, does the operations staff grouping, probably reinforced by the recent experiences of the South Atlantic campaign, though there remains a question-mark about the degree to which detailed work, calling for a depth of single-Service expertise, should be carried out centrally, rather than in the Service Departments or in the Commands themselves. This question raises in turn the general issue of the level to which single-Service expertise has to be provided in the centre and whether such posts can be filled with any confidence by officers from another Service. The problem is at its most acute in the field of operational requirements. It is here that a Chief of Staff most directly influences the future shape of his Service. While broad concepts may be set out by the central staff and be generally accepted, the negotiations and arguments are likely to be much tougher when performance parameters are being determined. This area is likely to be the most sensitive, yet, formally, the executive control has moved to the central Defence Staff. Finally, there is a miscellany of tasks in the personnel and logistic field which have been tucked into parts of the centre, very much with loading rather than with logic as the paramount consideration.

The scope for change therefore remains. So, regrettably, does the temptation, as this is such a high-visibility area. Two hopes can be expressed. The present structure, whatever its pros and cons, should be allowed time to show its worth. Any further change should be analysed on the principle of its advantage for the ultimate product in the field rather than appearances in Whitehall.

SEPARATE SERVICES AND THEIR INDEPENDENT COMMANDS

There seems to be little prospect of achieving organisational change and apparent simplification as a result of the abolition of alleged triplication of management resources derived from the continued existence of the three Services. The Canadian experiment of one unified Service has found little support in any country which has sizeable armed forces. Logical arguments about different roles and specialisations, and emotional but still valid arguments about leadership, loyalty and tradition, most recently vindicated by the performance of units in the South Atlantic campaign, all lend weight to their continued separate existence. Management arguments about the value of clear lines of executive command, exercised by staff who are respected professionals in their special field of expertise, also point in the same direction. The passionate arguments, very noticeable in the 1930s and the 1950s, about the dismemberment of the RAF and its redistribution between the Royal Navy and the Army have died down, although occasional mumbles may continue to be heard, particularly when there are severe pressures on resources. Concentration of roles within NATO, where allied forces have a similar three-Service structure and where the Command chain is for operational reasons based on single Services, has contributed to this decline in overt interest. That is not to say that there may not be calls for changes at the margin within the existing three Service structures. This could arise in two ways. Question-marks could be raised against those areas where there may appear to be some duplication of role: e.g. the RAF Regiment, the Royal Marines, the Infantry. Separately there may be further extensions in the field of rationalisation whereby the present practice of leading on a specific sub-function could go further and take over a whole Corps. But such changes would not in themselves have any profound effect on the higher organisation of the Ministry.

At the Command level, with the decline of major national commitments outside Europe, the case for unified Headquarters has diminished from the highpoint of the Mountbatten era of integration and the line of thinking exemplified in the Geraghty Report. Moreover, the nature of the structure of the forces of our NATO allies, and the geographical and tactical degree of separation between the major NATO Headquarters of SACLANT and SACEUR, have reinforced the continued need for single-Service Command Headquarters dealing, at least for management directions, with their respective single-Service departments in the Ministry. At the same time, there will be collocations and perhaps an increasing degree of integration where it is called for by particularly close sea–air and land–air involvements as at Northwood and Rheindalen. But, for the most part, evolutionary changes at the Command level in the latter half of this period have been directed at reducing within each Service the number of individual headquarters. The resultant concentration in a few big and powerful headquarters does not affect the basic line of executive control from the Service Department, but it heightens the likelihood of duplication between the Ministry and Command HQs.

Further changes will therefore be most likely to be made in the precise allocation of detailed work as between the Ministry and Command Headquarters as the degree of duplication becomes more blatant, particularly if each Service is able to concentrate its UK forces into one Command. The political thrust is likely to be in the direction of eliminating tiers of detailed work at the middle and lower staff levels from within the Ministry where there is the greatest risk of overlap with Command HQs. Organisational changes would then flow from fewer posts and lead to wider spans of control at the higher levels.

PROCUREMENT

The Procurement Executive, following the fundamental develop-ments of the Rayner Report and the subsequent partial degree of still closer integration into the Ministry as a result of the Management Review, seems to have been accepted as a logical structure. It offers benefits from the concentration of professionalism within it, and from providing a unitary point of contact for industry at home and also for the broadly comparable structures in other major countries such as the USA, West Germany and France. Theoretically, major changes could occur in two quite different directions. On the one hand, flowing from a fundamental political concept about the relations between Government and industry, there could be a major restructuring of central government as a whole to provide one all-embracing Ministry for dealing with the major industries. On the other hand, there could be a move towards splitting up the Systems Controllerates between the three Service Departments. There is no evidence of any effective head of steam to proceed in this way. It would cause either duplication or awkward major user arrangements in such key project areas as aircraft and guided weapons. It would be much less compatible with the centralisation that has occurred in the handling of operational requirements in the Defence Staffs and in relations with British industry.

The absence of any likelihood of major change does not signify a high degree of satisfaction with the products of the Procurement Executive. There has been frequent criticism in Parliament, in the media, and in the Services themselves. It concentrates on late delivery, on high, even uncontrolled costs, on inadequate clarity of policy as between indigenous production and off-the-shelf purchase, on poor overseas sales performance. But the effect of these criticisms has been, and is likely to continue to be, to direct attention to weaknesses in the determination of requirements, to the absence of sufficient professional depth and industrial experience within the staff of the Procurement Executive, and to failures of cooperation at both ministerial and official levels between the various Government Departments involved in industrial policy. Possible consequences of the criticisms will be discussed further later but they are unlikely to affect the basic internal procurement organisation as such.

PERSONNEL AND LOGISTICS

The personnel and logistic areas have tended to be grouped together in these two decades, following the creation of the post of DCDS (P & L) in 1964. The conjunction is perhaps a little artificial, for, although there is the common factor of single-Service management in the field, the problems and issues posed at the Ministry are significantly different except where they overlap in the rather neglected field of works services and accommodation.

Given the continuation of the separate three Services the scope for further change on a radical scale on the personnel side is limited possibly to one particular issue. While further savings may be found in the collocation of recruiting and training this is unlikely to affect the HQ organisation of personnel. Pay is already centralised in its basic issues through the existence of the Armed Forces Pay Review Board and the Top Salaries Review Board and the associated machinery of central staffs supported by central Committees that was set up over a decade ago to respond to the recommendations of these Boards. Within broad pay settlements there will still need to be sub-specialisation by skills and roles (e.g. pilots, submariners) which will call for single-Service requirements to be identified. The bread-and-butter work of personnel management in the field of postings, promotions and discipline will still be run on a single-Service basis.

The one potential area of change of real magnitude and sensitivity remains the question of a single list for senior officers. The Jacob/Ismay recommendations were strongly in favour of such a 'purple' list but it has never been followed up in any sustained way. Indeed in the subsequent first decade the level and powers of the newly created Defence Services Secretary were reduced. Since then there has been a move towards a greater combined consideration across the three Services of senior appointments, linked with the increased powers of the Chief of the Defence Staff. It is too soon to judge whether this system of consultation will be adequate to produce staff qualified to fill the larger number of central staff posts, in particular those posts where knowledge of more than one Service's professional skills are involved. If it were decided that a more planned and directed postings policy were to be needed to man the higher posts or even all tri-Service staff posts, a possible machinery would be to create an executive Defence Services Secretary reporting to the CDS and responsible for all senior postings and the selection processes designed ultimately to fill them. Such a change would be a major one going much further than the 1984 reorganisation and reducing the responsibilities of the Naval Secretary and his colleagues. A very contentious sub-issue would be the position of the single-Service Chiefs of Staff *vis-à-vis* such a central post, and in particular whether they could exercise a veto over any or all appointments.

The logistics area, like the personnel area, remains predominantly one for single-Service management. Rationalisation in the supply field has rather laboriously and somewhat haltingly worked its way through the major range of common-user items. There has been no attempt to go down the American road of setting up a fourth wheel in the form of a central Defence Supply Agency which covers the common non-specialist stores. This would seem to be an expensive solution for the UK's circumstances as it would not obviate the need for three specialist supply services with their associated headquarters staff.

There have been charges levied over the years, notably by Parliamentary Select Committees, of slow and reluctant progress towards unification and even rationalisation in both the personnel and logistic fields. Whatever the validity of these charges, changes have undoubtedly been constrained by two interrelated factors: the strict annuality of the financial system (the recent modest degree of annual flexibility that has been granted may be of some help), and the separate existence of the Property Services Agency (PSA). It is easy to make fun of the continued existence of three separate units for the manufacture of false teeth, which is a recent *reductio ad absurdum* example. It is less easy to recognise that their historical origins were sensible, and that to change here, while it would almost certainly in the long run result in financial savings and a release of real estate, would require initial capital expenditure to provide a properly equipped centralised location. The conventional financial wisdom of the discounted cash flow technique does not always result in an immediately convincing case: there are pressures against additional new expenditure; it is more difficult to have a coherent policy when two Ministries with differences of emphasis and priorities are involved. This is but a small example. There is frequent criticism of the lack of responsiveness on the part of the PSA in works maintenance and in estate management. Organisational changes by transferring the defence tasks of the PSA back to the MOD could be beneficial. (It is not simply a return to a status quo ante situation. When the Services had their own works departments it was on an individual basis and before the 1964 unification. Indeed they lost them in 1959 upon the creation of what became the Ministry of Public Building and Works.) Therefore a transfer to the MOD could give rise to an organisational concept more on the line of the Procurement Executive than separate groups, triplicating skills, in the Service Departments. But such a step could in turn give rise to wider organisational questions about the areas of work reporting to the Principal Administrative Officers. There is not a great deal in common between works and supply matters and there is less fundamental unity within the task of a PAO than there is within the task of a PPO. The case for the dismemberment of the PAO could arise. Based on the argument of the cradle-to-grave unity of the equipment of the Services, it could be proposed that the in-Service supply functions of the PAO should be joined to the development and production responsibilities of the Systems Controller, thus giving the opportunity for better pay-offs between production and maintenance costs. If works responsibilities then went to a Property Executive (and whether such a department would be organised by function or by Service would be a separate and controversial question), the residual tasks would hardly justify a Board member's charge. There could then be the further argument in favour of uniting all the day-to-day support management of the Service in both the personnel and material fields under one Board member.

THE SERVICE BOARDS

Such a change would highlight one further consequence. Recent years have seen a diminution of the uniformed element within the Service Boards: the Deputy-Chiefs' posts were disestablished in 1968 and the Vice-Chiefs went as part of the most recent 1984 changes. At the same time the Boards and their associated Executive Committees have continued to be the main and effective tool of management of each Service. Indeed they have probably been more effective in this role than as the mouthpiece of their Service in the struggle for resource allocation. But there has been growing concern about the balance of representation on the Boards, with the uniformed element declining and the political and civil-service element increasing as a consequence of the multiplication of functional posts. There must inevitably be a feeling that there cannot be the same degree of commitment from functional members to the affairs of an individual Service. Any further reduction in the uniformed membership would accentuate this disparity. A possible development, which would not only rectify the balance of representation but might also be to the benefit of each Service, would be formally to bring Commanders-in-Chief on to the Boards. Such a step has been made much more practical by the reduction in recent years of the number of Commands. There might be the further incidental benefit of increasing the amount of contact between Ministers and Commanders in Chief, which has inevitably fallen away with the functionalisation and reduction in the number of ministerial posts.

Another approach, which would significantly modify the thrust of the 1985 reorganisation, would be to bring back the single-Service Vice-Chiefs of Staffs, while still leaving the centralisation of the policy, operations and operational requirements staffs untouched under the Vice-Chief of the Defence Staff. The arguments in favour would be that such a post would free the Chief of Staff for his important task of getting out and about from Whitehall in his capacity as head of his Service, and would provide him in his absences with continuity at the appropriate level to negotiate with senior members of the Defence Staff. Against such an argument would be the apparent erosion of the 1985 concept as well as the unwelcome growth in that top hamper, though this latter point would be invalidated if the PAOs were simultaneously to disappear.

PERMANENT SECRETARY'S DEPARTMENT

Finally there is the Permanent Secretary's Department. Within the Service Departments there seems to be little reason for any change in the civil service structure other than as a direct consequence of change within the PPOs and the PAOs themselves. The removal of the remaining secretariat and financial staff would undermine the essential complementariness of their roles alongside their military colleagues and the high degree of collaboration that exists between military and civilian staff. There may indeed be a case for improving the linkage with the centre by coopting the DUS (P & L) at least to the Executive Committees of the Service Boards. But much will depend upon the degree of effective budgeting delegation to the Services that may be granted.

The new Office of Management and Budget (OMB) needs time to prove its concept and efficacy, notably the formal separation of 'policy' within the Defence Staff and the budget within the OMB. Now that the Defence Staff report to PUS as well as CDS, there is a case for the programme being handled in its budgetary as well as its capability terms in the Defence Staff, with the OMB having a more discrete interrogatory and monitoring role. But working practices may develop pragmatic sensible arrangements between the two groups and avoid the risk of one set of financial staff interrogating another group. It would be preferable to see the system tested against a major review of the programme.

THE DEFENCE COUNCIL

The very shape of these previous paragraphs brings out one general organisational question. Individual areas have been discussed seriatim. There would seem to be a general view that the Service Boards and their Executive Committees have worked effectively, particularly in their managerial role. The Procurement Executive Management Board has gradually established a corporate identity. The PPO and PAO Committees have had some coordinating value and have probably helped rather than hindered greater coordination and economy of effort in their fields and the moves towards rationalisation. The Chiefs of Staff Committee has still a clear role in operations even though the frequency and level of work has fallen off. It is less clear what use will be made of it on wider issues, given the new powers of the CDS and the central Defence Staff and the now well-established role of the Financial Planning and Management Group (FPMG) in the financial and resource fields. But, at the very centre of the whole Ministry the Defence Council has not gained any permanent position as the key policy body. Central leadership has depended, perhaps unduly so, on the Secretary of State himself. His ability to get the views of the Department has depended almost entirely on direct personal contact with senior officers and officials. This may have had the unintentional side-effect that the department and particularly the uniformed officers have felt that they were, in a sense, fighting ministers simply because they could not see any visible participatory system, but rather that policy was handed down in a series of ukases. While this is not a fact, it is nevertheless very difficult to produce any sense of belonging in such a vast organisation, particularly when the natural loyalty is to the individual Service.

This is not any easy issue. The fact that a series of recommendations about either restructuring (proposals for a smaller Defence Board) or greater use of the Defence Council have all fallen by the wayside must be attributed in part to ministerial reluctance and in part to fears of an apparently unwieldy structure. But if the Cabinet can meet regularly and if most major companies can operate some form of board system it should not be impracticable to use the Defence Council on a regular basis. There must be some grounds for believing that it could help in the most difficult field of resource allocation now that ministers have been functionalised. Moreover if it was seen by the staff to be an effective focal point this could make some imponderable contribution to a sense of unity.

THE PROBLEM OF DEFENCE RESOURCES

These comments have covered specific areas and their central coordination. A common thread running through them and affecting many of those working in the various groupings discussed above, whether politicians or military or civilian staff, has been the determination and allocation of defence policy and resources. This task has produced the greatest and most vocal dissatisfaction, primarily because of the repeated failure to reconcile with any general approval the apparently permanent gap between tasks and financial resources. Four main approaches have been tried during the period, sometimes simultaneously, to close the gap: economy drives within the Services; policy changes; rationalisation; more effective purchase of equipment.

The first line of approach did not require organisational change. Individual Service Boards and their executive Committees provided an adequate machinery for the identification of possibilities and the

momentum for running such drives, coupled with the position of
authority exercised by the single-Service Chiefs of Staff over their
individual Commands. Such drives have usually produced useful
savings within the framework of the individual Service. They could
not be expected to tackle cross-Service rationalisation, and sometimes they were criticised for conservatism towards internal change.
The other three approaches have had an erratic record. For all of
them, organisational changes, some of them more outwardly effective than others, have been tried as a catalyst towards the policy
solution. Possible targets for further organisational change have been
identified earlier in this chapter. But it is a tediously well-known
truism that an organisation can only be as good as the quality of the
staff which operate it. This period has seen much criticism of the
quality of the personnel working in central government: their insu-
larity cocooned from commercial realities and industrial experience;
their lack of professional qualifications and of job-related training;
the shortage of tours in certain key areas where continuity would
appear to be a prerequisite; the loss of breadth of vision occasioned
either by the inadequate use of outside academic and professional
institutions, or by the unduly restricted employment within Government of able people with different but relevant experience to offer
from the outside world. For the Civil Service one major vehicle of
criticism was the Fulton Report, subsequently supplemented by
various White Papers on the workings of Government. For the
Armed Forces, Select Committees have been the biggest source of
criticism and have tended to concentrate on the operational requirements and projects fields, and to comment, adversely, on the short
tours of officers contrasted with the practice in, for example, the
United States.

THE STAFF THEMSELVES

Efforts have been made, some more sustained and successful than
others, to respond to these criticisms. But it is arguable that more
could be done and that it would be timely to put more effort into
the manning rather than the changing of the organisation. These are
broad generalisations. They are likely to be accepted as having some
relevant validity if they can be seen to apply particularly to the
last three of the four areas just identified: namely, policy changes,
procurement, and rationalisation.

Policy changes call for a difficult amalgamation of cool objective scrutiny and the uncertain skill of futurology. Scrutiny can be helped by modelling and by operational analysis. This work has traditionally been carried out in the Ministry of Defence by scientists, supported by military officers, some located in the Service Departments or Command Headquarters, some employed at the Defence Operational Analysis Establishment under the policy direction of the Chief Scientific Adviser. There have been some charges that DOAE has been disappointingly ineffective over this period. In some major issues this is understandable. While DOAE can rightly be expected to make a valuable input on whether a tank in Europe can best be dealt with by another tank, a gun, a guided weapon (land-based, helicopter-borne or aircraft-borne) or a bomb, their problem becomes much greater, if not insoluble, if they are asked to make judgements on the basis of measurable facts between the value of the UK defence contribution to the continental or the Atlantic battle. But, leaving aside these wider aspects, the Department has not seemed to have made sufficient use of this in-house capability to resolve its major problems. Indeed, until recently, the analytical effort by MOD scientists appears to have been devoted more to providing single-Service staffs with apparently rational and objectively reputable arguments to support their proposals than to provide the central staffs with effective and, what is vitally important, timely advice. The 1984 reorganisation has, yet again, reappraised and re-emphasised the role of DOAE and has located it firmly as a tool of the central staffs. It would seem sensible to try to make use of it before embarking on further organisational change.

The sponsor and policy director of DOAE has been the Chief Scientific Adviser – now, following 1984, formally subordinated for the first time to the Permanent Secretary. While it has been made clear that this in no way impedes his direct access to the Secretary of State, it seems presentationally dubious. The CSA is the nearest approach to an independent source of advice, perhaps in a loose sense of the term almost a 'political adviser' to the Secretary of State. It is noteworthy that in such a large Department, where successive Secretaries of State have felt isolated, there has been no sustained attempt to provide an alternate source of policy thinking. Mr Healey, for a short time only, tried his Programme Evaluation Group, but even that was mostly manned by insiders. Since then, little effective grit has been introduced either by other Government Departments or from outside. One reason may be the limited scale of the academic interest in the politico-defence complex. It is regrettable that praise-worthy initiatives by the Ministry of Defence over the creation of Defence lectureships and the funding of defence fellowships have had, with some noteworthy but all too few exceptions, such a poor response. These comments are not directed at finding an alternative primary source of advice on defence policy to the Chiefs of Staff supported by the now strengthened defence staff. But future defence policy is a notoriously difficult problem which makes great demands on national income. When major reviews are undertaken there would seem to be advantage in involving from the start the best and independently placed brains both from other governmental departments and from outside Whitehall, either at universities or at institutions such as the RUSI and the IISS.

The contributions required from the staff in the procurement area have a different emphasis. Timely delivery, cost control, acceptable but not over-elaborate performance, are key factors. They are also essentially practical issues calling for both user and industrial experience. The multi-disciplinary teams which now largely manage projects – and their creation is a welcome development – tend to be formed from administrators, scientific research specialists, and officers fresh from operational units for a short tour. At the higher, directing staff level it is now much more likely that the incumbents will be on at least their second tour in the Procurement Executive. But the lack in particular of industrial or engineering experience is still widespread. Research scientists do not necessarily make good project management staff, and tend to be released too late and often with reluctance from a career in the Research and Development Establishments. Engineers have been for the most part segregated into a self-contained career in the Royal Ordnance factories, and few now remain in the Ministry. Uniformed officers, notwithstanding repeated Select Committee reports, usually serve only two-and-a-half to three years with a project whose life-cycle to bring it into operational service may be several times longer. The US Forces have solved some of the career aspects of this problem by being prepared to promote *in situ* during a lengthy tour of duty, rather than demand all-round experience and therefore a rush of short postings as a prerequisite of being considered in the field for promotion. Within the civilian administration group there have been major attempts to provide greater depth of experience as a result of a system of moderate sub-specialisation introduced in the 1970s. While the experience is most marked in the contract, project management and quality assurance fields, it still lacks one essential ingredient of direct industrial experience. The opportunities of learning by direct industrial experience as a result of secondment or exchange are still deplorably infrequent. While the defence industries as a body accept the principle, there has been only very limited success in achieving practical results with the few interested firms. A sustained high-level drive to increase expertise in all these categories could pay considerable dividends.

A BALANCE SHEET

The earlier paragraphs have identified areas which might be the target for further change, though not necessarily implying any recommendation on the need for change. The later paragraphs have suggested ways in which the efficacy of personnel might be improved within the organisation. Both need to be put in a wider context.

The Armed Forces have a high reputation for their professional competence. They have acquitted themselves well in operations. They have shown discipline and tact in their involvements in civil disobedience. In NATO evaluation exercises their results are very good. Their safety record is excellent. Their training makes them highly sought after either as managers or craftsmen in the civilian world. All this must reflect back in part on the policy and executive guidelines and instructions that emanate from the Ministry. Commands can do much, but they are more likely to be successful if the initial guidelines issued to them are sound and if the central machinery has by virtue of its policies over the years equipped them with competent, well-motivated staff. Their strong point may be efficiency rather than cost-effectiveness. One of the main thrusts in recent years has been to increase the return on the investment in experience, equipment and training. This would seem to be an area calling for continued attention. The scheme of responsibility budgets will take time to be introduced and tried. It should be given that time.

Similar considerations apply to the products of the Procurement Executive, where the record has been more erratic. Here, confusion of policies may have been at least as responsible for failures as deficiencies in organisation. To collaborate or not to collaborate; to stay in a very expensive area of high technology or to buy off the shelf or, seemingly worst of all, to opt alternately in and out and to expect intra-mural research and industrial development and production easily to catch up years of neglect. These issues call for central clarity of policy at the governmental level. Lower down within the organisation the policies need to be supported by greater toughness and skill in the control processes.

There is one other aspect which often calls for comment. The Ministry, irrespective of its organisatonal shape is often considered to be still too big. One solution, long discarded, is the unification of the three Armed Forces. There are still two continuing possibilities within the existing organisation. One is further delegation to the Commands. The reduction in the number of Commands must make it more feasible to go further down this road and give them lead roles (e.g. repair or training policy). Another is the elimination of over-elaboration, not just in detailed workings but also in policy thinking. The Ministry could in its policy areas still be concerning itself unduly with the whole range of the world and its possible roles in the world, whereas political realities would suggest concentration on a more modest canvas. Such considerations go outside the Ministry itself into the wider framework of central government which determines national policies.

These wider points may be considered to be irrelevant to the central organisation in the form of the shape of the Ministry of Defence. This is not necessarily so. The last twenty-five years have seen many changes, some clearly improvements, but at the price of much turbulence and perhaps undue concentration on the organis- ation itself rather than its policies, and on resource questions rather than the Services themselves. For a time it may be desirable to reverse the emphasis and see if the organisation as it has evolved can find the solutions. A period of structural stability could lead to greater economy and efficiency. Coupled with better training and longer tour lengths, the result could be better returns on the huge investment in defence and a more cost-effective defence effort. The Ministry would then pay its way handsomely.

Appendix A Chronology of Major Events

1924	–	Formation of Chiefs of Staff Committee
1936	–	Appointment of a Minister for the Coordination of Defence
1940	–	Prime Minister assumes additional title of Minister of Defence
1947	–	Formation of a Ministry of Defence
1958	–	Creation of post of Chief of the Defence Staff
1963	–	Jacob/Ismay Report
1964	–	Incorporation of the Admiralty, War Office and Air Ministry into the Ministry of Defence
1965/6	–	Geraghty Committee
1967/9	–	Gradual introduction of functional posts in the Administration and Equipment areas
1969/72	–	Headquarters Organisation Committee
1970	–	Reorganisation of Vote Structure
1971	–	Rayner Report
1972	–	Formation of Procurement Executive within the Ministry of Defence under a Chief Executive and abolition of the Ministry of Aviation Supply
1975/6	–	Management Review
1977	–	Concentration of Accounting Officer responsibilities on PUS and CDP
1981	–	Functionalisation of all ministerial posts and abolition of single-Service Parliamentary Under-Secretaries of State
1982	–	Increase in powers of CDS
1983	–	Initial application of MINIS procedures to the Ministry of Defence
1984	–	Publication of consultative Defence Open Document, 'MINIS and the Development of the Organisation for Defence'
1985	–	Introduction of the expanded Defence Staff and the new Office of Management and Budget. CDS and PUS made the two principal advisers to the Secretary of State. Abolition of single-Service Vice-Chiefs of Staff and DUSs

Appendix ▌

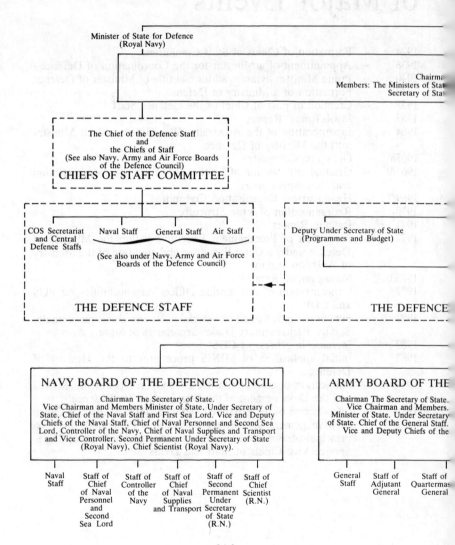

THE MINISTRY Oⁱ

Minister of State for Defence
(Royal Navy)

Chairmaⁱ
Members: The Ministers of Staⁱ
Secretary of Staⁱ

The Chief of the Defence Staff
and
the Chiefs of Staff
(See also Navy, Army and Air Force Boards
of the Defence Council)
CHIEFS OF STAFF COMMITTEE

COS Secretariat   Naval Staff   General Staff   Air Staff
and Central
Defence Staffs

(See also under Navy, Army and Air Force
Boards of the Defence Council)

THE DEFENCE STAFF

Deputy Under Secretary of State
(Programmes and Budget)

THE DEFENCE

NAVY BOARD OF THE DEFENCE COUNCIL

Chairman The Secretary of State.
Vice Chairman and Members Minister of State, Under Secretary of
State, Chief of the Naval Staff and First Sea Lord. Vice and Deputy
Chiefs of the Naval Staff, Chief of Naval Personnel and Second Sea
Lord, Controller of the Navy, Chief of Naval Supplies and Transport
and Vice Controller, Second Permanent Under Secretary of State
(Royal Navy), Chief Scientist (Royal Navy).

Naval Staff	Staff of Chief of Naval Personnel and Second Sea Lord	Staff of Controller of the Navy	Staff of Chief of Naval Supplies and Transport	Staff of Second Permanent Under Secretary of State (R.N.)	Staff of Chief Scientist (R.N.)

ARMY BOARD OF THE

Chairman The Secretary of State.
Vice Chairman and Members.
Minister of State. Under Secretary
of State. Chief of the General Staff.
Vice and Deputy Chiefs of the

General Staff	Staff of Adjutant General	Staff of Quartermas General

Cmnd. 2097 July 1963

EFENCE (at 1st April 1964)

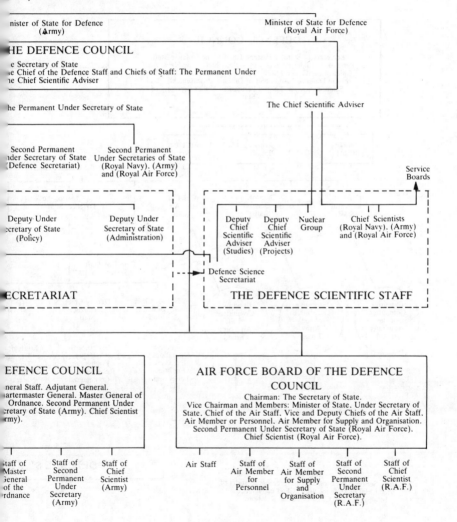

cretary of State for Defence

nister of State for Defence
(Army)

Minister of State for Defence
(Royal Air Force)

HE DEFENCE COUNCIL
e Secretary of State
e Chief of the Defence Staff and Chiefs of Staff: The Permanent Under
e Chief Scientific Adviser

he Permanent Under Secretary of State

The Chief Scientific Adviser

Second Permanent
nder Secretary of State
(Defence Secretariat)

Second Permanent
Under Secretaries of State
(Royal Navy). (Army)
and (Royal Air Force)

Service
Boards

Deputy Under
cretary of State
(Policy)

Deputy Under
Secretary of State
(Administration)

Deputy
Chief
Scientific
Adviser
(Studies)

Deputy
Chief
Scientific
Adviser
(Projects)

Nuclear
Group

Chief Scientists
(Royal Navy). (Army)
and (Royal Air Force)

Defence Science
Secretariat

ECRETARIAT

THE DEFENCE SCIENTIFIC STAFF

EFENCE COUNCIL
neral Staff. Adjutant General.
artermaster General. Master General of
Ordnance. Second Permanent Under
cretary of State (Army). Chief Scientist
rmy).

AIR FORCE BOARD OF THE DEFENCE
COUNCIL
Chairman: The Secretary of State.
Vice Chairman and Members: Minister of State. Under Secretary of
State. Chief of the Air Staff. Vice and Deputy Chiefs of the Air Staff.
Air Member or Personnel. Air Member for Supply and Organisation.
Second Permanent Under Secretary of State (Royal Air Force).
Chief Scientist (Royal Air Force).

taff of
Master
eneral
of the
rdnance

Staff of
Second
Permanent
Under
Secretary
(Army)

Staff of
Chief
Scientist
(Army)

Air Staff

Staff of
Air Member
for
Personnel

Staff of
Air Member
for Supply
and
Organisation

Staff of
Second
Permanent
Under
Secretary
(R.A.F.)

Staff of
Chief
Scientist
(R.A.F.)

Appendix C

DEFENCE COUNCIL

Secretary of State, Ministers, Chief of the Defence Staff, Permanent Under Secretary of State, Chief of the Naval Staff, Chief of the General Staff, Chief of the Air Staff, Vice Chief of the Defence Staff, Chief of Defence Procurement, Chief Scientic Adviser. Second Permanent Under Secretary of State

Admiralty Board

Army Board

Air Force Board

Chief of the Defence Staff

Chief of the Naval Staff

Chief of the General Staff

Chief of the Air Staff

Vice Chief of the Defence Staff

Defence Services Secretary

Chie Pub Rela

Chiefs of Staff Secretariat

Executive Committee of the Admiralty Board

Executive Committee of the Army Board

Executive Committee of the Air Force Board

Deputy Chief of Defence Staff

Deputy Chief of Defence Staff

Deputy Secretar

Commitments Operations Exercises Logistics Policy and Plans

Operational Concepts, Equipment Requirements. Command, Control, Communications and Information Systems

Strategic and Long Term Policy. Nuclear Issues

Single-Service Executive Staffs

DEFENCE STAFF

Note
1 Single Service Chiefs of Staff have access to staffs of
   Vice Chief of Defence Staff, Chief of Defence
   Intelligence and Chief of Public Relations

Organisation
Chart 1985

OF THE MINISTRY OF DEFENCE

SECRETARY OF STATE

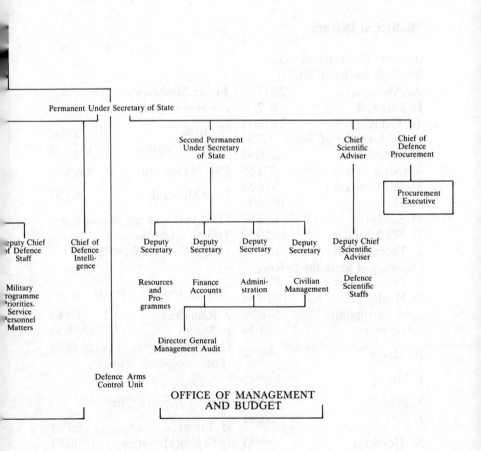

Permanent Under Secretary of State

Second Permanent
Under Secretary
of State

Chief
Scientific
Adviser

Chief of
Defence
Procurement

Procurement
Executive

Deputy Chief
of Defence
Staff

Chief of
Defence
Intelli-
gence

Deputy
Secretary

Deputy
Secretary

Deputy
Secretary

Deputy
Secretary

Deputy Chief
Scientific
Adviser

Military
Programme
Priorities.
Service
Personnel
Matters

Resources
and
Pro-
grammes

Finance
Accounts

Admini-
stration

Civilian
Management

Defence
Scientific
Staffs

Director General
Management Audit

Defence Arms
Control Unit

OFFICE OF MANAGEMENT
AND BUDGET

Appendix D List of Ministers

DEFENCE MINISTERS 1946 TO 22 MAY 1986

Minister of Defence

(became Secretary of State
for Defence from 1/4/64)

A. Alexander	20/12/46	
E. Shinwell	28/2/50	
W. Churchill	28/10/51	
Earl Alexander of Tunis	1/3/52	
H. Macmillan	18/10/54	
S. Lloyd	7/4/55	
Sir W. Monckton	20/8/55	
A. Head	18/10/56	
D. Sandys	13/1/57	
H. Watkinson	14/10/59	
P. Thorneycroft	13/7/62	

Secretary of State for Defence

P. Thorneycroft	13/7/62
D. Healey	16/10/64
Lord Carrington	20/6/70
I. Gilmour	7/1/74
R. Mason	5/3/74
F. Mulley	10/9/76
F. Pym	5/5/79
J. Nott	5/1/81
M. Heseltine	6/1/83
G. Younger	1/86

Junior Ministers

Parliamentary Secretaries

N. Birch	28/2/52
Lord Carrington	18/10/52
Earl of Gosford	26/5/56
Lord Mancroft	18/1/57

(This post was left vacant from
11/6/57 up to the
reorganisation of 1964)

Min. of Defence (Army)

J. Ramsden	1/4/64
F. Mulley	19/10/64
G. Reynolds	24/12/65

(Post abolished 7/1/67)

Min. of Defence (Air)

H. Fraser	1/4/64
Lord Shackleton	19/10/64

(Post abolished 7/1/67)

Min. of Defence (Navy)

Earl Jellicoe	1/4/64
C. Mayhew	19/10/64
J. Mallalieu	19/2/66
(Post abolished 7/1/67)	

Min. of Defence (Administration)

G. Reynolds	7/1/67
R. Hattersley	15/7/69
(Post abolished 19/6/70)	

Min. of Defence (Equipment)

R. Mason	7/1/67
J. Morris	6/4/68
(Post abolished 19/6/70)	

Min. of State

Lord Balniel	23/6/70
I. Gilmour	5/11/72
G. Younger	8/1/74

Min. of State (Procurement)

I. Gilmour	7/4/71
(Post abolished 5/11/72)	

Min. of State

W. Rodgers	8/3/74
J. Gilbert	10/9/76
Lord Strathcona	5/5/79
Lord Trenchard	5/1/81
(Post abolished 29/5/81)	

Min. of State (Armed Forces)

P. Blaker	29/5/81
J. Stanley	13/6/83

Min. of State (Defence Procurement)

Lord Trenchard	29/5/81
G. Pattie	6/1/83
A. Butler	11/7/84
N. Lamont	?/9/85
Lord Trefgarne	22/5/86

Min. of State

Lord Trefgarne	9/85
(Office abolished to become M of S (Defence Support) 11/85)	

Min. of State (Defence Support)

Lord Trefgarne	11/85
(Office abolished 22/5/86)	

Under-Secretaries

Army

P. Kirk	1/4/64
G. Reynolds	20/10/64
M. Rees	24/12/65
D. Ennals	6/4/66
J. Boyden	7/1/67
I. Richard	13/10/69

Air Force

J. Ridsdale	1/4/64
B. Millan	20/10/64
M. Rees	6/4/66
Lord Winterbottom	1/11/68

Navy

J. Hay	1/4/64
J. Mallalieu	21/10/64
Lord Winterbottom	6/4/66
M. Foley	7/1/67
D. Owen	3/7/68

Under-Secretaries

Army

I. Gilmour	24/5/70
G. Johnson Smith	7/4/71
P. Blaker	5/11/72
Lord Brayley	8/3/74
R. C. Brown	18/10/74
B. Hayhoe	6/5/79
P. Goodhart	5/1/81

Air Force

Lord Lambton	24/6/70
A. Kershaw	5/6/73
Lord Strathcona	8/1/74
B. John	8/3/74
J. Wellbeloved	14/4/76
G. Pattie	6/5/79

Reorganisation 29/5/81

Navy

P. Kirk	24/6/70
A. Buck	5/11/72
F. Judd	8/3/74
P. Duffy	14/4/76
K. Speed	6/5/79

Armed Forces

P. Goodhart	29/3/81
J. Wiggin	15/9/81
Lord Trefgarne	13/6/83
(Office vacant 9/85 to 22/5/86)	
R. Freeman	22/5/86

Def. Proc.

G. Pattie	29/5/81
I. Stewart	6/1/83
J. Lee	18/10/83

Appendix E List of CDS, PUSs and CSAs

CHIEFS OF THE DEFENCE STAFF, PERMANENT UNDER-
SECRETARIES OF STATE AND CHIEF SCIENTIFIC
ADVISERS SINCE 1964

CDS	PUS	CSA
1964 Admiral of the Fleet Lord Mountbatten (from 1958)	Sir Henry Hardman	Sir Solly Zuckerman
1965 Field Marshal Sir Richard Hull		
1966	Sir James Dunnett	
1967 MRAF Sir Charles Elworthy		
1968		Sir William Cook/ Professor Cottrell (Post temporarily divided)
1969		
1970		
1971 Admiral of the Fleet Sir Peter Hill-Norton		Sir Herman Bondi
1972		
1973 Field Marshal Sir Michael Carver		
1974	Sir Michael Cary (Died in post)	
1975		
1976 MRAF Sir Andrew Humphrey (died in post)	Sir Frank Cooper	
1977 Admiral of the Fleet Sir Edward Ashmore (Feb–Aug)		Professor Mason
1978 MRAF Sir Neil Cameron		
1979 Admiral of the Fleet Sir Terence Lewin		
1980		
1981		

1982 Field Marshal Sir
Edwin Bramall
1983   Sir Clive Whitmore   Professor Norman
1984
1985 Admiral of the Fleet
Sir John Fieldhouse
1986

Appendix F Defence Budget Trends

DEFENCE BUDGET SHARES

Shares by Service				Shares by Principal Headings		
	RN	Army	RAF	Personnel	Equipment	Other
1964	26	30	28	37	43	20
1965	27	30	29	37	44	19
1966	29	29	27	39	43	18
1967	30	30	27	41	40	10
1968	31	30	27	44	38	18
1969	30	30	28	45	36	19
1970	27	31	28	47	33	20
1971	27	33	29	53	30	17
1972	26	32	27	49	34	17
1973	26	32	32	46	37	17
1974	25	34	31	46	36	18
1975	25	35	29	46	34	20
1976	26	35	28	46	35	19
1977	27	34	28	45	37	18
1978	28	35	28	43	40	17
1979	28	33	29	42	41	17
1980	28	32	29	42	40	18
1981	29	32	30	40	44	16
1982	29	31	31	38	46	16
1983	29	31	31	36	46	18
1984	29	31	31	35	46	19
1985	29	31	31	35	46	19
1986	29	30	30	36	45	19

The balance to make up 100 per cent covers R & D and other services not readily attributable.

From 1974 onwards DOE staff on defence work were included under 'Other Expenditure'. Before, they had been included under Personnel.

Appendix G Manpower Figures

MANPOWER STRENGTHS (in, 000s)

At 1 April	Service Manpower	UK-based Civilians	LECs	MoD HQ	MoD HQ Revised basis of calculation
1964	423 000[1]	285 900	114 300[4]	20 500	
1965	432 000	278 300	100 200	19 800	
1966	418 000	274 700	98 900	19 500	
1967	417 000	274 900	94 500	18 900	
1968	405 000	273 200	82 300	13 700[5]	
1969	383 000	263 300	74 800	13 200	
1970	373 000	257 900	68 700	12 800	
1971	368 000	253 500	63 800	19 300[6]	
1972	371 500	275 100[2]	48 500	18 300	
1973	367 000	272 700	47 000	16 800	
1974	349 500	267 100	47 500	16 000	
1975	338 500	266 600	50 000	16 300	
1976	336 500	266 200	44 600	16 000	
1977	330 500	258 700	42 200	15 000	25 400[8]
1978	320 700	250 400	40 000	14 100	24 700
1979	315 000	247 700	32 200	13 200	23 000
1980	320 500	239 800	36 400	12 700	22 700
1981	333 700	229 600	35 300	12 500[7]	21 500
1982	327 600	216 900	34 800		20 500
1983	320 500	208 900	33 800		19 800
1984	326 000	199 100	33 400		19 400
1985	326 200	174 100[3]	32 400		19 500
1986	322 500	169 500	32 200		18 700[9]

Note 1. Over this period the RN/RM strength went down from 97 600 to 67 900 – a reduction of 29.5 per cent; the Army from 189 400 to 161 400 – a reduction of 14.8 per cent; the RAF from 136 000 to 93 200 – a reduction of 31.5 per cent.

Note 2. Reflects the additional R & D Establishments transferred from DTI to MOD on the creation of the PE.

Note 3. ROF staffs are excluded on their change of status.

Note 4. Locally engaged civilians overseas were mostly employed in the Middle East, Near East and Far East, and the large reductions are associated with the withdrawals from these theatres. There have also been savings among the LECs employed in Germany, Gibralter, Cyprus and Hong Kong. These staffs called for very little staff effort in the MOD; their administration was almost exclusively carried out by the relevant Command HQ.

Note 5. Reflects a change in convention whereby some of the Ministry staff deployed out of London (notably at Bath) were to be regarded as outstation staff.

Note 6. Reflects the transfer of the HQ staff from DTI to the MOD on the formation of the Procurement Executive.

Note 7. A further reclassification in 1981 led to all staff outside London who were part of MOD Directorates being included in the Ministry's number count. This reclassification added back more than just the staff who were excluded in 1968.

Note 8. The column going back from the 21 500 in 1981 to 25 400 in 1978 is purely an illustrative extrapolation to show the comparative strengths.

Note 9. While it is impossible to make a precise comparison between 1986 and 1964, an adjustment of the 1964 total to allow for the subsequent addition of the PE numbers and the most recent categorisation would suggest that the real reduction in the size of the Ministry between 1964 and 1986 would amount to not less than 40 per cent.

Bibliography

The main developments in the organisation have been set out either in special White Papers or in the annual 'Statement on the Defence Estimates'. The extent of public comment on them, by serving as well as retired service officers and officials, has increased in recent years and has mostly taken place in the forum of the RUSI. The following bibliography, which is selective rather than exhaustive, is divided into three parts: the key official documents, major articles and seminars, and more general publications, in particular biographies of those directly involved.

OFFICIAL PUBLICATIONS

Annual Defence White Papers: Statements on the Defence Estimates 1963–1986.

Central Organisation for Defence: Cmd 6923 (October 1946).

Central Organisation for Defence: Cmnd 476 (July 1958).

Central Organisation for Defence: Cmnd 2097 (July 1963).

The Reorganisation of Central Government: Cmnd 4506 (October 1970).

Government Organisation for Defence Procurement and Civil Aerospace: Cmnd 4641 (April 1971).

First Report from the Expenditure Committee, Session 1974/75: Central Management of the Services. HC 220 (February 1975).

First Report from the Expenditure Committee, Session 1977/78: Joint Training of Servicemen. HC 86 (November 1977). (NB. This report includes the text of the report by the Steering Committee of the Management Review of Ministry of Defence).

Second Report from the Defence Committee, Session 1981/82: Ministry of Defence Organisation and Procurement. HC 22–I, II (2 vols) (June 1982).

Ministry of Defence Organisation and Procurement: Observations by the Secretary of State for Defence . . . Cmnd 8678 (October 1982).

Third Report from the Treasury and Civil Service Committee, Session 1981/82: Efficiency and Effectiveness in the Civil Service. HC 236–I, II, III (3 vols) March 1982.

Efficiency and Effectiveness in the Civil Service: Government Observations . . . Cmnd 8616 (September 1982).

Ministry of Defence Organisation (Statement by the Secretary of State for Defence. Hansard, House of Commons, 12 March 1984, cols 22–30.

MINIS and the Development of the Organisation for Defence. (Defence Open Government Document 84/03) (March 1984).
First Report from the Defence Committee, Session 1983/84: Statement on the Defence Estimates. HC 436 (May 1984).
Defence Staff Centralisation Debate. Hansard, House of Lords, 13 June 1984, cols 1157–93.
Central Organisation for Defence: Cmnd 9315 (July 1984).
Third Report from the Defence Committee, Session 1983/84: Ministry of Defence Re-organisation. HC 584 (Oct 1984).
Third Report from the Defence Committee, Session 1985/86: The Defence Implications of the Future of Westland plc. HC 518 (July 1986).
Fourth Report from the Defence Committee, Session 1985/86: Westland plc: The Governments Decision-Making. HC 519 (July 1986).
Westland plc . . . Government Response to the Third and Fourth Reports of the Defence Committee. Cmnd 9916 (Oct 1986).

ARTICLES AND LECTURES

Bell, M. J. V., 'Management Audit in the Ministry of Defence', *Public Administration*, vol. 63(3), Autumn 1984, pp. 311–21.
Bramall, Field Marshal Sir Edwin, 'The Contribution of the Chiefs of Staff to UK Defence', *RUSI Journal*, Sept. 1986, pp. 6–10.
Chichester, Michael, 'British Defence Organisation: The New Look', *Navy International*, Jan. 1985, pp. 504–6.
Cooper, Sir Frank, 'Perhaps Minister: Political and Military Relations Today and in the Future', *RUSI Journal*, Mar. 1983, pp. 3–6.
Cooper, Sir Frank, 'Power to the Centre: A Review of the MOD Reorganisation', *Armed Forces*, Apr. 1985, pp. 130–2.
Hastie–Smith, R. M., 'The Tin Wedding: A Study of the Evolution of the Ministry of Defence', *Seaford House Papers 1974*, pp. 25–42.
Hobkirk, Michael, 'The Heseltine Re-organisation of Defence: Kill or Cure', *RUSI Journal*, Mar. 1985, pp. 45–50.
Howard, Michael, *The Central Organisation of Defence* (Royal United Services Institution, 1970).
Howard, Michael (Chairman), *Does the Present Central Organisation of Defence Meet the Requirements of the 1970s?* (Report of a discussion held at RUSI, 13 Jan. 1971) (Royal United Services Institution, 1971).
Lewin, Admiral of the Fleet Lord, MOD Re-organisation: A Personal Perspective', *Jane's Naval Review 1985*, pp. 107–13.
Omand, D. M., 'MINIS in MOD', *Management in Government*, (4) 1983, pp. 261–73.
Taylor, Brian, 'Coming of Age: A Study of the Evolution of the Ministry of Deference Headquarters 1974–82', *RUSI Journal*, Sept. 1983, pp. 44–51.
Whitmore, Sir Clive, 'Ministry of Defence Re-organisation', *RUSI Journal*, Mar. 1985, pp. 7–12.
Wiggin, Jerry, 'Changes at the Ministry of Defence', *The Hawk* Mar. 1985, pp. 45–56.

GENERAL BACKGROUND

Burridge, Trevor, *Clement Attlee* (Cape, 1985).
Campion, Sir Gilbert, *British Government Since 1918* (Allen & Unwin, 1950).
Cloake, John, *Templer: Tiger of Malaya* (Harrap, 1985).
Fisher, Nigel, *Macmillan* (Weidenfeld & Nicolson, 1982).
Fry, G K, *The Administrative Revolution in Whitehall* (Croom Helm, 1981).
Hamilton, Nigel, *Monty: The Field Marshal 1944-76* (Hamish Hamilton, 1986).
Hobkirk, M. D., *The Politics of Defence Budgeting* (National Defense University Press, 1983).
Jennings, W. I., *Cabinet Government* (CUP, 1947).
Johnson, F. A., *Defence by Ministry 1944-74* (Duckworth, 1980).
Macmillan, Harold, *At the End of the Day* (Macmillan, 1973).
Owen, David, *The Politics of Defence* (Cape, 1972).
Slessor, MRAF Sir John, *The Central Blue* (Cassell, 1956).
Ziegler, Philip, *Mountbatten* (Collins, 1985).

Index